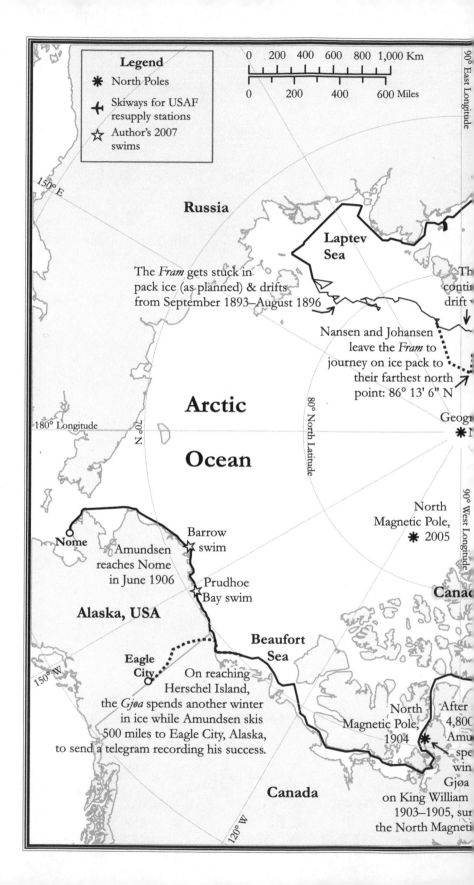

Legend
* North Poles
+ Skiways for USAF resupply stations
☆ Author's 2007 swims

0   200 400 600 800 1,000 Km
0   200   400   600 Miles

90° East Longitude

150° E

Russia

Laptev Sea

The *Fram* gets stuck in pack ice (as planned) & drifts from September 1893–August 1896

Th
conti
drift

Nansen and Johansen leave the *Fram* to journey on ice pack to their farthest north point: 86° 13' 6" N

Arctic

80° North Latitude

Geogi

* N

Ocean

180° Longitude

70° N

90° West Longitude

North Magnetic Pole, 2005 *

Barrow ☆ swim

Nome   Amundsen reaches Nome in June 1906

Prudhoe ☆ Bay swim

Cana

Alaska, USA

Beaufort Sea

150° W

Eagle City   On reaching Herschel Island, the *Gjøa* spends another winter in ice while Amundsen skis 500 miles to Eagle City, Alaska, to send a telegram recording his success.

North Magnetic Pole, 1904 *

After 4,800 Amu spe win Gjøa on King William 1903–1905, sur the North Magneti

Canada

120° W

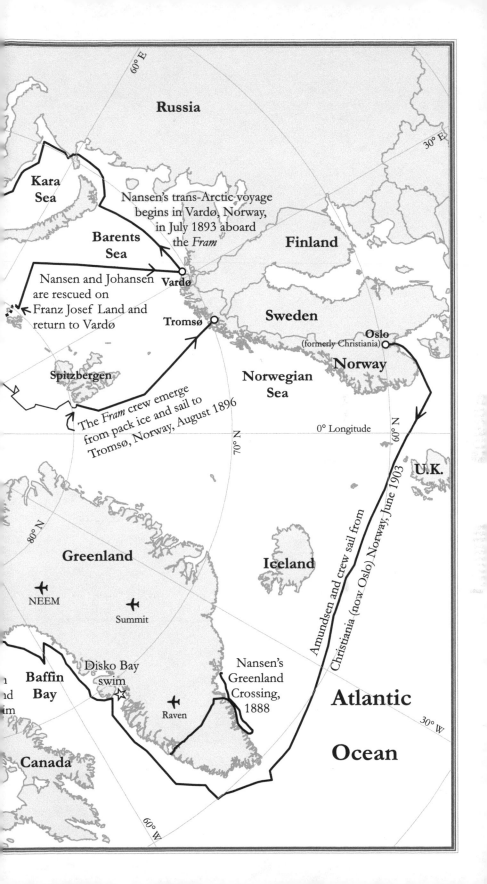

Russia

60° E

Kara
Sea

Barents
Sea

Nansen's trans-Arctic voyage
begins in Vardø, Norway,
in July 1893 aboard
the *Fram*

Finland

30° E

Vardø

Nansen and Johansen
are rescued on
Franz Josef Land and
return to Vardø

Tromsø

Sweden

Oslo
(formerly Christiania)

Norway

Spitzbergen

Norwegian
Sea

The *Fram* crew emerge
from pack ice and sail to
Tromsø, Norway, August 1896

70° N

0° Longitude

60° N

U.K.

80° N

Greenland

Iceland

NEEM

Summit

Amundsen and crew sail from
Christiania (now Oslo) Norway, June 1903

Baffin
Bay

Disko Bay
swim

Raven

Nansen's
Greenland
Crossing,
1888

Atlantic

30° W

Canada

Ocean

60° W

SOUTH
WITH THE
SUN

SOUTH
WITH THE
SUN

Roald Amundsen,
His Polar Explorations,
and the Quest
for Discovery

Lynne Cox

ALFRED A. KNOPF   NEW YORK   2011

THIS IS A BORZOI BOOK
PUBLISHED BY ALFRED A. KNOPF

Copyright © 2011 by Lynne Cox
Maps copyright © 2011 by Diana McCandless
All rights reserved. Published in the United States by Alfred A. Knopf,
a division of Random House, Inc., New York, and in Canada by
Random House of Canada Limited, Toronto.

www.aaknopf.com

Knopf, Borzoi Books, and the colophon are registered trademarks of
Random House, Inc.

Portions of this work were published in slightly different form in
The New Yorker.

Library of Congress Cataloging-in-Publication Data
Cox, Lynne.
South with the sun : Roald Amundsen, his polar explorations, and the
quest for discovery / by Lynne Cox.
p. cm.
"A Borzoi Book."
Includes index.
ISBN 978-0-307-59340-5
1. Amundsen, Roald, 1872–1928. 2. Explorers—Norway—Biography.
3. South Pole—Discovery and exploration—Norwegian.
4. Antarctica—Discovery and exploration—Norwegian.
5. Amundsen, Roald, 1872–1928—Travel—Antarctica. I. Title.
G585.A6C69 2011
919.8'9—dc22   2011008637

Jacket image: Sled dogs sitting on the snow at the South Pole,
Dec. 14, 1911, from an album inscribed "Original photos taken at
South Pole by Capt Amundsen Dec. 14th 1911" and "Films developed
and printed by E. W. Searle Mar. 12, 1912." Courtesy of the
National Library of Australia.
Jacket design by Gabriele Wilson

Manufactured in the United States of America
First Edition

You knew of marathon. It could be won,
after drafts were drunk from milky fountains of
quest; where star-eyed falcons stun
those frozen seas—adrift until you would
wrest them, with sail of snow and sun.

—Ronnie J. Smith, *The Only Road*

CONTENTS

Contents

ILLUSTRATIONS

ix

Illustrations

ACKNOWLEDGMENTS

There were many people who contributed to the research for this book, who gave generously of their time and knowledge, and who always gave a little more, to make sure that I had all the information and helped me in any way that I needed. I would like to thank everyone who helped as they come to mind, in no particular order. Thank you to Vicky Wilson, my editor at Knopf, who gave me free rein and the best editorial direction, and thank you to Martha Kaplan, my agent, who was enthusiastic about the book from the start and encouraged me all the way to publication.

Thank you especially to Nina Korbu, Special Collections Reading Room, and Anne Melgard, Manuscripts Collection, at the National Library of Norway, who opened the world of Amundsen and Nansen to me and allowed me to see their original letters, documents, and journals. Thank you to Guro Tangvald, Picture Collection, the National Library of Norway, who helped me discover some of the images in the book. Thank you to Oddvar Vasstveit, expert on Amundsen's sled dogs, now retired from the National Library of Norway; Dr. Harald Dag Jolle, University of Tromsø, expert on Nansen; and Geir Klover, managing director of the *Fram* Museum, for information on the *Fram, Gjøa,* Amundsen, and Nansen. Thank you to Helen Olsen in Norway, who provided me with background and insights about her country.

Thank you to Janike Rod and Mogens Jensenius, M.D., who hosted me in their home in Oslo. Janike spent days with me in the National Library translating Amundsen's and Nansen's letters and journals, and Mogens introduced me to the Viking ships and Norwegian culture.

Thank you to the British Library Manuscript Collection,

for research information on Robert Falcon Scott; Cambridge University, Scott Polar Research Institute, Huw Lewis-Jones, art curator; Len Bruno, Library of Congress Manuscripts Collections in Science and Technology; Laura Kissel, polar curator, Byrd Polar Research Center Archival Program, Ohio State University; Dr. Peter Jakab, associate director for Collections and Curatorial Affairs, Smithsonian Air and Space Museum, whose Wright Brothers' exhibition and the exhibitions about flight helped me write this book, and Melissa Keiser, chief photo archivist, National Air and Space Museum, Smithsonian Institution; Miriam Tuliao, assistant director of the Central Collection Department, New York Public Library; and Jim Delgado, president of the Institute of Nautical Archaeology.

Thank you to Tom Pickering, former undersecretary of state for political affairs, U.S. ambassador to the United Nations, Russia, India, Israel, El Salvador, Nigeria, and Jordan, and former assistant secretary of state for oceans and international environmental and scientific affairs, for his wise counsel and unwavering support, and for opening diplomatic doors.

Thank you to Michael Donley, secretary of the U.S. Air Force, and Captain Angela Web, USAF, and Technical Sergeant Rebecca Danet, USAF, for granting me approval and unit support for the book project. Thank you to the chief of staff of the air force, General Norton Schwartz, and Lieutenant General Lloyd Utterback for their inspiration, and to Major Samuel Highley, USAF, for supporting the book project.

A very special thank you to Brigadier General Anthony German and the men and women of the 109th Airlift Wing of the New York Air National Guard at Scotia, New York, who helped me understand the very special mission they do for the United States. Thanks for the added instruction to Lieutenant Colonel Kurt Bedore, navigator, triathlete; Lieutenant Colonel Johnson, pilot, triathlete; Major Paul Berconni, pilot; Lieutenant Colonel Mark Armstrong; Lieutenant Colonel Joe Hathaway, pilot; (retired) Lieutenant Colonel Lloyd East, pilot; Master Sergeant Roy Powers, loadmaster, triathlete; Captain Wayne

Brown, pilot; Lieutenant Colonel Bruce Jones, maintenance officer, pilot; Major Frank Medicino, pilot; Lieutenant Colonel John Panoski; Major Chris Sander; Chief Master Sergeant Rodney Begin; Lieutenant Colonel Fabio Ritmo; and Technical Sergeant Candace Lundin. Thank you to New York Air National Guard public affairs for coordinating the Greenland trip and thanks to Colonel Kimberly Terpening, Technical Sergeant Brian Terry, Master Sergeant William Gizara, Lieutenant Colonel Robert Bullock; and thanks to Captain Gregory K. Richaert, M.D., Operation Deep Freeze, for his help with hypoxia information.

There were people in the United States Air Force and the Air National Guard who inspired and informed my writing. Thank you very much to Major General Susan Y. Desjardins, currently Director of Strategic Plans and Programs, HQ U.S. Strategic Command, Offutt Air Force Base, New England; Colonel David Fountain, HQ New York Air National Guard, Albany, New York; Scott McMullen, deputy director, Strategic Plans, Programs, and Requirements, HQ Air Mobility Command, Scott Air Force Base, Illinois; Brigadier General Michael Stough, deputy director, Strategic Plans, Programs, and Requirements, HQ Air Mobility Command, Scott Air Force Base, Illinois; Colonel Thomas (T.J.) Kennett, Air National Guard Advisor to Air Mobility Command, Scott Air Force Base, Illinois; Brigadier General (Dr.) John Owen, Air National Guard Advisor to the Surgeon General, Air Mobility Command, Scott Air Force Base, Illinois.

Thanks to Lieutenant Tim Casares, dive officer, dog team supervisor, flight mechanic, USCG; Jenn Casares, HS2 second-class (retired), USCG; Christopher Shane Walker, ASTC, rescue swimmer, USCG; Paul Terry, rock climber; Kyle Smith, rock climber, who helped me develop the safety swim harness for my Arctic project; and June McKernan who designed the rescue harness.

Thank you to Brownie Schoene, M.D., pulmonary and wilderness medicine specialist, who helped me prepare to swim in 28.8-degree-Fahrenheit water; Laura King, M.D., dermatologist, for advice on preventing skin and nerve damage; and to Charles Nagurka, M.D., internist, for general advice. Thanks to William Poe, DDS, for protecting my teeth and ear canals from the cold. Thank you to Barry Binder, who has supported my projects. Thank you to J. J. Marie, Zodiac boats, and to Antoine Bourel and Andrea Fleischer Bourel for test swim support off Long Island.

For giving me great insights into the C-17 mission in Antarctica, thank you to Lieutenant Colonel Bill Eberhardt, pilot; Chief Master Sergeant Jim Masura, at Tacoma/McChord; and Staff Sergeant Paul Garcia, with the 446th Airlift Wing.

Thank you to Jean Chamberlin, vice president, Boeing; Lee Whittington, project analysis director; Colonel Jim Schaeffer (retired), director of Mobility Requirements, Boeing; Major James T. Schueler Jr. (retired), C-17 production test pilot, Boeing; Joe Brown, FOD program office and world-class tour guide, Boeing; Margee Ralston; Ted Ralston, director, Advanced Maritime Awareness, Boeing (retired); and Suzanne Weekley, director of program management and operations, C-17, Boeing.

Thank you to Trish Roberts; Lieutenant Commander John Shalis USN (retired); Lieutenant Colonel Steve Murray (retired), who flew LC-130s and flew with the Blue Angels.

"HOOYAH Navy SEALs!"

And thank you to all the following: Glenn Helm and James A. Knechtmann from the Department of the Navy Library, Naval Historical Foundation Archives, for all their research recommendations about the *Jeannette* expedition.

Friis Arne Petersen, Danish ambassador to the United States, who took my Greenland project seriously and introduced me to the embassy's Greenland expert, Jakob Alvi, who supported my research and swim.

David Remnick, Dorothy Wickenden, and Cressida Leyshon, my editors at *The New Yorker*, who encouraged Amundsen's story.

Billy Ace-Baker and Gus Shinn, Old Antarctica Explorers Association, Pensacola, Florida.

Acknowledgments

The National Naval Aviation Museum, Pensacola, Florida, and specials thanks to Billy Suckow, naval aviator, for taking Gus Shinn and me to see the *Que Sera Sera*.

Carmela Veneroso and John Odling-Snee for their hospitality in Washington, D.C.

Emmy Griffin, Amanda Mittleman, Kathleen Fessenden, Raylene Movius, and Barry Binder for idea discussions, and Kathy Kent for photo editing. And to Estelle Cox, my first reader.

For computer and tech support, Davey Cox, David Cox, Christine Cox, Laura Cox, Kenny Hawkins, and Vicky Guilloz.

Ed Salazar, U.S. State Department (retired), for advice and help with embassy contacts.

Craig and Cissy Pfeiffer and J. J. Marie for boat support and training support in Long Island Sound, and to Jack Deshales and Albin Power for their support on the Pond Inlet swim.

Special thanks to Diana McCandless for creating the maps of the Arctic and Antarctic.

And finally, thank you to the Knopf team: Kathy Hourigan, Andy Hughes, Michelle Somers, Sue Betz, Gabriele Wilson, Carmen Johnson, Chris Gillespie, Kathleen Fridella, Roméo Enriquez, Virginia Tan, Pat Johnson, and Sonny Mehta.

SOUTH
WITH THE
SUN

Preface

I gazed into the black sky at the canopy of stars, watching constellations climb across the heavens as the earth spun through space at a tilt, pulled by the moon and tugged by the sun. I felt a connection to the earth, and to the depths of the universe.

There are waypoints in life—people, places, things from the past that are guides, as true and dependable as the stars, the planets, and the sun that guide great navigators across the earth, seas, and heavens. These markers emerge from the past and guide us on our life's journey, giving us hope, inspiration, and warning, and show us we are on our way. They are not always evident; sometimes it takes time to see them, sometimes it takes reflection to understand, and then these signs become as clear as the stars and planets illuminating a dark velvet sky, or as bright as the southern sun on a summer's day.

This wasn't the path I thought I was supposed to take; it was one that I was pulled toward. Something compelled me to follow his path. His name was Roald Amundsen. He was one of the greatest polar explorers, the first man to reach the South Pole. I had heard about him one evening many years before, during a workout. Helen Olsen, a friend who grew up in Norway, told me about Amundsen when I was fifteen years old. I imagined what it must be like to reach the South Pole. Then I began to wonder: How did he get there? How did he start out? How did he train? Where did his greatness, his inspiration, come from? How could I learn from him? He stayed with me in the back of my mind, but something inside kept telling me to look at him, to examine his life; he was one of those waypoints, a star closer than the sun.

And so I looked back to see ahead, just as the navigators look into the heavens at stars that are light-years away, at light that has taken millions of years to reach the earth.

Though a hundred years separated us, time didn't matter; that kind of time was just a wink in the time of the universe. Trusting my impulse confirmed for me the connections within the universe, that there would be signs, people, places, and things from the past that would guide me. I needed to trust this because the things I had done before, the things I was doing, had never been done before, and I knew I needed to look at others to see how they had found their way across uncharted waters, unexplored continents, unknown skies. They would be my guides and my inspiration, ways to trust my own direction in life. We are all explorers, trying things we have never done before, entering into the unknown of our lives and we all need to trust those impulses that stay with us, and to look for hope, inspiration, and direction in others who might be able to help show us the way.

CHAPTER I

Siberia and U-2

The nose of the Aeroflot TU-154 aircraft parted long feathery white strands of stratus clouds that whorled past the cockpit, the captain continued his descent, and suddenly, the whole world opened below. An ancient Siberian taiga, a forest dark and dense with fir, spruce, larch, and pine, rose on craggy hill-tops and descended deep into shadowed valleys.

Strong shafts of sunlight focused by the clouds lit the groves of Berioska—white birch—and transformed them to yellow flames. The world below suddenly changed, and all the forest was gone; just stumps remained, and death, and naked brown earth, for miles. The earth was eroding quickly into rivers and streams, turning them from clear blue to muddy brown. But on the horizon another evergreen taiga appeared and a sliver of deep lapis blue: Lake Baikal—the deepest lake in the world, four hundred miles long, an average fifty miles wide, one-quarter of the world's fresh water. This was the blue jewel of Siberia. It was 1988, a year after my Bering Strait swim, which had opened the border between the United States and the Soviet Union. I wanted to swim Lake Baikal. I had no idea how much the Soviets appreciated my Bering Strait crossing or the upcoming Lake Baikal swim until we landed in Moscow and later in Siberia. There were crowds and press everywhere, and people recognized us on the streets. We were told when we reached Irkutsk that the Siberians had been waiting for a group of famous Americans to visit them ever since the time of President Eisenhower. They had constructed new roads for his visit, and a new hotel, but when the U-2 incident occurred, when the U.S. spy plane piloted by Gary Powers was shot down over the Soviet Union in 1960, President Eisenhower was no longer welcome. The relations between the United States and the Soviet Union disintegrated, and the cold war grew colder and grimmer. But our Soviet hosts told us things had changed. We were the group of Americans that the Siberians had long been waiting for.

Our Siberian officials arranged tours of cities, took us to basketball games and other special events, and fêted us at dinners and church celebrations. After flying through thirteen time zones, and two days of constant motion, we were weary, and my focus needed to be on the upcoming swim: planning it out, figuring out the currents, and talking to the local pilot so we could work together. I would be swimming in three days. That wasn't much time to recover or figure out the course of a swim.

Early one morning, before anyone was awake, I slipped out a back door, and went for a long walk along Lake Baikal's shores. I climbed down some boulders, to the Angara River. This was the only river that flowed out of the lake, and here the currents were strong, the water flowed fast, probably three or four knots. I studied the movement of the water as it flowed along the shore. It was like one massive drain out of a swimming pool. If we got caught in that, we'd move out with the river. We would need to keep a distance of a mile or two, or I'd never make it across the lake.

A Siberian woman with high Slavic cheekbones and tanned skin, probably in her seventies, wearing a bright scarf on her head, a blue jacket, and a skirt well below her knees, scrambled across a quarter mile of river rocks. She stood up excitedly and waved. Holding her hand was a young man who looked like her son. He was taller and leaner, but he had the same blue eyes, the same nose, and the same-shaped smile.

When they reached me, she was barely out of breath. She immediately said that she had been waiting for me. Her son translated my English for her. He had studied it in school as a child, and he had never used it before to speak to an American. He was thrilled. The elderly woman said she had a dream the night before that we would meet on the Angara River. She was so excited. Her blue eyes were full of light. She told me that I was welcome there. And then she said something I didn't understand. She said that I was like George Washington De Long, an American hero to all of Siberia.

I had never heard of George Washington De Long before. I was perplexed. Maybe I misunderstood. Did she maybe mean to say George Washington? I asked.

No, Captain George Washington De Long. Hadn't I heard of him? The man translated. He seemed very disappointed. But his mother put on a smile and said that I was welcome there, and welcome to join them anytime at their home.

With all that happened during the next days, and all the political challenges, and the swim across Lake Baikal, which was moved up a day and was completely successful, I forgot this conversation. It faded deep into memory, but one day when I was reading about Roald Amundsen, drawing inspiration from his life, and from the lives of other polar explorers, I kept seeing references to a ship called *Jeannette*. Finally I decided I needed to know more about the ship and saw that the ship's captain was George Washington De Long. He was Amundsen's inspiration and was one of the very first polar explorers. I had to find out about Captain George Washington De Long to understand Amundsen's path and to gain inspiration and direction for my own.

CHAPTER 2

North

On the soft foggy gray horizon of San Francisco Bay, a brown dot bounced on navy blue waters. The dot grew in size and became the form of a ship—the USS *Jeannette*. She plied through the rough, salty, white-capped waters on an epic journey.

It was July 8, 1879, and Lieutenant Commander George Washington De Long and his crew were attempting a historic voyage to become the first expedition to reach the North Pole via the Bering Strait.

De Long stood at the helm dressed in full navy uniform with Emma, his wife, beside him on the bridge. His sky blue eyes behind round eyeglasses scanned the water; the colorful escort boats ablaze with signal flags and masthead flags accompanied him as he sailed past Alcatraz Island and toward the distant headlands of San Francisco Bay. The hum of the *Jeannette*'s engines vibrated through the De Longs as they steamed west together.

George and Emma had met in France, and he had fallen in love with her immediately. But she had another commitment, to a young man who was dying. George wrote to her and waited for her and, when her friend passed, convinced her that he loved her. Emma's father set up conditions. He insisted that they stay apart and out of communication for two years, and if after that time they still felt the same, he would permit them to be together. They had endured and married and now had a young daughter, Sylvie.

More than anything, Emma wanted to sail with George. She had worked alongside him lobbying the U.S. Navy and James Gordon Bennett, a New York newspaper publisher—and owner of the *Jeannette*—and President Rutherford Hayes to provide the support to refit the *Jeannette* and fund this expedition.

Lieutenant Commander De Long, and the thirty-two-man crew of the USS *Jeannette,* a 420-ton bark-rigged wooden steamship, were attempting to become the first American ship to reach the North Pole through the rough waters of the Bering Strait. This journey was meant to be one of exploration, of scientific research, and of discovery, for in 1879 sailing north into Arctic waters toward the North Pole was like flying to another galaxy.

Thousands of people from all over the Bay Area came to see the *Jeannette* off. It was a day to celebrate the possibility of solving one of the world's great puzzles, of reaching the North Pole, and of making great discoveries. The jubilant San Franciscans lined the waterfront. They stood on wide wooden piers, along the curve of Market Street, on top of Telegraph Hill. They lifted children on their shoulders so they could see above the heads in the crowd. They stretched their necks to catch sight of the *Jeannette.* As she sailed past, they cheered wildly, dogs barked excitedly, and roar upon roar rose from the crowd that followed the *Jeannette* along with a great wave of humanity on foot, bikes, and in horse-drawn carriages, as she headed west.

The *Jeannette* passed what would one day become major San Francisco landmarks: Alioto's and Capurro's restaurants and the Argonaut Hotel. She powered by what would become the South End Rowing Club and the Dolphin Club, and the Buena Vista Café and Ghirardelli Square. She sailed past what would become the beautiful St. Francis Yacht Club, and the exquisite Palace of Fine Arts Theater and the Exploratorium. She slipped toward what would become the majestic spans of the Golden Gate Bridge and the entrance to San Francisco Bay.

Cool moist gusts of wind funneled through brown bone-dry hills above San Francisco and pushed the bay into two-foot-high waves. Boats of all sizes—tugs, launches, fishing boats still smelling like fish from the morning catch, and yachts all decked out with brightly colored flags and banners from the San Francisco Yacht Club—steered toward the *Jeannette*. People on the boats sounded the ships' horns and blasted the whistles. They clapped, waved, cheered, and shouted "Good luck" as the *Jeannette* sailed near the Presidio and Fort Mason, where the U.S. Army honored the captain and crew of the *Jeannette* by firing off a farewell salute.

Bound for the north, into unexplored waters and lands that were mostly uncharted, with almost complete uncertainty about what lay ahead, the *Jeannette* was loaded to the gunwales with provisions, coal, and supplies in case the worst happened and the ship was lost, and the crew had to take to shore and somehow survive.

The *Jeannette* sailed with her hull low in the water. She lumbered almost painfully toward the entrance to the Pacific. Her own construction made her heavy. She had been reinforced with thick oak timbers and strong iron transverse beams that were meant to protect her from the deadly pressure of the sea ice in the Arctic waters. The sea ice was something the *Jeannette* would most likely encounter on her way to the North Pole.

The movement of this sea ice was unpredictable, frightening, and could be deadly. It snared sealing ships and whaling fleets and like an anaconda squeezed the life out of ships and sent them down to the ocean depths.

Shortly before Lieutenant Commander De Long left the port of San Francisco, he was given a new set of orders. Baron Nils Adolf Erik Nordenskiöld—the Finnish-born Swedish scientist, geologist, and explorer—had been sailing his ship, the *Vega*, along the northern edges of the Siberian coast, in an attempt to become the first person to find the Northeast Passage.

Finding the Northeast Passage would open new ocean freeways to the world. If Nordenskiöld succeeded, he would discover a more direct sea route from the Atlantic Ocean to the

Pacific Ocean, a route that would increase world trade and open the world to further exploration and understanding. But it had been months since anyone had heard from Nordenskiöld. It was feared that his ship was locked in the sea ice or that it had been sunk. De Long was ordered by the U.S. Navy to alter his course. Instead of heading directly north through the Bering Strait bound for the Arctic Ocean and North Pole, De Long would first search for Nordenskiöld and, if he found him, come to the aid of him and his crew.

This change wasn't what De Long wanted; he knew that this delay could disrupt all of his plans, plans he had worked so hard on for many years, and with the shortness of the summer season in the Arctic, the delay would increase the *Jeannette*'s chances of being caught in the dangerous ice and diminish their chances of reaching the North Pole. But it was his duty to help Nordenskiöld. That was what happened in those days. When ships were late returning to port, especially in waters known to be dangerous, other ships and crews were sent out to search for and rescue them.

On board the *Jeannette,* Emma De Long stood near the helm and watched her husband. Emma had done everything she could to help him reach this point. She had rallied and convinced politicians, and James Gordon Bennett Jr., the publisher of the *New York Herald,* to support this venture, and she realized De Long could succeed in reaching the North Pole, as he had dreamed of, or they could die.

The *Jeannette* rocked and heaved between the north and south headlands. Emma and George De Long climbed down from the ship into a small boat.

The boat carried them to a yacht, one that would receive Emma and transport her back to the harbor. When George said good-bye to Emma, she threw her arms around his neck, and she kissed him good-bye.

Her act completely startled George. Until that moment George hadn't fully realized what was happening. Emma would not be beside him as she had been for all of those days they had worked on and planned this project together. He had been so immersed in the worries of the day, this realization had completely escaped him. George was stunned.

They parted. Emma climbed aboard the yacht, and George took the small boat back to the *Jeannette*. The vessels were beside each other, but facing in opposite directions.

They waved good-bye and they continued waving to each other until George and Emma blended into the two different dark gray horizons.

As the *Jeannette* entered the Pacific Ocean, the air grew saltier, and the wind whipped the waves into reeling and rolling crests that slammed into the sides of the ship and tossed her like a toy boat to and fro. The crew was becoming seasick. Their faces first turned white, and as the waves grew to three and four feet high, and the *Jeannette* rolled and spun, their faces turned a grayish green.

De Long was worried. The ship was sailing so low in the water that waves were breaking over the gunwales, and sheets of water were washing across the deck. He feared that the *Jeannette* would capsize and toss everyone into the Pacific Ocean.

De Long turned the *Jeannette* into the waves, so she would cut across the wave top at an angle, and this he hoped would prevent the *Jeannette* from being rolled over by incoming waves.

The weather did not improve, and De Long and his crew suffered as they sailed slowly all the way north along the California coast, north past Oregon, and north beyond Washington.

After twenty-three days of sailing through rough seas, the *Jeannette* stopped off of Unalaska, in the Aleutian Islands, and De Long was told that the Bering Strait was free of any large ice floes. Seven days later he hove to at St. Michael, a U.S. military post on the Norton Sound, about 125 miles southeast of Nome, Alaska. De Long checked with the local people to see if there was any news about Professor Nordenskiöld from sailors who had been traveling in the Bering Strait area. But there was none.

While in St. Michael, De Long decided to hire two Inuit dog-sledge drivers for the journey and brought them, their sledges, and their forty dogs on board.

De Long continued his search for Professor Nordenskiöld as he sailed west by northwest. Once De Long reached Siberia's Cape Serdtse-Kamen, he learned from the local Siberian villagers that Nordenskiöld, who had first set out from Göteborg, Sweden, had sailed along the waters north of Siberia, and in September the *Vega* had reached 180 degrees longitude and became stuck in the ice. Through the long winter, Nordenskiöld traded with the local Chukchi Inuit.

In July, when the ice broke, Nordenskiöld became the first man to sail through the Northeast Passage.

Relieved by the good news that Nordenskiöld was doing well, De Long refocused on his goal to be the first to reach the North Pole, but it was early September, late in the season, and he had traveled far west to Siberia to search for Nordenskiöld instead of sailing directly north through the Bering Strait toward the North Pole.

De Long wondered if he would be able to reach the pole before the *Jeannette* got stuck in the winter ice pack. If that happened they would be locked in ice until the following spring or summer. There was a theory that there was a powerful warm-water current in the Pacific Ocean, called the Kuro Siwo—Black Stream. The Kuro Siwo, it was hypothesized, originated off the coast of Japan and flowed north, like the Gulf Stream in the Atlantic. Some scientists believed that the Kuro Siwo flowed through the Bering Strait and into the Arctic Ocean, warming the polar waters.

De Long sailed north; he believed that the warm current would melt the sea ice and enable him to reach the North Pole. He believed the Kuro Siwo would move through the Bering Strait and into the Arctic Ocean and warm the polar waters.

This warm current, De Long hoped, would keep the ice

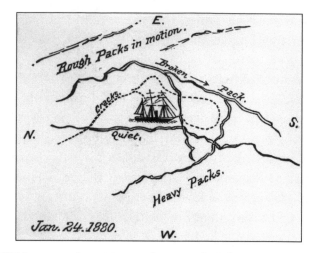

USS Jeannette*'s position in the ice pack, Siberia, January 24, 1880. Engraving after a sketch by expedition naturalist Raymond L. Newcomb. Copied from* The Voyage of the Jeannette, *published in 1884.*

away, and he would be able to reach the pole before winter fell. Quickly De Long learned that this theory was horribly wrong.

De Long, who had been moving along the Siberian coast, decided to turn the *Jeannette* and sail about two hundred miles north toward Wrangel Island. He knew whalers had observed the island, but no one had walked along its shores. It was uncharted. Some geographers believed that it was like a second Greenland, and other scientists thought that Wrangel Island was a part of Greenland, and that Greenland was attached to the North Pole.

De Long decided to get as far north as he could and sail for Wrangel Island. At first they made headway. They managed to maneuver through the light ice floes, but within hours everything changed. The *Jeannette* was fighting her way through the ice pack, zigzagging and forcing her way through it with as much speed as she could draw from the steam engine and sails. There was no Kuro Siwo, no help from any warm current. The onslaught of ice began.

De Long and his crew continued their maneuvers through the ice, weaving when they could into open channels, and

Crewmen from the Jeannette *and their dogs return from a hunt with fresh polar bear meat. Woodcut engraved by George T. Andrew after a design by M. J. Burns.*

then pushing their way through the ice. De Long felt an enormous responsibility for his crew, and he was worried. On September 6, 1879, the *Jeannette* was frozen into the Arctic ice pack. De Long maintained his optimism. He hoped that the ice pack would carry him and his crew of thirty-two men to the North Pole, but he also feared that the ice would crush the ship.

Some days were calm, and magical, and the *Jeannette* was frozen in an exquisite world of crystalline beauty. Her masts, rigging, and decks were covered in frost that shimmered in the moonlight, and the sky swirled with phosphorescent light of green, blue, or rose and charged the air with energy and a crackling sound. But there were days and nights when the ice smashed into the *Jeannette* with so much force that the energy waves reverberated through the ship and jolted De Long and his crew. The sled dogs howled, and pinned their tails between their legs. When the ice pressure increased with the speed and force of the wind, the ice pack smashed together so hard that it sounded like bursts of artillery fire.

For twenty-one months, the *Jeannette* drifted slowly northeast toward the North Pole, and then on June 12, 1881, ice floes closed in on the ship with such force that its hull was crushed.

Huge hummocks—hills and ridges of ice and snow—formed up to ten feet high. Nerves were frayed. No one could sleep. The ice pack slammed into the *Jeannette*'s hull over and over again like a giant car door. The wood used to fortify her was resilient at first—the ice bounced off the hull—but as the ice pressure grew, like nature's vise, it wrenched the planks open.

The crew worked frantically, pumped the frigid water out of the hold, and filled the spaces between the planks with a mixture of moss and oatmeal. For a time this kept the *Jeannette* afloat, but on June 13, 1881, the ice pack dramatically shifted. The ice squeezed the *Jeannette* with so much force that it popped the pins and plugs that held the planks together, wrenched the wood apart, and split her hull. They removed everything they could—the sledges, whaleboat, two cutters, equipment, journals, diaries, and provisions—and on the morning of the thirteenth, the *Jeannette* sank.

For the next three months, the men trudged across the sea ice, with the hope of reaching the open waters off northern Siberia. They dragged the three heavy boats and their equipment on sledges, up over massive hummocks, across broken

The sinking of the USS Jeannette *after being crushed by Arctic ice, June 1881. Engraving by George T. Andrew after a design by M. J. Burns.*

ice and constantly moving ice floes, and covered about one mile a day.

They endured great and relentless hardships: they fell through the ice into the frigid water, cut themselves on large ice shards, wrenched their backs and their bodies, and in the wet shredded clothes, with icy winds and blowing snow, their skin and muscles and the blood in their feet froze. The blood crystallized, and the cells ruptured. The nerves in their feet died, but when their feet warmed the pain was so intense that they wanted to shake them loose from their bodies. Their feet turned black from the frostbite. The muscles died, and chunks of their feet, cut by ice, fell off. They hobbled forward. Their provisions dwindled. Unable to feed both themselves and the sled dogs, they shot the dogs, except for Snoozer, the ship's mascot.

When the ice gave way to water, they divided into three crews and climbed into the small overladen boats. One group went with Lieutenant Commander De Long and Snoozer in the first cutter, the second group joined Lieutenant Charles Chipp in the other cutter, and the remaining men climbed into the whaleboat with Chief Engineer George Melville. The men jumped into the overladen boats, rowed when they had to, and sailed when they could toward the Lena River. This was the closest landfall. They hoped to find food and shelter there, but the Lena River delta was uncharted. It was a labyrinth of multiple river mouths and fingerlike projections of land that divided the water into confusing inlets and bays. There were constantly shifting sandbars and strong, unpredictable currents where ships were lost forever.

Winter comes early to the high latitudes. On the moonless evening of September 12, 1881, an Arctic front descended upon the ocean and De Long's men. The winds grew to gale force and roared. As waves grew larger they broke in all different directions. There was no way to tell where the waves would hit them, and there was no way out of the storm.

De Long signaled to his men and tried to keep them and their boats close together, but the waves kept crashing into the boats, and the men were frantically bailing out the frigid water and rowing as fast as they could to gain a position and find some kind of a balance before the next wave hit.

When Lieutenant Commander De Long and Chief Engineer Melville looked back to check on Lieutenant Chipp, they realized that he and his crew were gone; the sea had taken them.

For more than two days, the storm raged on. De Long's boat and Melville's were separated, but both groups managed to find the Lena River delta and headed inland for help. Most of the men in De Long's crew were injured to the point where they could not move. They were starving. They ate the soles of their shoes and shot and ate Snoozer.

Blizzards hit the region. The Lena River froze, and deep snow covered the tundra. De Long stayed with the crew and sent two of the strongest men off to find help.

Chief Engineer Melville and his thirteen crew members were far more fortunate. They managed to reach the village of Little Borkhia in Yakutsk. Melville immediately gathered a rescue party—a combination of his crew and the Russian people

The Jeannette's *crewmen drag their boats over the Arctic ice, attempting to reach Siberia, June–August 1881. Engraving by George T. Andrew after a design by M. J. Burns.*

from Siberia. They found two survivors from De Long's crew, and with their directions took off to search for the others.

They found Lieutenant Commander De Long and his men. All had died.

De Long and his crew had mapped uncharted areas of northern Siberia and became heroes to the Russians and Americans. The survivors brought back scientific data about the flora and fauna. It seemed like a huge price to pay, but something else happened, far beyond the realm of man, something wonderful and mysterious.

As spring came to the north, the Lena River thawed, and the water in the river shallows warmed quickly in the constant Arctic light. The river flowed north, gathering strength as the tundra thawed, and more water traveled farther north and quickly melted the Arctic ice pack.

Timbers, planks, equipment, torn clothes, and other artifacts from the *Jeannette* rose up to the ocean's surface on the spring currents and drifted across the vast polar seas. These pieces of life from the *Jeannette* would become clues for Arctic exploration.

CHAPTER 3

Nansen Returns

The earth rotated closer to the sun and warmed the Norwegian mountains and the deep fjords. The saltwater inlets between the mountains and the warm breezes swirled and carried the high twitters, chirps, and songs of birds through the tall white birch and fuzzy evergreen forests, and the islands of snow on the steep Norwegian farmlands melted into silvery rivulets of sweet water that softened the earth and swelled the seeds in the soil. The sun's energy pulled the seeds from their jackets, and the land grew bright and fragrant with pink roses and delicate wildflowers and tender green wild grasses and grains. Roald Amundsen stood at the head of the Christiania, now Oslo, Fjord.

It was May 30, 1889, and Amundsen was waiting for the return of Fridtjof Nansen, who, along with his five-man crew, had been the first to cross from east to west the unexplored regions of the Greenland ice cap. Amundsen's heart was pounding in his chest. He was not alone. The entire city of Christiania, now Oslo, had come out to welcome Nansen home. It was a high holiday in Christiania, all shops and businesses were closed, and the city was ablaze with decorations.

Crowds of people rimmed the edges of Christiania Fjord, making more visible from the sea the small scalloped-shaped bays, wavering inlets, and rocky points. People waited and talked excitedly as they strained to see Nansen. Amundsen could hardly contain himself. He had been fascinated by polar exploration, since the Arctic during his lifetime was as remote and unknown as outer space is today.

Amundsen had read about all the early forays into the polar regions in accounts by the polar explorers. At age eight or nine, Amundsen became interested in John Franklin, a British explorer, who had attempted to be the first to sail through the Northwest Passage, a sea route that linked the Atlantic and Pacific. Amundsen studied John Franklin's accounts of his attempt: "I read them all with fervid fascination which has shaped the course of my life."

Amundsen was enthralled with Franklin's stories about the blizzards he and his men endured, their hunger that became starvation, and the resolve Franklin exuded that encouraged his crew to survive. Amundsen began dreaming of becoming a polar explorer, but he kept his dreams secret, especially from his mother. She had other plans for her son; she wanted him to study medicine and become a doctor.

In order to become an explorer, Amundsen knew he had to prepare and train. At every opportunity, he skied long distances along the hills and over the mountains around Christiania. He strengthened his muscles and increased his endurance. He slept with the windows in his bedroom wide open during the coldest nights of the Norwegian winters and was considered to be a freak for doing so. His mother questioned his motives. He told her that he liked the cold fresh air and didn't tell her that he was conditioning his body to endure the extreme cold. She would not have understood. But he sensed that Nansen would. He became a great fan of Nansen's, and he learned all that he could about him.

Nansen was tall, lean, flexible, and strong. He was blond and blue-eyed, with a deep intensity. His face was oval, his complexion fair, and he had an appealing smile. Nansen was born in Store Frøsen, near Christiania, on October 10, 1861. His father was a prosperous, respected attorney, with a personal sense of duty and unwavering integrity. His mother ran the household. She was athletic and strong-minded. She spent her free time reading and learning, always wanting to improve her mind. She was the one who encouraged Fridtjof and his brother Alexander, and Nansen's half brothers and sisters, to love the outdoors.

Fridtjof Nansen was a natural-born athlete, and he excelled at every sport he attempted. He was a great swimmer and tumbler, but he attained a level beyond any other athlete in skating and skiing. Nansen broke the world record for the mile in skating, and he won the national cross-country skiing championships twelve times. He also showed a great capacity for endurance and self-confidence. In one day, with limited gear and only his faithful dog, he skied fifty miles through the pine forests and open fields of Norway.

From the very start, Nansen was fascinated by the Arctic. In 1882, when he was twenty-one years old, he was invited along on a sealing ship, the *Viking*, and during his time on board, he recorded observations of ice floes, ocean currents, winds, and polar animals. They sailed off the coast of Greenland, an island that seemed to always be veiled in fog. When Nansen got one glimpse of Greenland, that was all it took. He knew he had to go there. He had to explore the island.

No one inhabited the east coast of Greenland at that time, and no European had ever crossed the interior ice fields. Nansen knew he had to attempt it. Most people thought Nansen was out of his mind—it couldn't be done, it was too dangerous, he would surely die—but he was confident and began to formulate a plan. He gathered together a team of strong, disciplined, athletic men from across Norway: Otto Sverdrup, a retired ship's captain; Oluf Christian Dietrichson, a first lieutenant in the Norwegian infantry; and Kristian Kristiansen Trana, a peasant from northern Norway, as well as Samuel Johannesen Balto and Ole Nielsen Ravna, two men who were Sami people—nomadic reindeer herders.

Nansen believed that the best way to cross Greenland's interior was *skilobning*—cross-country skiing. He selected special skis for what he thought the snow would be like, and paired the skis with *lauparsko*—Norwegian boots. The soles of the boots were composed of pliant leather that was turned up along the

Fridtjof Nansen, Bergen, Norway, 1887. Nansen studied zoology, researched nerve anatomy, and designed the Nansen bottle for collecting water samples. He studied the movement of currents in the Arctic Ocean and life within the northern waters.

sides and toe and covered the upper area of the foot. His team wore well-shrunk thick woolen stockings and, over them, goat's-hair socks as a way to keep the feet warm and repel the moisture outside. He also brought Norwegian *truger*—snowshoes that resembled tennis rackets. He redesigned them to make them smaller so they could be used later in the spring.

Nansen also redesigned the sledges. These were what his team would use to carry all of their equipment and provisions, and they needed to be lightweight, maneuverable, and strong, but also flexible. He studied those that had been used on previous expeditions and made improvements on the Norwegian *ski kjaelke,* a low hand sledge on broad runners that was strong and light and moved well on all kinds of surfaces. He added elements from the sledges used to rescue the Greely expedition a few years before.

His sledges were made of wood; the runners on the bottom

were elm or maple covered with thin steel plates. They were nine feet six inches long and one foot by eight inches wide. The front and the back of the sledges were turned up to add strength and flexibility. Each sledge weighed twenty-eight pounds.

Nansen knew that the sledges would need to be steered on the ice and snow and around crevasses when they were moving fast downhill, so he added central line plates that were like a keel. These keels worked as long as they lasted, but they would be torn off by rough ice.

He had two small boats constructed for landing onshore.

For provisions, Nansen chose food that would be light in weight. He brought pemmican, dried meat; pea soup; Gruyère cheese; sugar; and a Swedish biscuit called *knäckebröd*. He also brought chocolate. Not just bars of chocolate, but meat-powder chocolate that when mixed with hot water served as a hot high-protein energy drink that warmed the body.

He believed that he and his team should live as naturally as possible, especially in an extremely cold climate where they would be physically exerting themselves. He thought artificial stimulants and narcotics might help the mind and the body for a period of time, but afterward, there would be a price to pay: the body would be artificially stimulated to do more work, but the following day it would be exhausted. He did pack some alcohol for medical purposes.

Nansen was concerned about snow blindness, or a temporary form of blindness caused by the sunlight's reflection off the snow. His friend Adolf Nordenskiöld, the Swedish professor whom Lieutenant Commander De Long had searched for in the Bering Strait and beyond, gave Nansen his thick goggles made of smoked glass that completely covered the eyes to protect them from the intense light reflected off the snow.

Water would be needed throughout the trip, so Nansen redesigned a cooker that would melt snow for water and warm the interior of the tent. He also had two three-man sleeping bags made out of reindeer skin. The men would share the bags on the expedition and would mutually benefit from one another's body heat.

He acquired the best sextant he could find for navigation and three compasses for testing magnetic deviations, a barometer, chronometer watches, a medical chest, and four sledges that weighed two hundred pounds each when they were fully loaded.

In June 1888, Nansen and his five men and two boats traveled as guests on board the *Jason,* a seal-hunting ship. After six weeks of seal hunting on the Arctic ice, Captain Jacobsen of the *Jason* sailed for Greenland. When Nansen saw the coast of Greenland, he said it was like going to a dance and "expecting to meet the choice of one's own heart." It would be a dance getting to land, but not anything like Nansen anticipated.

Nansen and his crew lowered their boats. The crew on board the sealing ship bid them an apprehensive farewell.

They thought they would quickly reach shore after rowing for two or three hours. But they got caught in a strong current they couldn't row against, and suddenly they were in ice floes that were ramming together and piling up on top of one another. Both of the boats were threatened with destruction. Sverdrup, the retired ship's captain, dragged his boat up on an ice floe, and Nansen headed toward one of the open pools. At every moment they were in danger of being crushed. Eventually, after considerable effort, they reached a large open pool of calmer water. They continued drifting, and Nansen and his crew weren't sure where they were.

They were near land, west of Sermilikfjord, and Nansen could see the rocks onshore and the mountainside. It seemed like a simple thing to get ashore, but there was more ice. Nansen and the crew dragged their boats onto an ice floe, and a sharp piece of ice cut through Nansen's boat. Sverdrup patched it as well as he could, but he wasn't sure if it would float, so Nansen and his crew remained on the ice floe. The skies grew dark and gloomy, and cold rain poured down upon them in torrents. They crawled into their sleeping bags and posted one man to stand watch in case the ice opened and they could row ashore.

But the current shifted from a westerly direction to the south and increased in speed and carried them farther away from shore. Nansen had known about the current but hadn't realized its strength, otherwise they would have put in farther east, off Cape Dan. They were twenty miles offshore. In spite of their challenges, Nansen sketched pictures of Greenland, and wrote about the glorious evening, the beauty of the northern lights, and the land that looked so near but, with the water currents, was so difficult to reach.

During the night the swell grew larger and began to break over the ice floe. The ice was shifting, grinding upon itself, and they were being carried out to sea. The floe beneath them had split in two. It was only about forty yards across. They moved camp to another floe, and the waves grew larger and columns of water were forming in the air. Nansen divided the provisions and ammunition into two boats in case one sank. Once again the evening became calm, and Nansen wrote:

> Beautiful it is, indeed with these huge long billows coming rolling in, sweeping on as if nothing could withstand them. They fall upon the white floes, and then, raising their green, dripping breasts, they break and throw fragments of ice and spray far before them on to the glittering snow, or high above them into the blue air. But it seems almost strange that such surroundings can be the scene of death. Yet death must come one day, and the hour of our departure could scarcely be more glorious.
> (*The First Crossing of Greenland*, 121)

For twelve days they drifted on the precarious ice until one morning they woke and saw open water and the shore. The water remained open the whole way except for two small sections of ice, and they landed on Kekertarssuak Island. Nansen wrote that it was as if they had escaped the sea and he now believed that they could begin their trek across the ice cap.

They were more than three hundred miles south of their initial position. They had to make up that difference, and they had to row north along the east coast of Greenland to be able to gain access to a route that would take them across the ice cap. They pushed north, chopped their way through the ice with axes, and used boat hooks to pull the icebergs apart to create gaps they could pass through. They had to move quickly and push the boats through the ice before the gaps closed and crushed the boats. They continued working their way north.

When they reached Cape Bille, north of Puisortok, they heard human voices and barking dogs. The Inuit, who were camped there, came out in kayaks and met them with big smiles, and a group of men showed them where to land. The Inuit invited them into one of their tents. Nansen was disgusted with the way the air smelled. And he was surprised to discover that inside the tents the Inuit wore few if any clothes. The Inuit were just as fascinated by Nansen as he was by them, but Nansen and his crew were exhausted. They returned to their own tent, and for the first time in a couple of weeks slept deeply on solid ground.

They continued to work their way north and stopped to have dinner off Mogens Heinesens Fjord. They found the ruins of two Eskimo homes and stretched out on the grass to sun themselves, then took some Greenland flowers to remember their evening there. They continued northward past huge icebergs, and, as they neared the Nagtoralik Islands, Nansen noted the beauty of the nearby icebergs that were hollowed out to the extent that a ship could pass through the hole. Nansen wrote:

> In these cavities were marvelous effects and tints of blue ranging to the deepest ultramarine in their inmost recesses. The hole formed a floating fairy palace, built of sapphires, about the sides of which brooks ran and cascades fell, while the sound of dripping water echoed unceasingly from the caverns at the base. When one comes across icebergs of this kind, which happens now and again, a wealth of beauty is found in fantastic forms

and play of colour which absorbs one's whole imagination and carries one back to the wonders and mysteries of the fairy-land of childhood.

On August 5, they struggled through the pack ice, which continued all along shore for as far as they could see. They passed Kutsigsormuit and stopped to take a sighting. Sixty feet ahead an enormous block of ice broke off from an iceberg and hit the sea with a thundering roar. If they had not stopped when they did, they would have perished.

On August 15, Nansen and his crew hauled their two boats out of the water and placed some food and ammunition in the boats, along with Nansen's description of their expedition so far, which would provide a note for those who might need to come searching for them. The sun was too bright during the daytime, and the snow was soft, so they traveled west in the sunshine of evening toward Christianshaab.

They dragged their two-hundred-pound sledges up the mountainsides to the top of the Greenland ice cap, and they traveled across rough ice and snowfields laced with bottomless crevasses. They suffered. The ropes they used to pull their sledges felt as if they seared their shoulders. Yet in spite of the enormous challenges, Nansen saw the uniqueness of this world and wrote about its exquisite beauty.

> Or when the moon rose and set off upon her silent journey through the fields of the stars, her rays glittering on the crest of every ridge of ice, and bathing the whole of the dead frozen desert in a flood of silver light, the spirit of peace reigned supreme and life itself became beauty.

They reached an altitude of 7,930 feet measured by barometer. If they ascended any farther, it would be difficult to continue their measurements, since they were enduring constant winds and bitter cold of up to minus 50 degrees Fahrenheit. And the ice from their breath covered their beards and faces, so it was difficult for them to open their mouths to speak.

There were days when the snow driven by wind fell so fast and heavy that they had to stay for as many as three days in their tents. Nansen used a sextant and map for navigation, and as he adjusted their course he decided to aim for Ameralik Fjord, to the south of Godthaab. Dragging the sledges each day was exhausting, so they made sails from pieces of the tent floor, rigged them to the sledges, and skied beside their wind-driven sledges.

On September 22, Nansen fell through a snow bridge into a seemingly bottomless fissure and would have been lost forever. The only thing that saved him was that the gap was narrow, and he was able to pull himself out. Finally, after a enduring a month of unfathomable physical and mental challenges, on September 24 they sighted water, climbed off the ice cap, and reached Ameralik Fjord. They had completed the first crossing from the east coast to the west coast of Greenland. Nansen

Fridtjof Nansen, Otto Neumann Sverdrup, Oluf Christian Dietrichson, and Kristian (Kristiansen) Trana after completing their forty-two-day crossing of the Greenland ice cap. They practiced using Greenland Inuit kayaks to explore the coastal area, 1888–89.

wrote: "Words can not describe what it was for us only to have the earth and stones again beneath our feet, or the thrill that went through us as we felt the elastic heather on which we trod, and smelt the fragrant scent of grass and moss." Thanks to that achievement, they were able to draw a more detailed map of Greenland, and gather a wealth of observations and scientific data about Greenland's ice cap, climate, and geography.

Nansen and his crew built a boat in Ameralik Fjord, and one of his crew successfully rowed north along the west coast of Greenland and reached Godthaab, a Danish and Greenlandic town.

The crew wintered in Godthaab, then sailed back on the *Hvidbjørnen* to Copenhagen on May 21 and then home to Christiania Fjord on May 30, 1889.

They were greeted by a flotilla of sailboats, a fleet of steamers, and crowds of people waiting at the head of the fjord, some holding on to dogs that were barking and wagging their tails expectantly. The air crackled with energy and warmth as cheer after cheer rose from the crowd. People pressed closer together and balanced on the sparkling slabs of granite rock that rounded the edges of the fjord. Deeper into the fjord, people climbed on top of black volcanic rock striated like the pages of a closed book. People stood on tiptoe, bounced up and down, twisted and turned, strained their necks to see where Nansen was.

CHAPTER 4

Amundsen's Inspiration

Seventeen-year-old Roald Amundsen was in that crowd. He wrote: "It was the day Fridtjof Nansen returned from his Greenland expedition. The young Norwegian ski runner came up the Christiania Fjord, on that bright sunny day, his erect form surrounded by the halo of universal admiration at the deed he had accomplished, the miracle, the impossible."

In those moments of seeing Fridtjof Nansen, the course of Amundsen's life suddenly became apparent to him. He knew what he wanted to do. Amundsen wrote in his memoirs: "I wandered with throbbing pulses amid the bunting and the cheers, and all my boyhood's dreams reawoke to tempestuous life. For the first time something in my secret thoughts whispered clearly and tremulously: If you could make the North West Passage!"

This was an enormous goal. For four hundred years men had attempted to find a better sea route to sail from the Atlantic to the Pacific. Many had died in the attempt. No one had ever successfully navigated through the Northwest Passage.

The attempts to find the Northwest Passage had helped map the uncharted coastlines of North, South, and Central America and segments of the Arctic.

Amundsen dreamed of finding this passage, but his mother diverted his dreams, and she landlocked him. Her husband and three other sons were in the shipping business, but she decided that Roald would be different. He would not be allowed to sail; instead, she insisted that he study medicine and become a physician.

Amundsen went through the motions and entered medical school and halfheartedly tried to live up to her expectations. But he held on to his dream and secretly began to train. He also kept close track of what Nansen was doing.

Something very significant had caught Nansen's attention. In 1884, before his crossing of Greenland, he had read an article by Professor Henrik Mohn, the director of the Meteorological Institute in Christiania, in the Norwegian *Morgenblad* that resulted in a theory of transpolar drift. Items from the wreck of the *Jeannette* had been discovered by an Eskimo near Juliane-håb, on the southwest shores of Greenland. The artifacts included a list of provisions signed by Lieutenant Commander De Long, a list of the *Jeannette*'s boats, and a pair of oilskin pants labeled with the name Louis Noros, one of the *Jeannette*'s crew. Professor Mohn thought that these items must have drifted right across the Arctic Ocean.

Nansen had a moment of great insight and clarity. He deciphered what the tall tales and Mohn's theory meant and wrote: "It immediately occurred to me that here lay the route ready to hand. If a floe could drift right across the unknown region, that drift might also be enlisted in the service of exploration—and my plan was laid."

Nansen proposed to the Christiania Geographical Society, one of his supporters, the idea that he could use the ice. Instead of fighting the ice barrier as other polar explorers had done, he would drift with the ice.

I believe that if we pay attention to the actually existent forces of nature, and seek to work with and not against them, we shall thus find the safest and easiest method of reaching the Pole. It is useless, as previous expeditions have done, to work against the current, we should see if there is not a current we can work with. The *Jeannette* expedition is the only one, in my opinion, that started on the right track, though it may have been unwittingly and unwilling. (*Farthest North,* 11)

What Nansen proposed had never been achieved; he knew that there would be many naysayers, but he saw there was a wealth of knowledge that could be attained just by venturing out into the unknown and doing it in a new way—using the ice to carry the ship north, rather than fighting it. Nansen wrote:

> Many people however, will certainly urge: "In all currents there are eddies and backwaters; suppose, then, you get into one of these, or perhaps stumble on an unknown land up by the Pole and remain lying fast there, how will you extricate yourselves?" To this I would merely reply, as concerns the backwater, that we must get out of it just as surely as we got into it, and that we shall have provisions for five years. And as regards to the other possibility, we should hail such an occurrence with delight, for no spot on earth could well be found of greater scientific interest. (*Farthest North,* 19)

Like almost anyone who attempted to do something new or different or creative or who wanted to explore the unknown, Nansen faced an onslaught of expert naysayers, including one of the world's most respected Arctic explorers, Admiral Sir Leopold Francis McClintock. Admiral McClintock was in the British Royal Navy, and he had been persuaded by Lady Jane Franklin to participate in a series of searches from 1848 to 1859 to find her husband, Sir John Franklin, a British Royal Navy explorer who had attempted to find the Northwest Passage.

Lady Jane Franklin had explored Tasmania and other parts of Australia at a time when this wasn't done by women. She had heard reports from Dr. John Rae, a physician and Arctic explorer who had also searched for the Northwest Passage, and who had received information from the Inuit living on King William Island, that Franklin and his men were dead, and that some men had reverted to cannibalism.

Lady Jane would not believe Dr. Rae's account, and she lobbied hard and also offered a reward to find out more about the fate of her husband and his expedition. Admiral McClintock set out on a series of searches largely financed by Lady Franklin. McClintock was only able to find the official record of Franklin's expedition. Both of Franklin's ships, the *Erebus* and *Terror*, were crushed by ice and sank in the Arctic waters off northern Canada. But in the course of McClintock's search he explored and mapped eight hundred miles of land that had been previously unknown. McClintock had had enormous experience in polar waters, and he had every reason to doubt Nansen's theory.

McClintock wasn't alone. Sir Allen Young also had extreme doubts. Young had assisted McClintock as the sailing master aboard the *Fox* from 1857 to 1869 and had helped search for John Franklin. After they completed these expeditions with little new information about Franklin's fate, Sir Allen Young decided to mount two subsequent Arctic expeditions in 1875 and 1876. He sailed on the *Pandora* in 1875 but made little headway. The *Pandora's* path in the Arctic was blocked by ice, and he and his expedition had to return to port. The following year, Young made a second attempt with the intended destination of King William Island, but the British Admiralty requested instead that he check on a depot for the British Nares expedition. So Young diverted his course and assisted the British scientific expedition.

The following year, James Bennett, the New York publisher, purchased the *Pandora* and refitted, reinforced, and renamed the ship—the *Jeannette*. The *Jeannette* would be the ship Lieutenant Commander De Long sailed in that ill-fated attempt to reach the North Pole via the Bering Strait. Young knew the *Jeannette* had been crushed in the icy waters off northern Siberia. He was concerned that Nansen might meet a similar fate, and at that time, no one knew if the North Pole was floating on the ice or if it was a part of the land.

Young wrote:

> Dr. Nansen assumes the blank space around the axis of the earth to be a pool of water or ice: I think the great danger to contend with will be the land in nearly every direction near the Pole. Most previous navigators have continued seeing land again and again farther and farther north. These *Jeannette* relics may have drifted through narrow channels, and thus finally arrived at their destination, and, I think, it would be an extremely dangerous thing for the ship to drift through them, where she might impinge upon the land, and be kept for years. (*Farthest North,* 23)

Another reputable polar explorer who doubted Nansen was Adolphus Greely, a U.S. Army general who led the Lady Franklin Bay expedition from 1881 to 1884, an expedition that was meant to establish a chain of meteorological observation stations as part of the First Polar Year and make astronomical and magnetic observations. Greely believed that Nansen was making a grave mistake. Greely and his crew explored the northwestern coastline of Greenland and crossed Ellesmere Island from east to west, but they were in desperate shape when their two relief ships failed to find them. Henrietta, Greely's wife, insisted that the search for her husband and the crew continue. The crew of the *Bear* found Greely on Cape Sabine. Of the twenty-five men who had been on Greely's expedition, nineteen had died from starvation, hypothermia, and drowning. Greely had endured great hardship, and in response to Nansen's idea, he wrote a bleak and discouraging article in 1891:

> It strikes me as almost incredible that the plan here advanced by Dr. Nansen should receive encouragement or support. It seems to me to be based on fallacious ideas

as to the physical conditions within the Polar Regions, and to foreshadow, if attempted, barren results, apart from the suffering and death among its members. (*Farthest North*, 23)

There were a few polar authorities who endorsed Nansen's plan; the most esteemed and helpful was the scientist Alexander Georg Supan, an Austrian geographer and editor of *Petermanns Mitteilungen*, who supported Nansen's ideas and lent some advice. Professor Supan believed that the prevailing winds in the polar basin would aid a person attempting to sail north.

Based on Professor Supan's theory and his own research, Nansen established an enormous and bold goal: to "investigate the great unknown region that surrounds the Pole, and these investigations will be equally important, from a scientific point of view, whether the expedition passes over the polar point itself or at some distance from it."

What was exceptional about Nansen was that he listened to his critics and considered what McClintock, Young, and Greely had written, and with those comments in mind, he developed a better plan. He believed it would take up to three years to achieve his goal, but decided to prepare a ship for men and dogs for a five-year journey. He also knew he needed plenty of warm clothing. Equally important to the success of the expedition was the ship he would use. On May 30, 1890, Nansen managed to gain support and funds for the expedition from the king of Norway and the Norwegian government, and he obtained sponsorship from private donors. He demonstrated his brilliance when he created a new design for the ship, one he believed could not be crushed by the ice—Nansen, along with shipbuilder Colin Archer, designed the *Fram* in the shape of an egg.

The bow, stern, and keel were rounded to prevent the ice from gripping the ship. And the *Fram* was small and light, but very strong in proportion to her weight, to be able to maneuver in and navigate through the ice. Nansen and Archer believed that the sides of the ship needed to be superstrong.

They chose Italian oak, and the thickness of the *Fram*'s sides were from twenty-four to twenty-eight inches as a way to externally resist the ice, and internally, the ship was reinforced with braces and stanchions and built so it would be watertight. A 220-horsepower engine powered the ship. In calm weather the ship could reach up to seven knots.

The living quarters were abaft under the half deck. In many ways the interior looked like a small floating hotel. There was a salon with a mechanical organ, a large dining room, and a drawing room in the middle of the ship and sleeping cabins on either side with electric lights. Nansen had also thought of how to make the ship warm and comfortable. The six very small shared bedrooms on the ship were arranged in a way to protect them from the cold environment outside. There was a large library on board and room for Nansen's collection of instruments used to gather data throughout the expedition.

While the *Fram* was being built, Nansen began selecting his crew, and everyone who applied had to be examined and deemed strong and healthy. There would be a total of thirteen members of the expedition including Nansen.

On June 24, 1893, the day Nansen was about to set off with his crew to attempt to reach the farthest north, he reflected heavily on leaving his home, his wife, and his daughter. He wrote:

> Behind me lay all I held dear in life. And what before me? How many years would pass ere I should see it all again? What would I not have given at that moment to be able to turn back; but up at the window little Liv was sitting clapping her hands. Happy child, little do you know what life is—how strangely mingled and how full of change. Like an arrow that little boat sped over Lysaker Bay, bearing me on the first stage of a journey on which life itself, if not more, was staked.

For the next month Nansen, Otto Sverdrup, and the eleven-man crew sailed through Norwegian waters, turned east at

Vardø, and then sailed through the Barents Sea and along the northern Siberian coast.

Before Nansen set sail, he contacted his friend Baron Edward von Toll, an Arctic explorer from St. Petersburg, Russia, to help him find dogs in Siberia for the expedition. Baron von Toll was organizing his own second scientific expedition to Siberia and the New Siberian Islands. Through contacts, the baron arranged for Alexander Ivanovitch Trontheim to find thirty East Siberian dogs, which were considered the best draft animals for the expedition, and the baron advised Nansen to create some depots on the New Siberian Islands that would hold provisions in case something happened to the *Fram* and the crew needed to return the way they had come. When the baron left on his own expedition to the New Siberian Islands, he put in three additional depots for Nansen.

On July 29 Nansen reached Khabarova, the village where he had prearranged with Trontheim to take on the sled dogs that they would use if something happened to the *Fram* and they needed to find their way home by way of the ice. A boat approached the *Fram* from shore. In German, Nansen asked one of the men, who had a kind face and a red beard, if he was Trontheim. He was, and along with him on the boat was a group of fine-looking Russian traders and pleasant-featured Samoyeds. Nansen's second question to Trontheim was about the ice in the Kara Sea. Trontheim said he thought it would be favorable, and some of the Samoyeds who had been seal hunting in the entrance to the Yugor Strait a day or two before thought it would be okay.

Trontheim took Nansen to the dog camp to collect the dogs for the expedition. Nansen wrote:

> As we approached it the howling and barking kept getting worse and worse. When a short distance off we were surprised to see a Norwegian flag on the top of a pole. Trontheim's face beamed with joy as our eyes fell on it. It was, he said, under the same flag as our expedition that

his had been undertaken. There stood the dogs tied up, making a deafening clamor. Many of them appeared to be well-bred animals—long-haired, snow-white, with up-standing ears and pointed muzzles. With their gentle, good-natured looking faces they at once ingratiated themselves in our affections.

After working with the dogs for a few days, they brought them aboard and put them on the forward deck. Captain Sverdrup noted the southern wind had been blowing for several days, and he was certain that they would be able to sail open waters all the way to the New Siberian Islands. On August 3, they set off and continued sailing east for three months, deeper into the darkness of November. Nansen worked side by side with his crew, but the days dragged by, and he was filled with self-questioning and self-doubt. He wrote:

Here I sit in the still winter night on the drifting ice-floe, and see only stars above me. Far off I see the threads of life twisting them into the intricate web which stretches unbroken from life's sweet morning dawn to the eternal death-stillness of the ice. Thought follows thought— you pick the whole to pieces, and it seems so small—but high above all towers one form. . . . *Why did you take this voyage?* Could I do otherwise? Can the river arrest its course and run up hill. My plan has come to nothing. That palace of theory which I reared, in pride and self-confidence, high above all silly objections has fallen like a house of cards at the first breath of the wind. Build up the most ingenious theories and you may be sure of one thing—that fact will defy them all. Was I so very sure? Yes, at times, but that was self-deception, intoxication. A secret doubt lurked behind all reasoning. It seemed as though the longer I defended my theory, the nearer I came to doubting it. But no, there is no getting over the evidence of the Siberian driftwood. But if, after all, we are on the wrong track, what then? Only disappointed human hopes, nothing more. And if we perish, what will it matter in the endless cycles of eternity? (*Farthest North*, 124–25)

The *Fram* drifted north and south within the ice pack, and Nansen's moods followed that drift. When the *Fram* drifted farther north he was happy; when it drifted south, he was despondent. He tried to focus on positive things; he read books, observed the natural beauty surrounding him, and continued to take depth measurements of the ocean. During these measurements, he discovered that the deep polar basin was an area where the waters could reach up to one thousand fathoms deep. In spite of his discoveries, Nansen was restless and homesick, and his heart ached to see his wife and daughter. The slow drift wore him down to despair.

Fridtjof Nansen beside the Fram *with dog skins and bearskins hanging out to dry, June 16, 1894.*

Almost another year has passed. The Fram *is still drifting in the Arctic Ocean with the ice into unexplored waters, but not toward the goal of the North Pole, March 1895.*

Nansen did not convey these thoughts to his crew. On May 28, 1894, they reached somewhere around 81 degrees, 34 minutes north.

Nansen calculated that the ship would not drift any farther north and they would not drift over the actual North Pole. He spoke with Otto Sverdrup and with his crew. They agreed with Nansen's new plan—Sverdrup should take charge of the expedition aboard the *Fram* and continue drifting, studying, and mapping the polar seas, and Nansen and Hjalmar Johansen would leave the *Fram* and attempt to reach the North Pole by dogsled.

On March 14, 1895, after two years of moving slowly with the ice pack, Nansen and Hjalmar Johansen left the ship. The weather was mild, only minus 41 degrees Fahrenheit, but on March 21, as they slept in a tent, the air became moist and their clothes froze and they crackled every time they moved. Nansen got frostbite, a sore opened on his wrist, and the wound grew deeper until it almost reached the bone.

The work of traveling across the ice, climbing over massive hummocks, and trudging beside the heavy sledges was exhausting. Sometimes Nansen was so tired, he fell asleep on his feet. The dogs did not always fare well, and one named Livjaegeren was the first to become ill. Nansen wrote: "This was the first dog which had to be killed; but many came afterwards, and it was some of the most disagreeable work we had on the journey" (*Farthest North*, 279).

The dogs endured more than the men, and Nansen reflected upon how hard Johansen had to work them to haul the sledges over the ridges of ice and how it was "undeniable cruelty to the poor animals from first to last, and one must often look back on it with horror."

Nansen calculated that they must be around the eighty-sixth parallel. The North Pole was at 90 degrees, a distance of 240 miles. But the ice conditions grew worse. There were endless moraines, ridges of rough ice, and high, vertical hummocks that stretched to the gray horizon. Even worse, it was becoming clear to him that in spite of their fortitude and ongoing struggle to go north, they were being carried quickly south by the wind and ocean current.

On April 5, Nansen was on the verge of complete despair, but he refocused and decided to continue north for one more day, hoping conditions would improve. Instead the ice grew even worse.

On April 7, Nansen and Johansen reached 86 degrees 13.6 minutes, the farthest north that anyone had ever traveled, but on April 8, after a day of trying to make progress, they were still quickly more or less at the same place.

On April 8, 1895, Nansen realized the North Pole was not possible. He quickly reshaped his plans and changed course to head south for Cape Fligely and Franz Josef Land. First he made a special banquet for Johansen of bread and butter and chocolate, berries, and hot whey drink. They slept in their sleeping bags and in the morning they began their journey home. On

*Sigurd Scott Hansen, Fridtjof Nansen, and Otto Neumann
Sverdrup aboard the* Fram, *drifting in endless days and nights
of light, June 16, 1894.*

*Fridtjof Nansen and Hjalmar Johansen leave the comparative
warmth and safety of the* Fram *and head out
into the frozen and unknown world with the hope of
reaching the North Pole.*

April 12 both Nansen and Johansen forgot to wind their watches. Knowing the time was essential to navigation—the key to figuring out where they were and where they were heading— Nansen wrote:

> The only thing I can now do to find Greenwich mean time is take a time-observation and an observation for latitude, and then estimate the approximate distance from our turning-point on April 8th when I took the last observation for longitude. By this means the error will hardly be great. (*Farthest North,* 290)

By June 14 they had been traveling for three months. It was a monotonous life, dull and depressing, but on June 22 Johansen sighted a bearded seal in open water. Nansen harpooned it and they ate the meat. They began to feel better. They climbed into the kayaks they had been carrying on their sledges and loaded the three dogs and provisions, then balanced the sledges on the kayaks and paddled into open water.

Finally, on July 24, Nansen and Johansen saw land, but they had no idea where they were. They pulled their kayaks ashore, hunted walrus and polar bears, cached the meat immediately, and built a hut from stones. They hung walrus skin from a log, and, for warmth, they slept in one sleeping bag, hibernating up to twenty hours a day. Thoughts of home kept them going.

Months later, when the world thawed again, they resumed their journey. They camped on many unexplored islands and continued paddling beside the ice. On June 12, after an entire day paddling in leaky kayaks, they climbed onto the ice to stretch their legs. Suddenly Nansen noticed that the kayaks were drifting away. Nansen ran to the ice edge, tore off his watch and clothing, dove into the icy water, swam as fast as he could go, and tried to get ahold of the kayaks. On board was everything they needed to survive. Nansen realized they were drifting away faster than he could swim. His arms and legs lost feeling. He became extremely tired. He rolled on his back and swam backstroke. He got a second wind and grabbed a snow-shoe on the kayak's stern.

Nansen managed to get a leg into the kayak and climbed on. The kayaks were tied together, so Nansen had to, with great difficulty, step into one kayak and take a few strokes, and then step into the other and paddle on the other side to keep them on course. He dragged them both to shore. By the time he reached Johansen he was suffering from severe hypothermia. Johansen stripped off Nansen's wet clothes, spread the sleeping bag on the ice, and covered Nansen with everything he could find to get him warm. Nansen shivered for a long time, but gradually he rewarmed.

Nansen and Johansen continued paddling, and on June 17 they landed on another island. Nansen decided to go for a hike and explore the island; he thought he heard a dog bark and a man's voice. He caught sight of the man. It was Frederick Jackson, the leader of the Royal Geographical Society's Jackson-Harmsworth Arctic expedition. Jackson and his crew had been exploring Franz Josef Land. He invited Nansen and Johansen to be his guests, and when the *Windward* came to pick up some of Jackson's crew, Nansen and Johansen sailed with them. On August 13, 1896, they arrived in Norway, and eight days later, Nansen read a telegram from Otto Sverdrup: "Fridtjof Nansen: *Fram* arrived in good condition. All well on board. Shall start at once for Tromsø. Welcome home! Otto Sverdrup."

Nansen read the telegram over and over again before he could believe it was true, and, he wrote, "and then there came a strange, serene happiness over my mind such as I had never known before." And on September 9 the *Fram* with all her crew sailed up Christiania Fjord, and they were given an unforgettable welcome home.

CHAPTER 5

Caves of Death

For two years, Amundsen endured medical school, but when he was twenty-one, his mother passed away. He was relieved that he no longer had to fulfill her wishes and dropped out of the university, but he had one further obligation, that of serving in the military. Amundsen was eager to do so; he believed that the military training would prepare him for life. Because his military service was limited to a few weeks per year, in his free time Amundsen decided to do an Arctic training exercise with his brother Leon as a way to prepare for future polar exploration. This first outing nearly killed both of them.

They skied west of Christiania to the Hardangervidda mountain plateau, four thousand feet high. The plateau extended to Bergen, and there were only two safe trails. In winter, the area was completely deserted. Amundsen was just twenty-two, and his big dreams did not match his level of experience.

Amundsen and Leon skied to the Mogen farmhouse, and the family was surprised to see them. No one ever traveled there at that time of the year. Amundsen planned to leave first thing in the morning, but a blizzard that lasted eight days forced them to stay until the weather improved. The family tried to discourage the two skiers from leaving, but they were set on making the attempt.

They believed they would achieve their goal in two days. They severely underestimated the time it would take and the food and equipment they would need. As they skied across the plateau, each man carried a reindeer sleeping bag on his back. They didn't think of bringing a tent. They had only a few crackers, some chocolate, butter, and a small amount of alcohol. For navigation, they carried a pocket compass and a map of the area. They didn't realize they were unprepared.

The plateau was flat and white, with no distinct landmarks. At twilight, about halfway across the plateau, they found a reindeer herder's hut, but the hut had been boarded up for winter. The air temperature began to drop to minus 10 degrees Fahrenheit. They worked quickly to open the hut and start a fire in the fireplace, but both got severe frostbite on their fingers. They managed to light a fire, but the ventilation was poor, and the room filled with smoke, making it difficult to breathe and to see.

In the morning the storm hadn't abated, and they were forced to stay there for a couple of days. When it stopped snowing, they decided to continue on to the Garden farmhouse, toward the west coast where they could ski down from the plateau.

A heavy wet snow began falling and turned their map to pulp. They could only navigate by compass. When it grew dark, they crawled into their sleeping bags, placed their provisions at the bottom of the bags, and planted their poles beside the sleeping bags as markers.

The blizzard continued all night, and the snow melted on their bodies and saturated their sleeping bags. Amundsen tried to find his bottle of alcohol in his bag. He believed that it would help restore his circulation, but if he had found and drunk the alcohol, he would have put himself in more danger. His body had reduced the blood flow to his extremities, and it had moved the blood to his core to keep his vital organs warm. Drinking the alcohol would have caused the blood to move from his body's core to its exterior. This might have made him feel warmer, but it would have caused him to lose heat more quickly and possibly have caused his death.

When it grew light, Amundsen and Leon decided to turn

around and get back to the farmhouse as quickly as possible, but it began to snow so hard that they could only see a couple of feet in front of them. But they kept moving, and by night they reached a small mountain peak where they decided to sleep in the protection of the mountain. Amundsen built a snow cave a little larger than his body.

He crawled in headfirst. During the night, the snow melted around his feet, and later in the evening, the temperature dropped, and the water froze across the opening of the cave. Amundsen woke up, but he couldn't move. He realized he was frozen in place. He started shouting at the top of his lungs, but Leon couldn't hear him. He began to panic. He wondered if they both were frozen in snow caves that had become snow coffins.

Amundsen heard Leon shouting. Fortunately, his brother had been too exhausted to build a snow cave himself. He dug for hours and finally in the middle of the night freed Amundsen. Neither of them could sleep. They decided to use the stars to guide them.

For a couple of hours they made progress, but Amundsen's brother suddenly disappeared. He fell into a precipice. He had landed on his back on his sleeping bag, and Amundsen managed to pull him out. They decided to wait until dawn to resume their march.

By morning, Leon was too exhausted to move. Amundsen left him and went for help. Amundsen noticed some ski tracks and followed them, and then he spotted a man in the distance. He shouted to the peasant farmer he had stayed with eight days before, and the peasant thought he had seen a ghost. The farmhouse was only an hour away, and so he returned to find Leon and bring him back.

When they reached the farmhouse they were greeted like strangers. It wasn't until Amundsen looked into a mirror that he recognized how much he had changed. His eyes and cheeks had sunken into his face, and his skin was a yellowish green.

A year later, Amundsen learned that the farmer who owned the farmhouse on the western edge of the plateau had noticed some ski tracks that headed toward his farm. Amundsen realized the tracks were theirs. At one point, they had been ten minutes from the farmhouse.

Amundsen's misadventure was one of the most important events to happen to him. It instilled in him the need to be prepared before he ever went into the polar environment again.

CHAPTER 6

Belgica

Amundsen began to develop the skills he needed to attempt the Northwest Passage. He worked on board the *Jason,* a sealing ship, for three summers from 1894 to 1896. In the relentlessly rough, ice-filled waters of the Arctic Ocean, he began to learn how to sail and navigate, and he started to earn his skipper's license.

In all the research Amundsen had done, he discovered that one flaw in every Arctic expedition was that the commander of the expedition was not the ship's captain. The commanders of the expeditions almost always depended upon experienced skippers to navigate and sail their ships. The problem that occurred and recurred was that the expedition team had two different leaders. And as a result there were always divisions within the expedition, with one group—the expedition leader and scientific staff—on one side, and the captain of the ship and his crew on the other.

He was convinced that he needed to be both captain of his ship and the leader of the expedition when he set out on the Northwest Passage attempt. He worked to hone his sailing skills.

During that same time, in the summer of 1895, while Amundsen was on board the *Jason* in the Arctic Ocean, Lieutenant Adrien de Gerlache, of the Belgian navy, was sailing with his friend Lieutenant Emile Danco to the east in the

Greenland Sea. They were testing out the *Castor*, a whaling ship, to see if it would be a suitable ship for an expedition to Antarctica.

Adrien de Gerlache was planning the first scientific expedition to Antarctica, called the Belgian Antarctic Expedition, to study the South Magnetic Pole, to make astronomical observations, and to chart unexplored lands and waters. What fascinated most explorers was the South Magnetic Pole, a migrating point on the earth's surface near the geographic South Pole. This was an area where it became impossible to use a magnetic compass for navigation. This meant that when explorers entered the areas around the South Magnetic Pole and geographic South Pole, they couldn't use the compass to tell them where they were or where they were going.

In areas that were mapped, the charts allowed the polar explorers to navigate with reference to the geographic North or South Pole, and the difference between the direction to the magnetic pole and the geographic pole is known as a variation.

In any case, a compass needle will align itself with the "local" magnetic force, a combination of the horizontal and vertical effects of the earth's magnetic field. In the polar regions the magnetic variation can reach 180 degrees, which means the compass can point in the opposite direction from the true geographic pole. This made navigation in Antarctica tremendously difficult and dangerous. Often the explorers didn't know where they were going, especially in the fog. The explorers hoped that by understanding how the earth's magnetism worked, especially in polar waters and on polar lands, navigation would be made safer.

During the time de Gerlache was testing the *Cantor* in the Greenland Sea to find out if it was suitable for the expedition, he noticed the *Patria*, sailing offshore. He immediately realized that the *Patria* would be a far better vessel for the expedition, and the following year he purchased it. He rechristened the ship the *Belgica*, and he had the ship refitted in the shipyard in Sandefjord, Norway. Amundsen had returned from his training in the Arctic and heard about de Gerlache's expedition to Antarctica. He immediately wrote asking if de Gerlache needed another sailor.

De Gerlache knew of Fridtjof Nansen and Nils Adolf Erik Nordenskiöld, the scientist who had sailed along the coast of Siberia in the *Vega*. De Gerlache was very aware that Scandinavians were tremendous athletes, scholars, inventors, designers, and scientists. He recognized that Scandinavian sailors were also known as terrific navigators and sailors in polar seas. De Gerlache checked Amundsen's references and accepted him as a second officer on the *Belgica*. Amundsen was thrilled. He knew that the expedition would give him the experience to get closer to realizing his own dreams, but he had no idea how much he would be tested or how much he would learn.

Amundsen is thrilled to have Nansen visit the Belgica *before departing from Sanderfjord, June 26, 1897. From left: Adrien de Gerlache (probably), Fridtjof Nansen, Frederick Cook(?), Henryk Arctowski(?), Roald Amundsen, and three unidentified men.*

On June 24, 1897, the *Belgica* sailed out of Sandefjord for Antwerp. Fridtjof Nansen made a special trip to Sandefjord to bid the crew of the *Belgica* bon voyage.

De Gerlache had gathered financial support from a number of sources: businesses, the scientific community, and the Belgian people. He also had found, interviewed, and pulled together a crew of twenty-three men, including officers, engineers, and scientists from Belgium, France, Norway, Poland, and Romania. But there were loose ends. At the last moment, the ship's doctor decided not to join the expedition; that, as it turned out, was a good thing. De Gerlache would find a far more experienced physician, one who would play a major role in de Gerlache's survival and that of his crew.

The *Belgica* sailed out of Ostend, Belgium, on August 16 but was forced to return the next day due to damage to the engine. They set off a second time on August 22. From Ostend, they made a brief stop in Madera, Spain, and then sailed across the Atlantic to Rio de Janeiro in fifty-two days, and in Rio they picked up Frederick Cook, a physician from Brooklyn, New York, who replaced the doctor who had decided not to join the expedition.

Dr. Cook was a rare physician. He had already had some polar experience. Cook had accompanied Robert Peary on Peary's 1891–92 polar expedition in northern Greenland. Peary's initial objective was to be the first man to reach the North Pole, but during a storm en route to Greenland, Peary's right leg was snapped just above the ankle by a tiller attached to the rudder when the ship slammed into ice. Cook set the leg and cared for Peary until he could walk again. The expedition members lived through the winter in a hut on McCormick Bay on the west coast of Greenland.

During that time Dr. Cook immersed himself in the lives of Greenlandic Inuit and focused on how they survived in a polar environment. Cook studied their physiology, their specially designed clothes—the anoraks, hooded parkas, and boots they made from fur that kept the Inuit warm in subzero temperatures in winter. He examined the way they designed their sledges, and he observed the way they worked their dog teams to pull the sledges. He also learned the Greenlandic Inuit language, sampled their food, and studied their customs. All of this experience Cook brought to the *Belgica* expedition.

The *Belgica* sailed south along the coast of South America from Rio to the Strait of Magellan. The area was relatively unexplored, and de Gerlache slowed the *Belgica* to enable the scientists to collect flora and fauna, gather species, and make meteorological observations. Cook took the opportunity to observe and care for some of the Ona and Yahgan Indians in the Tierra del Fuego region who lived a traditional life of fishing and hunting. With Dr. Cook, Amundsen attended to a group of very sick children at a mission and saw the effects of disease that had been transmitted by settlers to the region. Amundsen noted: "It will not be long before the Indians will only be a legend here. The evil of civilization has reached them and it won't stop until the very last one has been wiped out" (*Belgica Diary,* 61). This experience for Amundsen profoundly affected the way he would think about his own expedition.

The *Belgica* sailed south across the stormy and rough Drake Passage toward the South Shetland Islands and then across the Bransfield Strait. The ship slowed once it reached the west coast of Graham Land, the dog-tail-shaped Antarctic Peninsula, which was still partially unmapped. De Gerlache and his crew spent time charting the coast. They discovered the Gerlache Channel and passed through it into the Pacific Ocean.

De Gerlache's original plan had been to have the majority of the crew sail back to South America once the summer research was completed. He planned to stay with a small group of men, including Amundsen, and winter on South Victoria Land, while Georges Lecointe, his second in command, sailed toward Australia and conducted oceanic research. Once he reached southern Australia, Lecointe and the crew would replenish the ship's provisions. But things did not go as planned. Winter came more quickly than expected. De Gerlache decided to keep the crew together and they sailed south toward Antarctica. One afternoon, Amundsen came out to relieve the commander for the watch and discovered that they were battling a gale. Snow was blowing across the decks, and the visibility was dropping to zero. Icebergs were all around. De Gerlache showed one nearby to Amundsen and explained that all during his watch he had been keeping the *Belgica* in the lee of the iceberg because it was protecting them from the strong wind and huge swells. The iceberg had kept them from being pushed off course. De Gerlache told Amundsen to continue doing this. Amundsen followed the orders and passed them on to the next man on watch.

In the morning, Amundsen noticed that the ship wasn't rolling in the swells as it had the night before. He went up to the bridge and discovered that the *Belgica* was floating in a small bay encircled completely by enormous icebergs.

Unable to see the iceberg in the darkness and the snowstorm, or to use a compass, the sailor hadn't noticed until morning that the *Belgica* had been pushed through an opening between two enormous icebergs. Amundsen believed it was a miracle they weren't heaved by large waves into the icebergs and smashed to pieces. They had escaped death, but the danger had not diminished. They managed to get themselves out and began sailing with the Antarctic sea ice on their westward side.

They were slammed by another gale blowing from the north, and the *Belgica* was in danger of being smashed into a wall of sea ice and frozen and imprisoned in ice. They were unprepared for the winter, lacking the clothes, equipment, or supplies to sustain the entire crew through an Antarctic winter as they drifted around uncharted polar seas. Years later, reflecting upon his life's experience, Amundsen wrote:

> The instinct of any navigator accustomed to the Polar sea would have been to use every effort to get away to the north and into the open sea. This we could have done. But at this juncture my two superior officers saw an opening in the ice field to the south of us and decided to ride before the storm into the opening. They could not have made a greater mistake. I saw and understood fully

the great danger they exposed the whole expedition to, but I was not asked for my opinion, and discipline required me to keep silent. (*My Life as an Explorer*, 25–26)

Amundsen's feelings were completely opposite when he was twenty-five. He couldn't understand why the scientists were afraid, why they didn't want to push farther south and explore uncharted waters.

De Gerlache and Lecointe discussed their options. They decided they needed to push farther south even if it meant being locked in the ice through the entire winter. They had no way of knowing the toll this decision would take upon them and their crew.

In the deep blackness of the Antarctic winter, the crew slept for up to twenty hours a day, and when they awoke they fought a constant battle with deep depression. Two men went insane. Another died from heart failure. The entire crew came down with scurvy.

They were not getting vitamin C in their diet. Their bodies were unable to synthesize collagen, the main component of cartilage, ligaments, tendons, bones, and teeth. It is important for strengthening the blood vessels and skin. Because of this, the crew got dark purple spots on their bodies, mostly on their legs. Their eyes became sunken into their heads, their noses and gums bled; they had nonstop diarrhea, suffered from depression, and then, when made immobile, they could have died. Cook knew the symptoms of scurvy from his previous expeditions with Robert Peary in the Arctic. Cook had discovered that the reason the Eskimo—which means "people who eat raw meat"—didn't get scurvy was because the raw meat they ate contained enough vitamin C to prevent it. Cook and Amundsen spent long hours on the ice in bitter cold, hunting for crab-eater and Weddell seals and emperor penguins to feed raw to the crew. Amundsen wrote on July 11, 1898:

The commander, Lecointe and Arctowski are very ill but they are not yet in danger. The penguin the doctor and I caught yesterday was eaten today. I ate my piece raw and it tasted excellent. I ate my piece raw of course in order to get the energy from the meat directly. It also improves the circulation of the blood. Lecointe, who felt very ill this morning, put his papers in order and explained them to me. He looks very ill but according to the doctor he is not yet in danger. His legs and face are swollen. In ten days' time the sun will return and if we last until then everything will be okay. (*Belgica Diary*, 118)

Amundsen listened to Dr. Cook, and he remained active, skied when he could, ate the raw meat, and sat by a warm fire on the ship to combat the effects of the darkness and its impact on his psyche.

They worked together, sometimes with another crew member, dragging the heavy wooden sledges miles across the uneven ice and snow, and over hummocks up to twelve feet high, searching for seals and penguins. When they managed to find the animals, and kill them for food and for their fur, they loaded the heavy seals and penguins onto the sledges and then had to drag them back to the ship. They were completely exhausted by their efforts.

But Dr. Cook was in tune with the environment, and he was ingenious. He observed the penguins and noticed that they were highly efficient in the way they slid across the ice on their bellies. Cook came up with the idea of attaching penguin skin to the underside of the sledge runners; these enabled the sledges to glide much more easily across the ice.

De Gerlache was completely repelled at the thought of eating raw meat and ordered the crew not to eat any either. The effects of scurvy took over the crew. They all took to their bunks.

Dr. Cook and Amundsen attended to them, and Amundsen admired Cook all the more; he would one day emulate him. Amundsen wrote,

He [Dr. Cook], of all the ship's company, was the one man of unfaltering courage, unfailing hope, endless cheerfulness, and unwearied kindness. When anyone was sick, he was at his bedside to comfort him; when anyone was disheartened, he was there to encourage and inspire. (*My Life as an Explorer,* 30)

Still, in spite of Dr. Cook and Amundsen's care, the crew, without a change in diet, became weaker. De Gerlache and Lecointe were immobilized in their bunks and made out their wills.

On Sunday, November 13, 1898, de Gerlache called a meeting. Amundsen, as third in command, believed that he would be put in charge of the expedition if something happened to de Gerlache and Lecointe. What Amundsen didn't know was that de Gerlache had signed a contract with his sponsors, the Geographical Society in Brussels, and, if something happened to him or to Lecointe, a Belgian sailor, the fourth in line to command, would take over.

Amundsen saw this contract for the first time that day. The contract read:

In the event that during the expedition I am no longer the commander of this ship and if Mr. Lecointe is unable to take over command then I will decide who succeeds me. My successor will be selected from among the Belgian officers or members of the scientific staff unless absolutely necessary to deviate from this rule. In the latter case command may be transferred to a seaman from a foreign country. Signed Adrien de Gerlache, Brussels, 19th March 1897. (*Belgica Diary,* 154–55)

Amundsen was furious. He was the only officer who had not seen or signed the contract. He felt that he had been treated unfairly because he was Norwegian, not Belgian, and that a less qualified Belgian officer would be selected over him if something happened to the commander and Lecointe.

The next morning I asked to talk to the commander. He asked me to wait a few days with what I had to say and I did. Today, Wednesday morning, I went to see him again and this time he received me. I said to him, "I wish to make my plans clear to you in a few words, Commander. Since learning of the contract between yourself and the Geographical Society I consider my position on this ship as no longer existing. For me this is no longer a Belgian Antarctic expedition, the *Belgica* is an ordinary ship, stuck fast in the ice. It is my duty to help the handful of people here on board. For that reason, commander, I will continue my work as if nothing has happened. I will do my duty as a human being." (*Belgica Diary*, 155–56)

De Gerlache apologized for the contract, and

he could not see what I could see but admitted that it had been wrong to sign such a contract. . . . Finally he said that he saw no way of solving this matter now but later on he would do everything possible. I replied that I entirely agreed with this. Not much can be solved here in the ice pack. (*Belgica Diary*, 156)

De Gerlache answered Amundsen with a letter and wrote:

I did suggest to you during our interview at Brussels that you take part in the expedition as 2nd officer. You accepted and I believe that since that day I have treated you as second officer. It never occurred to me that the 3rd officer—be he Belgian—would have the right of command of the expedition above a 2nd officer and it is without doubt that this case is one of those that the authors of the contract include under "absolutely necessary." (*Belgica Diary*, 158–59)

Amundsen accepted the letter, but the hard feelings did not go away. Despite that, Amundsen, as always, drew something from the situation. This experience would not be repeated on his future expeditions.

*Amundsen caught three penguins and assisted Dr. Cook
on his rounds attending to the sick captain and the crew.
He fed them penguin and seal meat and had them sit half
naked by a hot stove for a few hours each day to replace the
solar radiation and help them recover from their depressed
physical and psychological state.*

De Gerlache finally agreed to Dr. Cook's recommendation
of eating raw meat. Amundsen and Dr. Cook gathered the few
healthy men together and dug the seal meat out of the snowbanks around the *Belgica*. They chopped the meat into steaks,
and sautéed it lightly in butter, being careful not to overcook
it and destroy the vitamin C. They fed the seal steaks to the
crew, and de Gerlache and Lecointe ate the meat as well. Their
health improved. Their energy came back. The constant oppres-
sive headaches de Gerlache and Lecointe had experienced began
to fade, and as sunshine returned, the crew began to dream of
sailing north.

Unfortunately, spring was slow in coming to Antarctica in
January 1899. The ice did not break, and the temperatures were
still below freezing. Faced with a new challenge, Dr. Cook
developed the idea of digging the *Belgica* out. On January 9,

1899, Cook and the crew began to dig two trenches to open a channel for the *Belgica* to sail out of the ice.

They tried using explosives to burst their way free. The explosive charges weren't strong enough, so they sawed and chopped their way through the trenches. The channels refroze, and so they returned and continued cutting and breaking the ice day and night. After more than a month's work, on February 13, Amundsen felt the ship starting to move, and on February 14 the *Belgica* shed her icy shackles and broke free from where she had been trapped for a long winter. They sailed about one hundred yards and were stopped again by the ice. But the following day the channel reopened, and the *Belgica* sailed for another month through the ice pack and then north toward South America. The *Belgica* expedition lasted for thirteen months. It was the first time an expedition had spent an entire winter in Antarctica. The *Belgica* would sail back to the Strait of Magellan and nearly sink in a gale and almost hit a reef. The scientists returned with a wealth of information about Antarctica, and de Gerlache and his crew charted new lands and seas. Amundsen sailed home aboard a fast passenger ship to work on his next set of challenges to prepare him for his own journey of exploration.

CHAPTER 7

Leaving Norway

Amundsen returned to Norway and completed his skipper's license. He began coordinating an expedition to the Arctic. He wanted to be the first to sail through the Northwest Passage; his objective was also to study the North Magnetic Pole. The North Magnetic Pole had the greatest influence on navigation in the Arctic regions. Knowing the North Magnetic Pole's position would allow sailors in any part of the world to get a better fix on their own position.

On June 1, 1831, Sir James Clark Ross, from Britain, had first discovered the North Magnetic Pole on Cape Adelaide on the Boothia Peninsula in Canada in his attempt to find the Northwest Passage. Clark and his crew nearly died of starvation.

Amundsen contacted Fridtjof Nansen, who by then had earned a doctorate and had become a world-renowned scientist. Nansen had done groundbreaking work on neurology and aerodynamics and was considered one of the fathers of oceanography. Wisely, Amundsen asked Nansen for his help, and Nansen not only endorsed Amundsen, but he also made contacts for him. Perhaps this was because Nansen had learned through his own studies and his collaborations with other scientists around the world the need to support others; there was also a strong friendship, a mentorship, between Nansen and Amundsen.

Amundsen needed to learn how to accurately measure the North Magnetic Pole and use new scientific instruments. He contacted the director of the British Observatory at Kew and asked for permission to study there but was refused, so he continued moving forward and contacted the director of the meteorological observatory in Christiania. Amundsen asked the director to introduce him to Geheimrath George von Neumayer, the director of Deutsche Seewarte at Hamburg, one of the most respected men studying magnetism at that time. Amundsen's chances of meeting Neumayer were slim, and his funding was very limited, but he believed that he had to meet him.

Neumayer agreed to meet, and Amundsen was escorted into his office. He was so nervous that his heart was pounding in his chest. He was taken by the gentleness in the elderly man's eyes, and he quickly gave Neumayer his background and explained that he wanted to learn how to make magnetic observations. Neumayer sensed that there was more to the story, and he encouraged Amundsen to explain. When Amundsen told Neumayer that he wanted to find the Northwest Passage and study the location of the North Magnetic Pole, the elderly man stood up and threw his arms around Amundsen and told him that his work would benefit all of mankind.

Neumayer took Amundsen under his wing for the next three months and taught him about the theory and practice of magnetic observation. Neumayer invited him to dine with him, and Amundsen was appreciative of Neumayer's kindness; he made a point of being at the observatory every day and learning all he could with great enthusiasm. After he completed his studies, Neumayer helped him gain access to the observatories in Wilhelmshaven and Potsdam.

Amundsen returned to Norway, raised money, purchased the *Gjøa,* the ship he would use in the Northwest Passage attempt, and spent a year training in the waters off Norway and Greenland and collecting data for Dr. Nansen as a way to thank him for his help. Before he set off on the Northwest Passage expedition, he wrote to Nansen and asked him what kind of research he would like Amundsen to do. Nansen was considered a leader in the field of oceanography, and in the early

1900s very little was known about the currents in the Arctic Ocean.

Happily, Fridtjof Nansen gave Amundsen a small black hardback notebook with sixty-five pages of what he thought Amundsen needed to know for the expedition and how he could help Nansen with his research. Nansen drew illustrations that depicted the instruments for water, snow, ice, and plankton sampling as well as the thermometer for taking water temperatures. Nansen gave Amundsen specific directions on the depths to take the measurements and the types of observations Amundsen could make for him, such as measuring currents and ocean ridges. Nansen was especially interested in the currents in the Barents Sea, Murman Sea, and the Gulf Stream and North Cape currents. He had a theory about the currents in the Kara Sea, but he wasn't sure if they were correct, and he was also very interested in the currents in the sea around Spitsbergen.

Nansen asked Amundsen to take as many samples as he could from the polar current on the east coast of Greenland because he believed they would solve many of the riddles about the current.

Nansen also asked Amundsen to pay attention to the color of the ocean, whether it was green, blue, or deep blue-green. He believed that the deep blue color indicated that it was water from the Gulf Stream; greenish or brown water could indicate a mixture of coastal water and polar water, and these both contained a lot of plankton. Jellyfish were also very important. He believed that they came from coastal waters, and he was most interested to see if Amundsen observed any jellyfish in the polar streams. Nansen asked him not to forget to draw a map in his journal and on every watch note the color, size, and number of jellyfish. Nansen also noted that in the holes on ice floes were colonies of brown algae that he believed could help determine the origin of the sea ice. And he also asked Amundsen to take as many soundings—depth measurements—as possible during the journey. He told him how to use tubes to sample water and plankton. And he asked Amundsen to see if he noticed a strange phenomenon that Nansen observed in 1893 when he was on the *Fram* in the Nordenskiöld Archipelago. Nansen had observed "dead water," which a Swedish scientist, V. Walfrid Ekman, described as a lighter layer of water resting on top of a denser, more salty layer of water. It had a strange effect on ships, reducing their speed and maneuverability, and sometimes made it extremely difficult to steer. Amundsen realized that taking these observations for Nansen would help Amundsen discover more about the oceans and navigate the Northwest Passage.

The following year, 1902–1903, Amundsen was exhausted from fund-raising from scientific societies and private sources. He interviewed and handpicked his crew: Godfred Hansen, first officer; Helmer Hanssen, second officer; Anton Lund, a former sealer; Peder Ristvedt, engineer; Gustav Wiik, second engineer, and Adolf Lindström, cook.

Amundsen worked frantically to prepare the *Gjøa* for the expedition, and a day before they were to sail, he faced the largest crisis of his career. One of his creditors was pressuring him to pay for the supplies for the expedition, and he threatened to have Amundsen arrested. Amundsen urgently called his crew together and explained the situation. They needed to take desperate action, and the crew supported his decision.

To avoid the creditors and an end to the expedition, at midnight on June 16, 1903, under the cover of a heavy rainstorm, Amundsen and his crew sneaked out of Norway. He wrote,

> When dawn arose on our truculent creditor, we were safely out on the open main, seven as light-hearted pirates as ever flew the black flag, disappearing upon a quest that should take us three years and on which we were destined to succeed in an enterprise that had baffled our predecessors for four centuries. (*My Life as an Explorer*, 36)

The *Gjøa* sailed across the North Atlantic through mostly smooth seas with little ice, and on July 24 reached Godhavn on Disko Island, halfway up the west coast of Greenland. The *Gjøa's* first stop was to load on board twenty Greenlandic sled dogs and supplies. Reaching Greenland was like finally taking flight or completing the first mile in a long swim. Amundsen knew that he was really on his way toward his goal. He had entered waters he had never explored.

CHAPTER 8

Greenland Shark

I had read about Amundsen as a teenager; I decided I would follow in his wake. When I first started considering Greenland as a place I would one day visit, I hadn't read yet about his Northwest Passage journey. I never realized how closely I would follow his path. I would go to Antarctica first, like Amundsen, then follow him to Greenland.

Now as we flew over Greenland, I pressed my forehead against the cool window.

In June 1972, on my way to swim across the English Channel, I flew on a 747 with my mother bound for London. It was one of the most exciting times in my life. I was fifteen years old, and I was on my first flight across the North Atlantic. The sky was clear and the water far below bright sapphire and darker shades of blue where the currents changed. All at once, the edge of Greenland, the world's largest island, most of it within the Arctic Circle, was rising up out of the ocean.

White glacial domes shimmered in the robin's-egg-blue sky; ribbons of fractured ice and snow clung to black rocky pinnacles; rivers of ice and snow, pushed by the force of gravity, creped and tumbled in wide S-shaped bands into the sea. I had never seen anything like this world before. I wanted to stop and explore. I had never felt so strongly about going anywhere as I did about Greenland. Something was drawing me there.

I looked thirty-five thousand feet straight down and held my breath. There was something oval and white floating on the dark blue water. It was an iceberg! It was the first time I had ever seen an iceberg, and it was as awe inspiring as seeing the North Star for the first time.

We continued our flight across the North Atlantic and landed at Heathrow, and I went on to swim the English Channel. I flew over again the following year when I returned to swim the Channel a second time. My dream of going to Greenland was even stronger, but I was only sixteen years old, and I had no idea of how anyone could swim with icebergs. I swam across various waterways, and eventually swam in colder waters. Finally I began to think about how to get to Greenland and swim there. No one I knew had ever been to Greenland but Robert Ballard, an oceanographer at the Woods Hole Oceanographic Institution who, like me, had attended the University of California, Santa Barbara, had. Robert Ballard was famous for discovering the RMS *Titanic,* the Olympic-class British passenger liner that had sunk in 1912 when the ship struck an iceberg in the North Atlantic south of the Grand Banks of Newfoundland.

Heart pounding, I called Ballard at Woods Hole in the late 1970s and told him everything in one breath—my background, that we both had attended UCSB, that because of his experience with the *Titanic* in the North Atlantic, he might know what I needed to learn to swim off Greenland: information about tides, current speeds, water temperatures, weather patterns, wind speed and direction during the summer months. Ballard knew of my background and was helpful and put me in touch with other people in his group who provided me with more details. The information, though, was not all that promising. The water temperature off Greenland in summer was, at the most, 38 degrees Fahrenheit and could be a lot colder.

I kept working at it, swimming in colder waterways, and just when I thought that I was ready to attempt a swim in Greenland, I heard about the Greenland shark. I was in Vancouver for a Canadian television program, and while waiting for the show, I watched a program called *Discovery Canada.* There was a shark expert answering question about polar sharks. I watched a huge fifteen-foot-long Greenland shark swim slowly across the television screen as the expert explained that the Greenland shark was very dangerous. It was known for being sluggish and for being cannibalistic, immune to the poison in other Greenland sharks' flesh. The Greenland shark ate salmon, crabs, flesh from dead whales, polar bears, and seals. Even the remains of reindeer were found in their stomachs.

Being smaller than most of those animals, I had second thoughts about swimming in Greenland's waters. But I needed to confirm with my shark expert friends how dangerous the Greenland shark really was to me; I didn't want to be scared off and, at the same time, was trying to figure out how to swim there safely. Friends suggested I swim in a net. The problem with that was there was drag, and I would be pulled along in the wake of the net, not making the swim under my own powers.

No one swam voluntarily in Greenland's waters, and I wasn't sure if there was a Danish coast guard that patrolled the waters, or a dive team. I just couldn't figure it out, and I was scared of the Greenland shark. Instead I decided to go south and swim in the cold waters off Antarctica. Without knowing it at that time, I was following Amundsen's path. He went south to go north, and I would be doing the same. What I didn't realize was that one of the biggest clues to figuring out if a Greenland swim would be possible would occur on the Quark expedition ship on my way to Antarctica in 2002.

Within the first few hours on board, I met Adam Ravtech, a documentary filmmaker who was working for *60 Minutes*. Adam looked familiar. He was of medium height, lean, nimble, with broad shoulders, and had dark brown wavy hair and a big smile. I thought I recognized his voice, and I remembered we had met at California State University, Long Beach, at the shark research lab.

It had been at least twenty years since I'd seen him. Adam had been doing research with Don Nelson, my shark expert friend, on little lemon sharks and small horn sharks. Adam had studied how sharks hunt and navigate by using the one hundred to fifteen hundred tiny black pores on their heads and snouts called ampullae of Lorenzini. He explained that the black pores are filled with electrically conductive jelly, and the bottoms of the pores are lined with hairlike cells called cilia. When fish or swimmers move past, they emit a weak electrical current, and this electrical current is detected by the shark's ampullae of Lorenzini. The cilia triggers at the base of the pores release neurotransmitters in the shark's brain, and the shark becomes aware of possible food in the water.

Adam explained that sharks are probably more sensitive to electric fields than any other animal. They can easily detect swimmers by their muscle contractions and perhaps the beating of their hearts, because humans and animals produce electrical fields when their muscles contract. But a shark can also detect weak electrochemical fields when its prey is paralyzed. Sharks are so good at using their ampullae of Lorenzini that they can even tell where prey is hiding in the sand.

Sharks may also use their ampullae of Lorenzini to detect the electrical fields that are produced by ocean currents that move in the earth's magnetic field and use these to orient themselves underwater and to navigate. And because their muscles contract when they swim, they can sense the electrical field in their own bodies. They may be able to use that to feel the earth's magnetic field and know which direction they are going.

The gel-like substance in the ampullae of Lorenzini has electrical properties that allow changes in temperature to be transmitted into electrical information that a shark can use to detect temperature gradients—temperature changes in different areas of the ocean.

What Adam told me made me think that the Greenland shark could probably detect the beats, the electrical impulses, of the human heart. This didn't make me feel more confident. But Adam assured me that the Greenland shark wouldn't be a problem.

Since he'd left the world of research, he had been working on documentaries about polar bears and walrus, and for twenty years he had been filming how climate change was affecting their survival.

When Adam mentioned that he had done a lot of underwater camera work, I asked him if he had ever encountered the Greenland shark. Not only had he filmed them, he had footage of one with him. We immediately went down to his cabin, and he pulled out a video and a small television screen and played the footage for me.

The shark Adam filmed was maybe sixteen feet long, with a massive head and stunningly sharp teeth. It was coffee-colored with a small dorsal fin. Adam swam close to the shark so that he could capture its head and face and then one of its eyes. I was squirming inside. I couldn't imagine ever getting that close to such a large shark. Adam must have been within a foot of it.

Adam pointed out the black pores, the ampullae of Lorenzini, on the Greenland shark's face. He captured a close-up of its jaw and large white serrated teeth. He explained that the Greenland shark's diet didn't include humans, and they wouldn't be interested in me.

Adam was somewhat reassuring, but it was hard to suddenly go from being scared of the immense shark to accepting what Adam told me. I had to weigh this with what Don Nelson, my longtime shark-expert friend and Adam's mentor, told me. He warned that sharks were unpredictable, and once when he had been out on a dive studying gray reef sharks, one of the sharks suddenly attacked him, even though it hadn't shown any sign of aggression.

Adam had spent at least twenty summers filming in Arctic waters, and he had been very close to the Greenland shark and had never had a problem. I was convinced. He smiled and said, "It's not the Greenland sharks you have to worry about, it's the walrus. They can be aggressive. One grabbed ahold of my diving partner when we were filming a documentary, and I had to grab the diver and pull him out of the water. But you should be okay, as long as you stay away from where the walrus haul out"—the places where walrus pull themselves out of the water onto the rocks or beach.

Adam offered to help me with contacts in Greenland, and I realized that my reason for going to Antarctica wasn't only to swim there, but was also to make this connection with him and take him up on his offer to help with a swim in Greenland. I verified the information I had been given twenty years before, about the water temperatures. Adam explained that in summer, on the warmer west coast of Greenland, water temperatures would be around 36 degrees Fahrenheit, but the water was warming up there, and it could be as high as 38 degrees Fahrenheit. In the spring, the water would be a lot cooler, in the high twenties.

Like Amundsen's first trip to Antarctica, mine would be to explore, learn, and work with my crew. I was also going to push myself further than I ever had before. If it worked, then I could go for Greenland. With amazing support from my crew, I swam 1.22 miles in twenty-five minutes in 32-degree-Fahrenheit water and completed the first Antarctic swim.

There were things that needed to be improved upon. We'd set up the swim with three Zodiacs (hard-shelled inflatable motorboats), three physicians, and three crew members who could pull me out of the water if there was a problem. Bob Griffith was in the lead boat out in front with a rope, Dan Cohen was in the Zodiac beside me in a dry suit, and Barry Binder was in the same Zodiac. If something went wrong and I couldn't get myself out of the water, Dan would jump in and swim over to me and pull me over to Barry's boat. If we needed more assistance, Bob would throw a lasso toward me, and Dan would loop it over my shoulders and arms, and Bob would pull me into his boat. As a backup, we also looped a small piece of rope through the back of my swimsuit and tied it, so that it could be grabbed if I needed to be pulled out. It was a good backup plan, but it needed to be improved on in case there were problems off Greenland.

Friends of mine were rock climbers, and I knew they wore harnesses when they climbed. Other friends were in the U.S. Coast Guard, and they showed me the harnesses coast guard rescue swimmers wore when they jumped into the ocean to rescue people. Their harnesses were elaborate. What we needed was someone who could create a hybrid. June McKenna could design just about anything, and Kyle, her son, was an avid rock climber. Together they created a simple, easily visible, cross-the-heart-and-back bright orange harness that I could wear with a carabiner, a clamp, looped through the harness, a place where another carabiner could be attached that was connected to a rope.

We didn't know where to place the carabiner, on the front or the back of the harness. It didn't seem like a big deal, but we wondered if it was easier to pull someone out more quickly one way or the other. I got in touch with Richard Galdish of the U.S. Coast Guard about doing a test swim with the harness in the Hudson River. Henry Hudson had discovered the river in his attempt to find the Northwest Passage, and it seemed like a great way to remember him, and a good place to gather with my crew to test out the harness. Rich told me that U.S. Coast Guard rescue swimmers wore swimming harnesses with a ring on the back to which a retrieving line could be fastened. Before the swimmer jumped into the water to make a rescue, the boat crew attached a long rope with a carabiner to the ring on the back of the rescue swimmer's harness. The rescue swimmer swam over to the victim, held on to him, and when the crew pulled them to the boat, the rescue swimmer and victim remained on their backs with their faces out of the water so they were able to breathe throughout the rescue. The harness did not provide any type of flotation; it only enabled the crew to pull them to the boat quickly and get them out of the water.

We decided to go with the U.S. Coast Guard model, and we needed to figure out how to use the harness-and-rope combination effectively. Friends with the swift-water rescue team with Long Beach Fire and Lifeguard Department in California invited Bob Griffith, one of my crew members, and me to join them in Long Beach and train with them.

The lifeguards had me jump into the water off the dive platform at the back of their rescue boat. They leaned over and clamped the rope to the carabineer on the harness and then looped the rope back and forth onto itself; each lifeguard grabbed an end, pushed the rope down and then up three times, gaining momentum each time; and on the third time they popped me out of the water. Bob Griffith learned the technique from them, and then we met with Bill Lee. When Bill and I were teenagers we swam for different swim teams and we competed against each other. He had played water polo at UCSB, and I had been the assistant coach for the men's water polo and swim teams. He had been a Newport Beach lifeguard and later became a director for Smith Barney.

When Bill heard that I planned to swim in Greenland, he immediately offered to be one of the support crew. Bill introduced me to his friend Gretchen Goodall from Citigroup. When Gretchen discovered that I was going to swim in Greenland, she offered to help by taking care of the logistics and whatever else might be needed for the trip.

We were from all different parts of the United States, and we decided to meet in New York City to test out the harness and have Bob Griffith teach Bill how to pop a swimmer out of the water. The water would be too cold in Greenland to do any kind of test there. My plan didn't work out. Because of the security concerns around Manhattan post-9/11, I couldn't get clearance to conduct a test in the Hudson or neighboring waterways.

Something better came along. When Bill found out that I was not making progress, he contacted Craig Pfiffer, the vice president of his company, and Craig suggested that we do a test swim off Long Island, where there weren't restrictions and the water would be cleaner. We got ahold of a prototype Zodiac 1800 boat for the test swim.

It all worked as planned. Our next step was to board the first historic flight on Greenland Airlines directly from Baltimore, Maryland, to Kangerlussuaq, Greenland.

CHAPTER 9

Greenland East and West

We arrived at Kangerlussuaq Airport on time for our flight to Ilulissat, but we were on hold because of rain and fog. Neither Bob, Bill, Gretchen, nor I could understand the announcements in Greenlandic or Danish, or even English over the PA system. We were afraid that we would miss the only flight that day to Ilulissat, which would throw off our plans. We had a meeting set up in Ilulissat with two local people who were going to help us decide the course of the swim.

Gretchen was busy checking with the agent at the airline counter. Bill and Bob were watching the tarmac for planes, and I was trying to figure out who else we could talk with who might know about our flight status.

I noticed a woman and a man, who had flight bags beside them with U.S. Air Force tags attached to the bags. They were sitting across from each other talking quietly. They looked relaxed, as if they were longtime friends. The woman was tall, athletic-looking, with a kind face softly framed with short wavy golden brown hair. She was speaking, leaning slightly forward in her chair, and the man was leaning back with his arms spread out along the top of the adjacent seat rests. He was totally open to the conversation, but they both looked a little tired, like two athletes after a long workout. They looked like they were recovering.

An announcement came over the PA system, words that were complete gibberish to me, but the woman and man lis-

75

tened momentarily and seemed to understand, and the man made a comment and they stayed in their chairs. They seemed very familiar with the airport and how everything operated. They could multiply our force—help us—but I wasn't sure about interrupting them.

To gather confidence, I remembered the time after my swim across Lake Titicaca. My support crew and I were on an airplane that lost an engine over Barranquilla, Colombia. The pilot was forced to make an emergency landing. The United States didn't have rights to land in Colombia, and diplomatic relations between the United States and Colombia were bad at that time.

Pete Kelly, one of our team members, who spoke fluent Spanish and had studied Latin American affairs for years, told me that we were landing in an unsafe place where there were three guerrilla groups fighting government troops in the jungles surrounding the airport.

The plane we were sitting in was a target. Pete made me realize that we needed to have a plan to get out of there. My first thought was that I hoped Bob Gelbard, a good friend who had been the U.S. ambassador to Bolivia and had helped us with the Lake Titicaca swim, would start to wonder why he hadn't heard from us about the swim.

For six hot, steamy hours we waited in the plane for engine parts to be delivered. Pete continued listening to the news updates. When he spoke, he tried to sound calm, but he was worried. He noted that there were no inbound flights, possibly because the fighting was nearby. In addition, the place we had landed was a major drug trafficking region.

When the airline pilot announced that the Colombian government had given us permission to leave the airplane and wait in the terminal, I didn't feel any more at ease, but as we disembarked, I noticed six men dressed in U.S. Army uniforms. They each looked agitated.

I remembered that Barry Binder, another member of our crew, had been in the U.S. Army. When we moved to a corner of the terminal, I told Barry what Pete had told me and asked him if he thought it would be a good idea for him and Pete to introduce themselves to the army men and, if they weren't aware of what was happening, have Pete tell them what he knew.

None of the army men were fluent in Spanish; they knew something was happening but didn't know exactly what. One of them, a captain, asked one of the team to use his radio and communicate with someone at a base somewhere. Pete let the captain know that he would keep them updated and that if they felt a need to leave, we would follow them. They asked if we knew of other Americans on the flight. We hadn't met any others, but our friend Deborah Ford was from Australia and was part of our team, and they said she'd be welcome to join them, too.

For the next three hours we waited in the terminal. The sun had set, and the jungle came alive with wild parrot calls and screeches and gunfire. Finally another American airplane arrived, and we charged into the plane, buckled up, and flew out of Colombia.

Waiting at the airport in Kangerlussuaq, Greenland, wasn't like being in Barranquilla, Colombia. It wasn't a critical situation, but maybe the U.S. Air Force would give us guidance. We were on such a tight schedule, with only five days to complete the swim. If we were delayed in Kangerlussuaq, our options for Ilulissat would be dramatically diminished.

The man rubbed his hand across his smooth face. Was he tired? Waking up? Bored? Would he want to talk, or would I be intruding? The woman stopped talking and smiled, and she seemed open. He inquisitively looked at me.

Start with the obvious and build, and see how far you can get: "Are you in the U.S. Air Force?" I asked.

They said yes.

"Are you busy?" I asked.

They shook their heads. I explained that I was with my friends waiting for the flight to Ilulissat and we couldn't understand anything over the PA system. We were afraid we'd miss our flight. The woman smiled and said that sometimes they had a hard time understanding the announcements too.

She said, "Don't worry, you're not going to miss your flight. The visibility is poor, and the wind's increasing." She looked across the tarmac at the wind sock. "And there are cross winds."

"It will be an hour or more before any flights can land or take off," she said.

For most people, talking about the weather was a way to socially engage, but in this case, it was what mattered most to me. I could tell she was aware that I was intensely interested. This wasn't the unusual response unless you worked in her world. She offered me a seat and introduced herself; her name was Samantha East and the man sitting across from her was Brian Gomula. He nodded and smiled. He was tall, trim, and tanned.

"What is the U.S. Air Force doing in Greenland? Are you based here?" I asked.

Samantha explained, "We're in the New York Air National Guard's One Hundred Ninth Airlift Wing, and we're part of the U.S. Air Force. We're based out of Stratton Air National Guard Base at Schenectady County Airport near Scotia, New York. Part of our mission is Operation Deep Freeze."

"Didn't that start with Admiral Richard Byrd, who competed with Lindbergh to become the first man to fly across the Atlantic? Wasn't Byrd the first man to fly to the South Pole and back? Didn't he set up some kind of stations in Antarctica?" I asked.

"Yes. McMurdo and the South Pole." She smiled and seemed happily surprised.

"I've been to Antarctica and I love history, reading about people who achieve things that most people would think impossible. If you're connected to a mission in Antarctica, why are you flying in Greenland?"

Samantha explained that the U.S. Air Force supported the scientists doing research in Greenland and in Antarctica. It was a joint mission between the air force and the National Science Foundation. She said that the air force flew LC-130s Hercules. They were nicknamed "Hercs" and "Skiers," because they were equipped with skis to land on snow.

The only cargo planes I knew of were C-17 Globemasters, built in Long Beach, California. They were massive aircraft, so large that I wondered how they got airborne. Often on the way to the beach, I pulled over to the side of Seal Beach Boulevard to watch them on their final approach for landing at the Los Alamitos military base.

The LC-130s were about one-third the size of a C-17, which enabled them to fly into more remote areas where the C-17s couldn't land. Samantha said that they trained in Greenland, landing on and taking off from the Greenland ice cap, to prepare them for the flights in Antarctica.

She explained that the C-17s were used in Antarctica to transport heavy cargo and people, but they just flew from New Zealand to McMurdo Station and back. McMurdo is the main base for the United States in Antarctica. The C-17 only has wheels so it can't land in the snow like the LC-130s. The C-17 also makes airdrops to far-reaching sites on the continent.

"Samantha, are you a pilot?" I asked.

"I'm the navigator. For the LC-130s we use a navigator. We have a flight crew that works together to fly the aircraft."

I thought for a moment, and said, "So as a navigator you give directions to the pilot and he listens to you?" This seemed unusual. Men aren't always good at accepting directions from a woman.

They smiled. They were amused by my naïve question.

"The air force is a professional organization and we're trained to perform our jobs and to work together," Samantha said.

"Brian, are you a pilot?"

"I'm a navigator, too," he said, and he explained that one navigator flew on the LC-130.

"But why do you need a navigator on an airplane? Aren't there navigation systems that you can use to guide the airplane?"

"Many of the navigational instruments don't work well or at all in the polar regions, and so we have to use different methods for navigation," Brian explained.

I wondered about the magnetic showers, the astronomical events Lindbergh wrote about in *The Spirit of St. Louis,* his story about trying to be the first man to fly from New York to Paris. He was flying somewhere off the coast of Greenland, and his magnetic compass stopped working. He was flying though the clouds and couldn't see anything. He wondered if something called magnetic showers were interfering with his compass. "Do your instruments not function well because of magnetic showers?" I asked.

Samantha nodded. "And also because of our close proximity to the North Magnetic Pole or South Magnetic Pole."

To read about this in Lindbergh's biography, and then to realize how much these forces of nature affect life and navigation, even today, was amazing to me.

I asked Samantha what it was like to be in an environment where she worked mostly with men.

She loved doing her job, and she said the men she worked with were completely professional.

"Are they good guys?" I asked.

"Yes, I married one of them," she said with a very big smile.

"Is he a navigator, too?"

"No, he's a pilot." She paused.

I laughed—a navigator marrying a pilot, what a great match. And she took his name—East. What a perfect last name for a navigator.

"We met in the chow hall at McMurdo Station in Antarctica."

"How romantic. Who would have ever thought!"

"Guess life takes you where you're meant to go," Samantha said.

Samantha East, self-portrait, 2007–8 season, Beardmore Camp, Antarctica. Altitude about six thousand feet, about 10 degrees Fahrenheit. The skiway is about two miles long, located at 84 degrees south latitude, or about 415 miles from the South Pole.

Samantha explained that from what she'd experienced the weather in Greenland in the springtime was very changeable, but the changes weren't as rapid or random as in Antarctica. Low-pressure systems swept across the Atlantic and were often accompanied by strong winds and snowstorms. The weather usually moved in and out pretty quickly, at least by the third day.

This was all good news. If the weather was bad, it could change quickly enough for me to get through the weather window and make a swim. Samantha realized that there was a real purpose for my questions.

I'd been thinking about how to tell her if she asked. If I started off by saying I was going there to swim, it would have given her room to have doubts about me, and so I told her my background, that I'd been doing long-distance swims for years. I'd swum across the English Channel and the Bering Straits, and I'd completed a 1.22-mile swim in Antarctica in a swimsuit, cap, and goggles. My interest was to figure out how to survive better in the cold, to find better ways of rewarming after cold exposure, research I'd been involved with for years with the hypothermia expert at the University of London.

The reason I choose Ilulissat, I explained, was that I was following in the wake of Roald Amundsen off Greenland and through the Northwest Passage. I wanted to write about him and compare his journey with mine, which would be about one hundred years later. But there was more to it. I wanted to see how far I could go, try something that caused me to reach further and explore the inner and outer worlds of what a human being could achieve. So I wanted to try to do a swim in Ilulissat, in waters that could be colder than in Antarctica.

Also I wanted to learn more about climate change, to see for myself and learn what was happening from people I met along this journey. What I'd read and heard was that the Arctic ice cap was melting, and the Northwest Passage, which had been such a challenge to navigate, was opening up. How would this affect the world and everything that inhabited it?

Samantha was surprised, and now she understood why I was so interested in the weather. She also mentioned that she was a triathlete and that she had always loved to swim. Of all the people to speak with in the U.S. Air Force, I discovered the swimmer. What were the chances?

Samantha explained that she and Brian were heading to Ilulissat, too, as representatives of the air force at meetings, but they would be flying on a different aircraft than me.

The low clouds were beginning to lift. We could see the base of the glacier. It was about twenty miles from where we were sitting. Her friends were training on that glacier, and I wondered if it could be the same glacier I saw on my first flight over Greenland. And I wondered what it would be like to land on a glacier. I so wished I could go there. I wished I could see how they flew there, how they landed, and what it was like to be on the surface of a glacier. I wondered what kind of research the scientists were doing.

There was an announcement over the PA system. Samantha said, "Your plane will be landing in twenty minutes."

I told Samantha I hoped we would meet again one day, and she agreed and wished me luck.

CHAPTER 10

Ilulissat

After all of that, we nearly missed our flight. Three planes landed within a few minutes of one another, and we couldn't tell which one was ours. We made the wrong choice, went to the wrong gate, and, once we realized our mistake, had to sprint across the runway with our luggage to reach the correct airplane in time. There were people on standby, and if we had been a few minutes later, we would have been bumped off the flight.

Out of breath, with sweat rolling down our cheeks, we ran up the stairs on the ramp, ducked through the aircraft door, and quickly found our seats. Gretchen sat beside me, and we watched to make sure Bob and Bill got on. We knew that if we missed that flight, we would have to wait for two more days for another flight if the weather held and longer if not, and there just wasn't extra time. We only had eight days to coordinate and attempt the swim. We had taken the last four remaining seats.

Within a few moments, the pilot started the engines, and I felt the hum of the airplane through my body. I loved to fly as much as I loved to swim, I loved everything about it, the take-off, the landing, and everything in between.

As a child, I used to go with my dad to the airport in Manchester, New Hampshire, and we stood near the landing field for hours watching the Cessnas and Pipers come in for a landing and take off. There was something so exciting about watching the airplanes and hearing their engines as they raced down the runway and suddenly lifted off. It was magic. But flight didn't work for humans; I knew that. I'd experimented a lot. I just couldn't run fast enough, and even with the boost of a maple tree, when I jumped from one of the low branches, I just went down, and it was never a good landing. I longed to fly in one of those airplanes, to see what it felt like, to see the world from above, like a robin. And then one day my uncle Edward's friend Mr. McGraw, who lived in St. Johnsbury, Vermont, asked me if I wanted to fly with him in his Cessna. Mr. McGraw gave my cousins rides, and now he was asking me.

From the moment I climbed into the airplane, I was smiling. I knew what was going to happen from watching the small planes take off, but being in the airplane was nothing like watching it. The engine roared, and the plane shook as we raced down the runway, and suddenly, the airplane lifted off and the ground got farther and farther away. I think I was so excited I forgot to breathe. There was nothing in the world that compared to this. We were flying. We were moving between the heavens and the earth. We were free, going higher and higher and flying over the treetops. I'd climbed to the top of trees, but I had never been this high before. Nothing short of a miracle. We were flying!

Mr. McGraw glanced at me with a concerned look on his face. "Are you okay?" he shouted. He was wearing earphones, and he pulled one of the ears aside.

I felt my body shift backward into the seat as we leveled off. We looked down on the backs of black-and-white cows. They were so small they looked like farm toys. We flew over Mr. McGraw's red barn and saw the roof and the top of the silo. There were bales of hay in the back of the barn. They looked like small squares of gold.

It was magic.

I never wanted this to be over. There was too much to see. I wondered what it would be like to fly beyond the horizon.

What would we find there? Was there an end to the horizon? Or did it just keep going? I knew I wanted to go there some-day—beyond the horizon.

We turned and I slid to the left in my seat and had to hang on. I could see the wing coming up. I hoped he'd turn again. I'd seen birds turning in flight: blackbirds, ravens, hawks, sparrows, robins, and seagulls. They were all different sizes and shapes, and they all turned, but they did it differently, some fast, some slow and with a long glide. I wondered how they turned without falling from the sky.

Mr. McGraw was looking at the gauges in front of him, and there were needles moving slowly up and down. It was a special language you had to see, to read, I guessed. The needles moved depending on how the plane was moving. There was something that looked like a compass, and there was a gauge with numbers and slanted lines and something else that looked like the gauge in my parent's station wagon.

"The gauge with the numbers on it is the altimeter, it tells you how high we're flying." And he said we were flying thousands of feet off the ground. How many thousands of feet would it be to the moon or the sun or the stars? I wondered.

"This is the fuel gauge. Looks like we're going to have to head back very soon. But we need to do something first," he said.

What could we do more than this? Could there be anything more to do in the world?

He smiled and asked, "Do you want to fly the plane?"

"Yes, I do! But I don't know how to fly a plane yet."

"That's okay, I'll help you. Put your hands on the yoke and I'll put mine on top of yours to help you steer."

I looked at him and thought, The yoke? He was pointing to the steering wheel. That must be the yoke. I put my hands on top of it, and felt the fast vibrations of the plane's engine through the yoke.

It was like the time I cupped my hands around a slow-flying bumblebee so I could feel the buzzing sound it was making. This time I could feel the plane's buzz, and I didn't have to worry about being stung. It was amazing. I waited, though, expecting him to put his hands on top of mine, and finally I had to say, "Are you going to help me fly the airplane?"

"You're doing just fine on your own," he said.

He was letting me fly the airplane on my own; I was eight years old and I was flying an airplane. I knew then that I was the luckiest kid in the whole world. I probably flew it all alone for five seconds, but it seemed so much shorter.

"I'm going to have to take the yoke now, so we can turn and fly over there."

We flew over Emerald Lake, and it changed color. It became the bright blue of the crystal-clear autumn sky, and it reflected the puffy white clouds sailing across the sky. What would it be like to fly through the clouds? Could we open our windows and reach out and touch them? What would they feel like? But I was distracted. I looked down into the mirror of the lake.

The whole world below was reflected by the lake—the forests of tall dark pine intermixed with snow-white birches topped with dazzling yellow leaves, and thick-trunked sugar maples capped with leaves the brightest shades of red, yellow, orange, burgundy, and yellow-green reflected at angles across the lake, and they rippled in the water. I knew my life would always be different now. I had seen something so special. I had seen the earth from the sky.

The engine sounds changed, and we descended slowly.

The world came up to greet us as Mr. McGraw lowered the plane onto the runway, and my dad and Uncle Edward were waiting for us.

My cheeks really hurt from smiling. My first flight was a freedom that I never felt on earth, and it was different from swimming. My life changed. I knew I would always want to fly to places I'd never been. And see world below and beyond the horizon.

Before leaving California I found it was difficult to get specific information about tides and currents in Greenland and where to find a support boat. I thought of Tom Pickering, a good friend who had been the U.S. ambassador to the United Nations and various other countries around the world, from India to Russia; he had also been the undersecretary of state. Once, when I was planning to swim across the Gulf of Aqaba and trying to get in touch with Queen Noor to get permission for the swim, I called Tom and told him that I had been trying to get permission through the Jordanian embassy but wasn't getting anywhere. But a friend who grew up in Pasadena had been Queen Noor's neighbor when she was growing up. Did it make sense to write a letter directly to the queen, I asked Tom, and he said something that I would always remember when I got stuck: "Use every channel you have." I don't know if he meant it to be a double entendre, but that made me smile. And in addition, he suggested writing to Ambassador Talhoum, a friend of Tom's who had worked at the Jordanian ministry in Washington, DC.

The queen gave her approval for the swim and arranged for a reception afterward.

For this trip, I thought of contacting the Danish embassy, but I couldn't quite figure out whom I needed to contact. Crown Prince Frederik of Denmark was a swimmer and a frogman, and he had spent some time in Greenland. He might know water temperatures in Greenland in the spring and if there was a coast guard base where I might be able to find out more about tides and currents. Being a swimmer, he might be willing to help. But what I was planning to do wasn't the usual, and this route required a lot of explanations and time. By the time my letter got through, he and his family were off on vacation. I kept trying to figure out what channel to use next and decided to go back to my mentor.

I called Tom Pickering, and as always, Tom was enthusiastic about the swims. He had traveled to Greenland, and his voice filled with warmth as he recalled the days he spent in Thule at the U.S. Air Force base. I asked if he would write cover letters for me to the Danish ambassador, to the prime minister of Greenland, and to the Canadian prime minister, for later swims. Tom wrote the cover letters and I attached mine and sent them off together.

A week or so later, I received a call from Jakob Alvi, the assistant economic adviser on U.S. relations to Greenland at the Danish embassy. Jakob was very excited about the project and willing to help. I got a number of contacts at the Greenland tourist bureau and at the offices of Greenland Home Rule. Greenland had been governed by Denmark, but had now become a self-governing Danish province. One of the main proponents of Greenland Home Rule was the former prime minister (from 1991 to 1997), Lars-Emil Johansen.

While waiting in line to board the Greenlandic airplane, I noticed that Lars-Emil Johansen was standing in line, only five feet from us. I shook my head with disbelief. Who would know more about Greenland than the former prime minister?

Lars-Emil was a compact and muscular man, maybe in his fifties, with a round face bronzed by the sun and a thin coarse white mustache. He wore thin metal-framed glasses that gave him a studious look, and when he spoke, in what I think was Greenlandic, his brown eyes lit up. He became animated. He looked as if he was approachable.

Upon hearing my story, Lars-Emil was intrigued. I asked him if he was an athlete; he nodded and said that he had been a soccer player and was great fan. He said that it was popular here and that we'd see kids playing late into the evening in summer because the sunset came late at night.

Talking about sports was always a great way to begin a conversation, as well as a great window into a different world, finding out what was culturally important in a different country, but I asked why he was visiting the United States. His expression completely changed. He said that he'd been in the United States to talk with officials about the rapid climate change occurring in Greenland. The glaciers that covered most of the country were melting at an alarming rate, and the air temperatures and ocean temperatures were getting warmer. The second part of his talk had been about cooperation among Greenland, Denmark, and the United States. Then he gave me a copy of his book. The title was *Tamatta Akuusa,* and he said it was about Greenland and how they had won home rule.

"Oh, you're the one who's known as the Daniel Webster of Greenland!" I said.

He seemed pleased that I knew that about him, but he nearly floored me when he quoted General John Stark.

" 'Live free or die,' " he said.

"You know that saying—the state motto for New Hampshire?"

From the inspiration of our American forefathers he must have developed his own ideas about freedom and leadership. Amazing. Who would have thought we would have this conversation standing in a line waiting to get on an airplane? "Are you and Jonathan Motzfeldt and Moses Olsen the ones responsible for creating a political party in Greenland?"

"Yes, it's called the Siumut Party. It is like the Whig Party during Andrew Jackson's time in office. The Whig Party was against the government's autocratic rule. The people wanted more of a say in their government, and we wanted more of a say in the way we are governed," he said.

Lars-Emil had invited us to join him at a reception that evening in Kangerlussuaq at a restaurant near the airport, and we accepted.

Bob, Bill, Gretchen, and I entered a lodgelike building along with VIPs from the United States, Denmark, and Greenland. We were pointed to a beautiful Danish and Greenlandic buffet. There was a magnificent variety of local meat and fish—musk ox, reindeer, beluga whale, bay shrimp, and cod—prepared in a large variety of ways, from roasted to boiled to sautéed. There were also many different salads: Waldorf, grated beets, tomato and lettuce, and shredded-carrot salad. It looked delicious.

We wanted to try almost everything. We were invited to sit at the table with Lars-Emil and his colleagues. We talked about his childhood in Greenland, where he hunted, fished, dogsledded, and played soccer. We talked about Greenland, the largest island in the world, and we talked about Denmark and how Greenland was still a Danish province. And we talked again about politics.

Bob Griffith joined the conversation. "Do you want your party to become more like the American Founding Fathers, Thomas Jefferson, Alexander Hamilton, and Thomas Paine? They fought for independence."

Lars-Emil smiled and pursed his lips. "It is the natural progression of things," he said.

"But there are only sixty thousand people who live in Greenland, and a lot of financial support comes from Denmark. How can you maintain your sovereignty?"

"These are questions we are finding answers for. The United States of America wasn't a large and powerful country when you gained independence from the British," he said.

We were having dinner with Greenland's former prime minister. I never expected to be discussing American history with Lars-Emil. I wanted to understand how people shaped their lives in a way that they could make a difference in the world. And now, here we were talking to Lars-Emil, who had studied American history, and those ideas that began with our Founding Fathers had not been forgotten; they were inspiring him and his friends.

The meal was so delicious, we went back for seconds. I was returning to a platter of reindeer with a local-berry sauce and took a small piece, and then continued on to the Waldorf salad and scooped out a spoonful and put it on my plate. The Danish chef, who had been watching us through an open window between the kitchen and buffet area, saw me. He was a tall man wearing a chef's white uniform and a cap. He gave me a nasty scowl, and he said something loud and angry in Danish and then in English, "No, you can't do that!" and he tried to reach through the window and grab my plate, but I was just out of reach, and so he sent his assistant, who grabbed my plate and whisked it away from me. "What's wrong?" I asked.

She explained that I was forbidden to put meat and Waldorf salad on the same dinner plate. She came back with the small piece of reindeer on a new plate for me. No one else made that mistake and encountered the wrath of the Danish chef.

Toward the end of the evening I asked Lars-Emil, "You want Greenland one day to become an independent country?"

"Yes, that is what happens. It is the nature of things. When you grow up you want to be independent," he said. "When you get to Ilulissat, make sure to meet with Hans Enoksen. He's an old friend of mine."

"The prime minister?" I asked. "We wrote to him. Can I just go up and talk with him?"

"Yes, he knows that you will be there. He received your letter and the one from Ambassador Pickering. Hans will be meeting with your Speaker of the House, Representative Pelosi, to discuss climate change, but he will probably have time between the meetings."

The next morning Gretchen, Bob, Bill, and I made it to the Greenlandic DH-7 just in time. And I think I was even more excited now than I had been on that first flight. I had previously studied Greenland from thirty-eight thousand feet, and now, finally, we would be flying lower over this magnificent island. Maybe we would have the chance to see Greenland up close, a land that I'd dreamed of exploring for so many years.

The flight attendant stood up in the front of the plane and gave us safety instructions in Greenlandic, Danish, and English. It was strange; I never expected Greenlandic to sound familiar, but the sounds that she made were very similar to people I'd heard speak on Little Diomede Island, in the Bering Strait.

We would be flying closer to the glaciers than I'd ever flown before, those glaciers that I had seen more than thirty years ago. And now we would be flying right over them, and over Greenland. What a dream this had been.

I couldn't help but think of Amundsen, and how he must have felt when he sailed out of Christiania Fjord, the excitement he must have felt when his crew cast off. That sense that, finally, this was the beginning of something he had dreamed of and thought about and worked for, for so many years.

Once they were beyond the city lights they celebrated and toasted their attempt to be the first men to sail through the Northwest Passage, a course that would take them to Greenland, across Baffin Bay, between the Canadian islands along the northern edge of Canada, across the top of Alaska, and into the Bering Strait.

The *Gjøa* was tiny, only seventy feet long, and it weighed forty-eight tons. It is hard to imagine that something so small could sail such vast, powerful, and unknown waters. But the *Gjøa* was what Amundsen needed to explore uncharted waters, places where the waters could be very shallow and where a larger ship might run aground.

The *Gjøa* had been used to fish for herring off the coast of Norway, and after that, a neighbor of mine had told me, her grandfather, who was Norwegian, had hunted seals from it in the waters off Norway and Greenland. When Amundsen purchased the *Gjøa*, he converted it for his expedition. He refitted it and reinforced it to withstand the forces of the ice. For the Northwest Passage attempt, the *Gjøa* would be powered by a thirteen-horsepower engine and sails.

Like the *Jeannette*, the *Gjøa* was heavy with provisions and equipment. Amundsen was worried that she sailed low in the water, but he wanted to make sure they had enough food and supplies so they wouldn't experience the horrors of the Arctic that Franklin and his crew tried to endure. They had died in the attempt.

The *Gjøa* sailed across the North Atlantic faster than the crew anticipated, then she moved south along the east coast of Greenland, around the southern tip of the large island, and up the west coast.

We were following the last segment of Amundsen's path, flying north above the west coast of Greenland.

The song of the propellors reached a heightened pitch. The

plane raced down the smooth runway, and we rose in a wide sweeping circle, sailed above the stark windblown area around Kangerlussuaq Airport, over the Quonset huts and small silver, white, and pale yellow buildings and dorms that composed the town, and flew immediately into thick woolly gray and white cloud.

I strained to find holes in the clouds, the portholes to the mysterious world below, but couldn't see beyond the thick gray clouds.

About an hour later, the aircraft descended through a world of white cotton-candy clouds, and there, to our right, was the rocky coast of Greenland and the wide, deep, dark blue waters of Disko Bay that separated Disko Island from the mainland. Large mountains composed most of Disko Island and they were covered in an enamel of ice and pure blue-white snow. The island radiated forbidding cold.

On July 24, 1903, five weeks after setting sail, Amundsen reached Disko Bay. He wrote, "A barrier of grounded icebergs seemed to block the entrance to Godhavn. But soon Nielsen, the governor of the colony, came out to us in a boat to bid us welcome and pilot us in. We met a violent squall and had to tack, as the motor could not manage it alone."

I had intended to swim off Godhavn, today called Qeqertarsuaq, because Amundsen had sailed there to take on dogs and provisions for the Northwest Passage attempt. But as I gazed below at the water, I could see the entire east coast of the island was blocked by thousands of icebergs. And they were all sorts of large shapes: squares, rectangles, ovals, triangles, and trapezoids. They were drifting on the dark rough blue-gray waters, and they looked different than the tiny white dots I'd seen in the North Atlantic on the way to English Channel so many years ago.

As the DH-7 descended, the icebergs grew larger. I thought, If I swim over there, it will be like swimming through a glass of water full of ice cubes. It could take a day or two just to sail across the bay and pick our way through the ice to reach Godhavn. We didn't have any extra days. This could cut down on the options I had for the swim. More than that, it looked like it would be a difficult sail just to get there. The town had about one thousand people, and it seemed remote.

Off to the right of the plane, the warm northern sun illuminated the spring snow that softened the edge of the island of Greenland. We descended to the base of the mountains, glazed with a shell of ice. We flew over the deep blue fjords and just above Ilulissat, a cozy city of five thousand people and five thousand Greenland Eskimo dogs. The homes and buildings were built on multiple layers of rock and painted the brightest colors of red, turquoise, canary yellow, purple, orange, and lime green, all of this intensified by the white layer of freshly fallen spring snow on the roofs and on the ground.

There was a series of both wide and narrow bays that could work for a swim, but there was one major problem: there weren't any beaches, just huge areas of upright rock with at least a four-foot distance from the top of the granite buttresses to the water's surface. That meant it would be hard to get into and out of the water. I hadn't thought to ask about this, hadn't realized it could be a problem. We would have to take time and find a place where I could start the swim safely without cracking my head on the way in or doing what I had done on the Bering Strait swim, slipping and scratching the whole back side of my leg on barnacles and having those open cuts bleed into the water. That had made me nervous, since I knew that there were two species of sharks in those waters, salmon sharks and great Pacific sharks; neither was known to attack humans, but humans didn't swim in those waters.

Here I might be swimming with Greenland sharks, and putting blood into the water for them would be bad. I hoped Adam was right about the Greenland sharks not being a real threat.

The plane rolled perfectly to a stop, and I felt a rush of energy. This was now our beginning. We gathered our gear and headed to the Hotel Icefiord van, and as we wound through the town built on high rocky hills and small flat rocky areas, I kept looking out the window to the bay, trying to see a cove or two where we could survey the area.

The town itself was strangely quiet. It was early afternoon, and no one was out. We discovered that the hours people kept were different than ours. It was spring, and the sun was finally coming back to this part of the world; people were celebrating, eating late, playing late. Children and teenagers would play soccer until midnight, when the sun started to go down, and they would get up early for school and come home and rest so they could stay out late and enjoy the light.

We had been given the names of Karen Filskov, who worked for a company called Destination Disko, along with her colleague Konrad Selbon. They had offered to help us work out logistics for the swim.

When we reached the hotel, Karen and Konrad were waiting for us in a light snowstorm and immediately guided us into the lobby.

We sat down around a wooden table with a map of Disko Bay spread out in front of us. Karen sat beside me. Her light-brown-and-honey fur-trimmed parka hood circled her face. She was the daughter of a Greenlandic mother and Danish father and was a beautiful and exotic blend of both, with the most extraordinary almond-shaped green eyes and soft auburn hair that fringed her cheeks. Her face was oval with a delicate nose, and she had high cheekbones and a big smile.

Konrad was equally exotic. His parents were both Greenlandic Inuit, and he had black hair and large brown almond-shaped eyes and a quick boyish smile with the whitest teeth. He was powerfully built, like a collegiate wrestler. His torso had a V shape, and his deltoids, triceps, and biceps were large and well defined even under his long-sleeved T-shirt. He seemed strong and had incredible balance. I had watched him walking to the hotel along the uneven road and cutting across a yard filled with irregularly shaped rocks, moving from one to another as if they were flat and even stepping-stones. Konrad probably had gotten strong from hard work, from hauling in seals or whales and pulling in fish from the bay.

This was good. If Konrad could haul a seal out of the water, he would be able to drag me out if I got into trouble and needed help.

We discussed the tides. I hadn't been able to find a tidal chart of Greenland's waters, but Konrad fished there often, and fishermen usually knew the most about the tides and currents. Konrad said that the tidal change was rarely more than a foot because the bay was very well protected. The speed of the current would not be more than half a knot.

We studied the map, calculated distances and time anticipated to swim, and considered the starting and, hopefully, the finishing point. There was one large bay near the northern section of town, and Konrad shook his head and explained that it was just below a shrimp-processing plant and that the inedible parts of the shrimp were dumped into the water. I pointed to another bay. Konrad shook his head. That was where the raw sewage pipe from town drained directly into the water. Konrad and Karen shifted into Greenlandic and Danish, speaking softly and discussing other options, and Karen translated their discussion for us. They suggested that I swim across Church Bay; it was near the town's center, and it was a distance of a quarter of a mile. The bay was just below Knud Rasmussen's home and the Zion church where his father had been the village vicar.

Knud Rasmussen was one of the most beloved and famous Greenlanders. His father was Danish, and his mother was Greenlandic Inuit. Rasmussen had led a number of expeditions by dogsled to Thule in the far north of Greenland. He explored and mapped much of Greenland and Arctic America. On his first expedition, the Danish Greenland Literary expedition, he had served as a translator for Ludvig Mylius-Erichsen, and translated the complex Greenlandic folk tales and myths into Danish.

Church Bay seemed like a good place to swim. Maybe I

would be able to see Rasmussen's home from the water and use that for inspiration.

Karen asked me, "When you swim, will you be wearing a wet suit or a dry suit?"

"I'll be wearing a swimsuit—a Tyr Lycra swimsuit," I replied.

It took a moment for my answer to register. Karen drew in a quick breath and said, "Are you crazy? Do you know how cold that water is?"

I'd thought she understood what we were doing.

"From the research I've done the water temperature could be between twenty-eight point eight to thirty-four degrees," I told her.

Konrad looked concerned. He asked Karen something in Greenlandic, and they spoke for a few minutes. Eventually, he said that he knew someone who had a Zodiac that we could use as an escort boat, in case anything went wrong and I needed to be pulled out of the water.

Before we decided on this as the starting point, though, we needed to check on entry and exit points for the swim. We walked out of the hotel into a light snow shower and followed the main dirt road that climbed into town. Dogs with long thick coats were staked in tiers along the steep rocky hillsides. When, at one point, a puppy bounded down to greet us, the adult dogs broke into loud, anxious barks and high-pitched howls. Karen warned us not to play with the puppy. These were working dogs, Konrad explained, not pets or companions. They were conditioned to withstand the harshness of the environment and they were strictly trained. There was no room on a sled for a dog that didn't listen. The result could mean death for the dog, the team, or the driver. These dogs could have been the descendants of Nansen's and Amundsen's and Rasmussen's dogs. What amazing dogs they were.

We walked along a narrow boardwalk that ran between the quaint houses and over spongy marshland. Here and there, the weathered boards had snapped or were about to, and the frame wobbled with every step, and the footing was unsteady. Every now and then a woman in her home would look out her window and wave and smile. They all seemed to know why we were there.

When we reached the southern end of Church Bay, we followed the cliff edge and decided on an entry point, an area of low rock that tapered gradually into the water. But the grass green algae that covered the rocks concerned me.

We walked below the Zion church, the small eighteenth-century wooden building where Knud Rasmussen's father had been a minister. The rocks around the church were covered by a foot of melting ice and snow. Below, a rocky ledge encircled the bay, but most of it was two or three feet above the water. If I were swimming, it would be too high for me to reach up and pull myself out.

The next morning, we scouted the northern part of Church Bay for an exit point. We watched a powerfully built Inuit man, of medium height, wearing thick black rubber boots and carrying two large plastic buckets, slip, slide, and swing his arms to catch his balance as he walked to the water's edge. If a local man had this much of a challenge to walk on the ice and rocks, what was I going to do? The man bent over and, with a groan, lifted a log-sized piece of clear blue ice from the water. He stuck it with a pick and split off chunks, which he dropped into the buckets. The ice had once been rainwater. It had fallen into the cracks of an iceberg and frozen there, and, when the iceberg broke up, the clear ice had floated away on the seawater. It was pure and sweet and would be used as drinking water.

I spent the days getting over jet lag. The cold water would have a greater impact if I was tired, so I needed to give myself a chance to be fully rested. This was not the ideal situation, though. I couldn't train in these waters, they were too cold, and I hadn't been able to train much over the past week, with all the preparations I had to make before leaving home. By the time I got into the water, it would have been nine days without training, but I reminded myself that I would just do the best I could and make it work.

The reason for going to Greenland wasn't only to swim, it was to explore, and for the next two days we wandered through town and visited the local art museum, which featured Emanuel Peterson's large canvas oil paintings with images from one hundred years ago, the time when Amundsen and Nansen sailed near these shores. The light on the bay, icebergs, people, fires and snow, and the Eskimo dogs all took you to a place that was long ago—and yet was alive within these paintings. Christian, the museum curator, was also the priest, and he took us on a tour of Zion Church. There was something so familiar about the space of the church that it felt strangely like home. The interior was painted white and sky blue, and behind the altar was a beautiful religious scene with Greenlandic words painted below.

The church was intentionally built in the shape of a ship to create a metaphor between the church and God and man. It was believed that like the church, each person is also like a ship, sailing on his or her journey through life.

It made me think of how often my body was a small boat as I crossed great waterways, and how often I felt most spiritual when I was out on the waters.

Christian asked why we had come to Ilulissat.

We told him we were trying to use the swim as a way to work with and connect with the people in Greenland, to understand them and their country a little better through the experience.

It was strange. It was as if he already knew, somehow, and he seemed to think it was important. He told us that Monday, when we planned to do the swim, was All Saints' Day, a highly spiritual day in Greenland, when people go to church in the morning and pray and give thanks. All schools and workplaces were closed that day. He asked us when we planned the swim, and he said that his colleague, a Greenlandic priest, would be giving the sermon, but he wanted to know if I might finish swimming after 9:00 a.m. so his congregation could come down and see the swim. He was so excited. He had to go to the jail to administer services there, but would race back for the finish. And he said that he would ask his friend to have the congregation say a special prayer during the service for the success of the swim, and they would come out of the church at 9:00 and welcome us if we reached the area.

Everything was set. Konrad would be able to get a Zodiac boat to escort me during the swim, and we had a plan in place, but we had to wait for a couple of days. Karen and Konrad were tied up in meetings translating for Hans Enoksen, the prime minister of Greenland, and for Nancy Pelosi, the Speaker of the House. I joked with Karen and Konrad that we had to share them—our crew—with the prime minister and Nancy Pelosi.

Waiting was always difficult, and it was especially challenging when the weather was perfect. The air temperatures in Ilulissat were in the forties, a hot white sun was illuminating the sky, and the water and the bay were a silky smooth silvery mirror of the heavens. Icebergs the size of battleships and ice-breakers had sailed in on the incoming tide, and they would have been a large obstacle to crossing Church Bay, but had drifted out with the outgoing tide. If we could have begun on that day, it looked like I could have swum straight across without having to swim around any icebergs. But we couldn't, we had to wait.

We met each day at the Hotel Icefiord in the lobby after Karen and Konrad had finished translating, and we discussed our plans in increasing detail, down to where our crew would be positioned; my main person to communicate with during the swim would be Bob Griffith, because he had been on my swim in Antarctica, and he had seen me swim in very cold water and knew how I responded.

We ate our way through those next two days, enjoying puffy fresh whole wheat rolls with paper-thin slices of buttery Danish cheese for breakfast. For lunch we ate tender halibut, delicate cod, and sweet bay shrimp from Disko Bay, and for dinner we tried musk ox burgers and chili that were far leaner than hamburger and delicious. We also ate Thai chicken and fish, since the main chef was from Thailand.

Trying to get rested and get over the jet lag, I went to bed at eight p.m., long before sunset.

I woke up around one a.m. and wiped the thick frost off my windowpane and looked outside. The crew was sitting on patio chairs two floors below my window. They were looking out across the silvery waters of Ilulissat Bay, watching the icebergs sliding by on the incoming tide and holding their hands up to their eyes now and then to examine the shapes of snowflakes lighting on their black gloves. They were huddled together, wearing their heavy winter coats, hats, and boots and wrapped up in navy blue woolen blankets trying to stay warm, and it was snowing harder. Big heavy wet snowflakes were swaying like tiny feathers falling from the sky. The wetness of the snowflakes meant the air temperature was growing warmer. And there was a shift in the air currents. Maybe by tomorrow the snow would have stopped. It would make it easier to swim, both psychologically and physically. Swimming in a snowstorm wasn't what most people did. But then there was something exciting about having the training and the focus to do it.

The storm was moving in. Snow was swirling with gusts of wind and falling more quickly now. Below my window my friends were covered from head to toe with an inch or two of fresh snow. They shook out their blankets and picked up their hot drinks, took a sip, and watched the snow falling into the water. They were like little kids; even though it was freezing cold, they didn't want to come inside. It would have been fun to join them, but it was late, and sleep was more important so I would be ready to swim in the morning.

CHAPTER 11

Coolest Crossing

A day later, on May 28, 2007, I put on my swimsuit and, for the first time, put on the bright orange harness and attached a carabineer to the back. My goal was to swim across Church Bay, about a quarter of a mile, and if I was doing okay my plan was to push farther. The distance would be decided by my reaction to the water temperature. I put on my sweat suit and gazed out of the window of the Hotel Icefiord, studying the movement of the icebergs. There were some that had returned on the tide that were larger than battleships. In 2002, just before I jumped into the waters off Antarctica, I had been overwhelmed by the thought of swimming among icebergs. Now, five years later, I was using the icebergs like buoys; they made the water currents visible.

Karen walked with me while the rest of the crew motored to the starting area in the Zodiac. They had taken the water temperature. It ranged from 28.8 to 29 degrees, 3 degrees colder than the water had been in Antarctica. I had asked them not to tell me the temperature. I knew the water would be cold, and I didn't think it would help me to know how cold it was. It could psych me completely out.

The bay was calm. There was no wind, and there weren't enough icebergs to make navigation difficult, but the tide was lower than we expected, and the exposed algae-covered rocks would be too slippery to walk across. We searched for another spot. A group of people from the hotel had come along as support and just to see the swim. One of the men, Sven, was a rock climber and mountain climber from Denmark. He helped us find a bare rock. It wasn't ideal—I would have to drop five feet off the rock cliff and hope that the water would slow my impact enough so that I could land safely on a craggy ledge two feet below the surface and give my body a few minutes to adjust to the temperature.

I handed my sweat suit to Karen and felt the cold 40-degree air against my skin. I put on my cap slowly, so my skin temperature would become the same as the air temperature, and the blood under my skin would race into my interior to keep it warm. I wrapped the elastic band of my goggles around my wrist so I wouldn't lose them when I hit the water. I looked over the edge and at the crew on the Zodiac boat. Gretchen was on the bow, Bob and Bill were sitting on the seat behind her, and Konrad was operating the motor. Bob was in his bright orange survival suit, Bill in his dry suit; all were watching the water for any Greenland sharks.

Bob was ready, holding on to a long orange-and-yellow nylon rope with a carbineer on one end and leaning slightly forward. Bill was clasping his hands and praying. The crew looked solemn.

"Lynne, are you ready?" Bob asked with a steady voice. I could just see his face under his parka hood. He would take the lead on this. He would be the one who communicated with me so I would just have one focus. If something else came up, Bill or Gretchen or Konrad would say something to Bob and he would speak to me. They knew that the water might be so cold that I might not have the air to speak to them. If that happened, I would lift my foot, and give them the Seal Beach wave, to let them know I was okay.

"Yes," I said.

We had discussed everything many times before. I looked down. I knew where to get in, but with the ebb tide, the water was lower than we expected. Would I be able to get out? I remembered: if I couldn't land, Bob would clamp the carabineers together, and they would bounce me out.

*I'm swimming across Church Bay, Ilulissat, Greenland, in
28.8-degree-Fahrenheit water, feeling the movement of fish
below. In the Zodiac, from left to right, are Konrad, Bob, Bill,
and Gretchen, all focused on me.*

I took a deep breath and stepped off the rock. My feet
touched the ledge, and in twenty seconds my arms, legs, and
torso were numb. The water felt colder than in Antarctica. I
licked my goggles to keep them from fogging, pulled them over
my head and over my eyes, pushed off the ledge, and started
swimming head up. I couldn't feel my arms and legs, just this
sensation of extreme cold, but I could sense that they were
moving against the water. My breathing was different than
what it had been in Antarctica. There, when I first hit the
water, I immediately started hyperventilating. That was the
normal response. The adrenaline kicked in, increasing heart
rate and breathing.

Dr. Brownie Schoene, my longtime friend and a pulmonary
expert who had climbed Mount Everest, and who had done
research on me to help me train to swim across Lake Titicaca,
explained that often in the cold the muscles that support
breathing become paralyzed, and so a person is only able to
take small and rapid breaths. But this time I was breathing
deep and fast and I couldn't get enough air. I was struggling

I'm wearing the rescue harness, breathing forcefully, and pulling hard through cold, dense 28.8-degree water.

from the moment I hit the water. I might have to get out, I thought. I was working so hard just to breathe. I was taking heaving chest breaths. My arms were turning over as fast as they could go. I tried placing my cheek and then my nose in the water to try to change my body position so my hips would float up and I would reduce the drag, but the water was too cold. I couldn't put my face into it. I couldn't hold my breath that long. I couldn't hold it for one second. This was harder than I thought it would be; so much harder than I ever expected. The water was like liquid ice, and I was fighting from the start, just to move fast enough to create warmth. This was like Lake Titicaca; at 12,500 feet, it had been really difficult to breathe, and I had to make a choice between swimming more slowly and breathing or not being able to swim. It was difficult to breathe in this cold.

Bob shouted, "Lynne, are you okay?"

I lifted my right foot, to signal that I was okay. But my breathing was becoming faster and more labored, my lips were pursed, and I was not able to catch up on the oxygen my body

Swimming backstroke as fast as I can, past a flat iceberg. My arms and legs are red and numb, and I can't really feel the water.

Unable to see where I am swimming, I trust the crew's navigation and the directions they give me.

was demanding. I had never started a swim this way before. Usually I was psyched up and ready to go, and I was nervous, and it took a mile or two to settle into my pace, but this was different.

I heard Bill's deep calming voice. "Lynne, we're right here."

I couldn't take the time to turn and look at him or the crew. All I could do was swim with my head up, focus on the forward path, and breathe, harder than I'd ever breathed before.

We had talked about my adding distance to the swim by flaring to the right and following the curve of the bay if I felt like I wanted to swim a longer distance, but the cold was seeping into my body, invading me. I wasn't sure I was even going to make it straight across, never mind adding distance. I couldn't get enough air. I thought maybe I'd have to get out. I tried to slow down my arm strokes, but that didn't work. I needed to keep up the heat production, or my internal temperature would plummet, and they would have to pull me out of the water. I heard Gretchen say, "You're looking great." I raised my foot to salute her.

Bob asked, "Do you want to swim farther—around the bay?" I didn't raise my foot. And I thought, I just have to keep moving in as straight a line as I can go. I can't veer off in any direction. I can't swim any extra. I just have to make it across.

Bob seemed to read my mind. We were in sync. That was good. "Do you want to go straight across?" Bob asked. I lifted my foot, but I thought, I might really need to get out now. I can't get enough air. It's hard to maintain this. It's so hard to keep going. Just keep moving your arms. You're almost there. But I can't breathe! I really can't breathe.

We were only two hundred yards from shore, but suddenly I couldn't go any farther. I heard the church bells tolling, saw the doors opening and the congregation stepping outside, climbing onto the snowbanks. I was sprinting, but suddenly I couldn't move. "Backstroke. Swim backstroke," I said to myself. "Roll over on your back and catch your breath." I did, and swam for about one hundred yards, and then rolled back over on my stomach. "Fifty yards."

"Over there, land right there." I could hear Bob, but I couldn't see where he was pointing.

I was pulling my hands right under my body so I could get more lift, and I could see above the waterline. My stroke was very short and rapid. Bill immediately noticed the change. We had swum together off and on for years. He knew how I moved through the water, the position of my arms, head, legs, body. He could tell from fifty yards away, from the other end of the pool, how I was doing. And what I was doing at that time was not normal.

Bill was beside me in the Zodiac, and he must have leaned farther over the pontoon, because his voice was right above me and he was speaking rapidly with an edge to his normally calm voice. "Lynne, are you okay?"

As much as I wanted to, I couldn't reply to Bill. I couldn't catch my breath. And I couldn't slow down. I couldn't take a moment to get an extra breath and recover. Worse, when I came to the rock where I was supposed to climb out of the water, the rock was too high.

I couldn't reach high enough and put my hands on the rock and press myself up and out of the water. Suddenly, I felt like a dog swimming in a pool, a dog that suddenly realizes she doesn't know where the pool steps are. She can't find her way out. She starts dog-paddling in a tight circle, frantically looking, turning her head from one side to the other, trying to find her way out. It was harder to breathe.

"Lynne." It was Bob.

Focus on his voice. Only that. Follow his directions.

"The ledge is too high for you here. We have to go farther. Fifty more yards. Do you think you can do it?"

I lifted my foot and dropped it quickly. I needed my foot in the water to give me more lift.

"Okay, Konrad is looking for a landing spot. Swim closer to the Zodiac. Just stay beside us. That's right." Bob's voice was calm, but suddenly it was filled with energy and excitement. "Look to your right side. You're almost there!"

For the first time since the swim began, I stopped for a moment and treaded water. I just had to see them so I could keep that image in my head. They were all leaning forward, Bob and Bill leaning so far over the pontoon they were just two arm lengths above my head. They were suddenly all pointing toward shore and directing me where to land.

Konrad pointed. "See the ledge? That's it!"

I nodded. I saw it. I swam for it. But as I got closer, I realized the ledge had grown in height; it was about three feet above my head. I couldn't get out there. I was too tired. I didn't have the strength to reach that high up and press myself out of the water. So I just kept swimming. Hoping they would find another option.

Bob said loudly, but in a controlled way, trying to figure out what was wrong, "You're missing the ledge, Lynne. You're swimming right past it!"

"Bob, it's too high for her. She can't reach that high," Gretchen said.

I lifted my foot. She understood.

I can't do this much longer. I need to land. I need to land now. Hurry. Please hurry.

"Lynne, we've got it. Just a little farther, just ten more yards. See, over there to your right. There's a ledge. It's an inch under the water. You can climb out there," Bill said.

Bill knew that if I couldn't get out of the water here, he and Bob would have to use the carabineer attached to the rope, clamp it onto the one on the back of my harness, and drag me out of the water. The swim would be over, and it wouldn't have much significance because I swim under the English Channel Swimming rules, and that means that I have to completely clear the water to finish. I wanted to complete it, but I really wasn't sure if I would be able to do it this time.

"Lynne, can you see it?" Bob said. His words ran together.

Konrad pulled the boat within inches of me. The Zodiac's gray pontoon almost touched my shoulder. I took a stroke and rolled onto my right side, and I looked up. Bob, Gretchen, Bill, and Konrad were pointing.

Yes! Finally. I saw it. The gray-speckled granite slab was at water level extending into the bay like nature's dive ladder. I swam to the rock and listened for the crew's directions. All I heard was their cheers. We made it.

I reached out and grabbed the edge of the rock and pulled myself onto the Greenland shore. I smiled. The rock felt foreign, hard, cold, and immobile after swimming freely through fluid. My skin was as cold as the bay, but the inside of my body felt warm.

As I pulled myself onto the rock and floated across it on my stomach, my face slid across a great patch of green slime. Globs of it stuck to my cheek and upper lip. I got up onto my knees and tried to figure out how to stand up in the slime without slipping and hitting my head. The green algae was more slippery than black ice.

"Hold on. I'll be there in a second," Bob shouted.

"I'm okay, Bob, I'll be out of here in a minute," I said. I didn't want him to try to help me. He could slip on the algae and hurt himself.

I tried to crawl across the rock on my hands and knees and sliced my knee on something sharp. My skin was numb, but somehow I felt the tear. Good thing Greenland sharks couldn't swim on rocks.

I crawled on the icy rocks. My right hand slid out from under me, and I went headfirst onto the rock. This was not good. I knew that the landing was going to be a challenge, that's why we had discussed it so much, but I didn't think I would not be able to stand. And I knew that this was a dangerous part of the swim. I was no longer exercising and creating heat. Being in the water like this was like being in a misty freezer in a bathing suit. I could feel a tremble rip through my body. And then I felt a second tremble. This was not good.

We had planned for Bob to help me up, and Gretchen and Bill would return with Konrad to the harbor with the Zodiac and meet us later. That way they would avoid walking on the rocks or snow and ice. But after I heard Bob's feet smack against rocks, I heard Bill land with a splash, and I realized Gretchen was talking. She was about to get out of the Zodiac, too.

I was worried about them. They could slip and split their heads open or fall into the water, and it would be difficult to grab ahold of them and pull them out.

Out of the corner of my eye, I saw him, in a glacial blue parka. It was the Iceman! It was the man we had seen a few days before gathering ice from the bay in buckets. He had come down to help. He was holding Gretchen's hand and helping her off the Zodiac. She would be okay. Bill was standing beside her. He looked like he was going to join Bob.

Bob was carefully working his way over to me. I heard his foot slip and saw him catch his balance. "Lynne, give me your hand," he said.

Oh no, if I try to stand and slip, I'll pull him over with me. No. I wouldn't take his hand there. "Bob, I'm okay. I can crawl out," I said, and something sharp gashed through the skin on my knee, but it didn't matter. I just needed to get out of there. "Bob, can you make sure the others don't try to come here, and they move back on the snowbank where it might be less slippery?" My lips felt like they were cold and swollen, and the words coming from my mouth sounded warped.

I crawled to the edge of the snowbank and tried to stand up on the icy rocks.

"Give me your hand now," Bob said. I looked up.

"Bob, I'm afraid I'll pull you over," I said.

"It's okay. I've got you," he said. Bob spread his feet out wide to give himself a solid base and grabbed my hand. I started to slide backward, but suddenly I felt a strong arm loop under mine and stop the slide. I looked over and saw a glacial blue parka. It was the Iceman! "We've got you," I heard him say, and I felt myself lifted by the two of them onto the snowbank.

The Iceman was smiling. His brown eyes held the light and glimmered like the icebergs. He shook his head and smiled.

Bob wrapped a towel over my shoulders. My skin was a little warmer, closer to air temperature, but inside my body, I could feel things starting to cool down.

Bob was calm, but there was an edge of stress to his voice. He knew that this was the time when my body was starting to cool down. And once I stopped moving, I stopped creating heat. He knew that I could get what was called an after drop, where my internal temperature plunged.

My lips felt a little larger than normal, but I wasn't slurring my speech. That meant I wasn't cooling down on the inside, but if I didn't start moving soon, I would.

Bob and the Iceman climbed the snowbank above me. Their legs were longer than mine. The embankment was too steep. I crawled up on my hands and knees.

And then I saw people leaving the church in small groups of twos and threes. They were walking down the church steps, but when they saw us they stopped in midstride and froze in place. They looked astonished.

Church bells were tolling loudly. What a great place in the world to land.

Bill was on my left side steadying me. Bob was on the right, handing me my sweat suit. The snow felt cold on my bare feet. I suppressed a shiver.

Bill was so excited. He hugged me and said, "Do you have any idea what the water temperature was?"

"It felt colder than Antarctica, but I couldn't tell by how many degrees," I said.

"It was twenty-eight point eight degrees!" Bill shook his head, and he wiped a tear away.

Gretchen joined the hug. "Bill was so worried, he was praying for you. You know I was, too," Gretchen said.

"I'm sure it helped. But I'm sorry I stressed you out."

"Are you kidding, we wouldn't have missed this for the world," Gretchen said, and Bill nodded.

"I saw it with my own eyes, and I still can't believe it," Bill said.

"It was pretty wild. This was the most intense swim I've ever done, Bill. How far did I swim? What was my time?"

"You swam a quarter of a mile in five minutes and ten seconds."

That was all? Five minutes? Really? It seemed like so much longer. How could that be? I thought back. It had been an all-out effort from the moment I entered that freezing-cold water—water that was below the freshwater freezing point. I had never worked that hard in my life or been on the edge from the moment the swim started to the finish. Never had I thought for every moment of the swim that I might have to get out. It was so hard.

Still, it was hard to believe that I'd only swum for five minutes. It had seemed like forever. There had been no escape from the intensity of those moments. No time to let my mind wander. No time to look at the sea or look down below. I couldn't even put my face in that water. It was so cold. It was an ice-cream headache the instant my forehead touched the water's surface. It was so cold I couldn't breathe. Maybe my body was telling me that the vagus nerve was overstimulated and that was affecting the beating of my heart. Maybe if had put my face in the water it would have slowed my heart down too rapidly. Maybe I needed the rapid heart rate to stay up with the speed my body was moving.

Five minutes. Only five minutes. I thought I could do better. But I'd never swum in 28.8-degree water. How could I do better, adjust my workouts, swim farther and for a longer time in the cold? How would it be possible to simulate this kind of energy use in my daily workouts? Where could I find water that was colder, but not so cold that I needed a support team beside me during workouts? What could be done to simulate the lack of oxygen I had experienced during this swim? Train more aerobically. Sprint more. The cold water had made me swim fast. That had enabled me to work harder than ever. That intensity had enabled me to generate more heat than I was losing. How would it be possible to sustain this level of activity?

People are born with different types of muscle fibers, which determine how fast muscles respond. There are people with a majority of fast-twitch muscle fibers—they are the sprinters, like Thoroughbred horses. And there are people who are born with a majority of slow-twitch muscle fibers; they are the distance athletes, like me—Clydesdales.

Everyone has what are called intermediate muscle fibers. These intermediate muscle fibers are trainable. It is possible to train them to become more like fast-twitch muscle fibers—for sprinting—or to train them to become more like slow-twitch muscle fibers to become more of a distance athlete. I was born with a majority of slow-twitch muscle fibers for long-distance swimming, and through the years I had conditioned the intermediate fibers to become more like slow-twitch fibers, but when I trained for the swims in Antarctica and the Arctic, I trained more like a sprinter. It had worked. I got myself to sprint. I would never be a Thoroughbred, though, just a faster Clydesdale. But if I didn't continue to work the intermediate muscle fibers to be like fast-twitch fibers, I would lose that training. I wondered if there was a way to develop these fibers better and get a better result. If I worked out harder, with more intensity, maybe I could sustain the sprint for a longer distance. Maybe that would be possible.

But at that moment, I needed to see if I had figured out a better way of rewarming after a frigid swim. I had tried the standard rewarming technique after my swim in Antarctica—passively shivering, with the crew huddling around me. It had seemed like a good idea. It worked for penguins, but it wasn't very effective for me.

Now I could try active rewarming. This might be the solution to rewarming more effectively and efficiently after cold exposure.

Christian, the priest, greeted us with great bear hugs. We talked with him for a few minutes, but I was afraid of letting my core temperature drop. I decided to rewarm by climbing the stair walkway to the top of the town and then walking back to the hotel. There I got into a cold shower and gradually added more warm water. Gretchen stayed close by to make sure that I didn't rewarm too quickly and pass out in the shower.

After about a twenty-minute shower the exterior of my

body was warm, and I felt great. This was so different than what I'd experienced after my swim in Antarctica. My swim in Antarctica had been twenty minutes longer, but the water there had been 32 degrees Fahrenheit.

When I first started swimming in water temperatures around 42 degrees Fahrenheit, I noticed the effects of the water temperature became more and more dramatic for each degree the water temperature dropped. The difference may have been only one degree lower, but it seemed to have an exponential effect on the body, like the logarithmic Richter scale used for measuring earthquakes; for each full degree that the temperature dropped, the effect felt ten times greater. There had only been a 3.5-degree-Fahrenheit difference between Antarctica and Greenland.

We celebrated that afternoon in the hotel lobby, along with new friends we'd made during our stay. Gretchen, Bill, and Bob couldn't stop smiling, and neither could I. We decompressed the next day, just relaxed and spent some time with Konrad and Karen taking in the sights and beauty of Ilulissat. We talked about wanting to return to explore Greenland more, one day.

I'm with (from left to right) Bob Griffith, Bill Lee, and Gretchen Goodall, each thrilled to complete the swim, about to walk past Greenland polar explorer Knut Rasmussen's historic home and pay a brief tribute.

I called an official to thank him for his help making some initial connections. He said, "I heard you only swam for five minutes. All of that work and you only swam for five minutes."

That surprised me, and I said that it was the first time I'd ever swum in 28-degree water. I had really extended myself. And I told him that if I hadn't swum for those five minutes, I wouldn't know what I could do. This was the beginning for something more. Sometimes it took time. Sometimes you had to build on experience. Often it didn't happen all at once.

When Amundsen left Disko Bay, he sailed north along the west coast of Greenland through dangerously thick drift ice and dense ice fog in Melville Bay, near what is now Thule Air Base. Amundsen described this area as the most dreaded and desolate part of the Arctic Ocean. He and his crew were fortunate. The water in Melville Bay was calm, and the ice was manageable. When the *Gjøa* reached Dalrymple Rock, Amundsen and his crew were suddenly surprised by two Inuit men emerging from the swirling cloud and fog and paddling directly for the *Gjøa*. Suddenly six more kayaks appeared; one was draped with a Norwegian flag, and another was covered with a Danish flag. In this group of six kayaks, Knud Rasmussen and Ludvig Mylius-Erichsen appeared.

Rasmussen and Amundsen, two of the world's great polar explorers, met joyously among icebergs at the top of the world at the beginning of their careers, and this meeting would begin a long-lasting friendship.

Mylius-Erichsen handed Amundsen a letter from Captains Milne and Adams, two Scottish whalers whom Amundsen had arranged to place provisions on Dalrymple Rock for Amundsen and his crew. The letter from the captains wished Amundsen success on his voyage. Amundsen and his crew were eager to continue their journey.

. . .

At the airport in Kangerlussuaq, we sat in the waiting area, in seats where we had sat only a week before. We were fortunate that the weather had been bad, or we never would have been stuck at the airport and met Samantha East and Brian Gomula, nor been able to gather weather information for the swim. We wondered how they had fared. Had they made their meetings in Ilulissat? Were they on their way to the Russel Glacier now? Just at that moment I turned to look out the airport window and saw them.

Samantha and Brian joined us. I think we were as excited about seeing them in the airport as Amundsen had been when he met Rasmussen in the Arctic Ocean. There is always something special that happens when travelers reconnect; perhaps it is just knowing that there are stories to share, and perhaps it was just because I had enjoyed meeting them so much before. In any case, it was great seeing them again.

"Did you swim yet? We didn't see anything in the papers," Samantha said.

"Yes, I did. I swam a quarter of a mile in twenty-eight-point-eight-degree Fahrenheit water in a time of five minutes and ten seconds. I think it's the fastest I've ever swum."

"Three point two degrees below freezing, it must have felt so cold," Brian said.

"It was," I said, and smiled and thought Brian knew freezing. He flew on the Greenland ice cap and in Antarctica.

Gretchen said, "We were freezing in the Zodiac. I was crouched down low in the boat, to use the bow to block the wind. I could feel the cold water radiating through the Zodiac's floor."

"I had no idea you were so cold. I thought you had on clothes that were warm enough," I said.

"That can happen with an LC-130 in a survival situation. The aircraft can cool down so that they become like giant freezers," Samantha said.

We swapped stories with Samantha and Brian, and Bob and Bill joined us, and we bragged about one another. I longed to hear more about what they were doing, but our plane was boarding. Samantha and I exchanged contact information, and I gave her a copy of my book to share with Brian. Samantha told me I didn't have to hurry, they were taking the same plane as us back to the United States. We sat beside each other, and for most of the flight Samantha asked me about swimming, and I asked her about flying. And when we reached Baltimore, I sensed that maybe someday we might meet again.

CHAPTER 12

Baffin Island

Bob, Gretchen, Bill, and I flew south to return to our normal lives, and for the month of June 2007, I worked out and waited for the Canadian Arctic to thaw. I trained differently and increased the intensity in my workouts to a level I had never reached before. I knew I had to do this if I wanted to be able to achieve something more significant. Each day I did hour-long spinning classes in the gym and then, for a second hour, a variety of other classes: moderate weights with high reps, yoga, Pilates, and a step class, or cardio. In the afternoon, I did only sprints in a backyard swimming pool for half an hour to an hour.

On August 17, 1903, Amundsen turned west, leaving Greenland behind, and crossed Baffin Bay. Often, I thought of him and how he had sailed across through those treacherous waters. On that five-day passage, the ship's magnetic compass, because of his closeness to the North Pole, stopped working, and they sailed into the unknown and for the most part blind. The feelings Amundsen had had when the *Gjøa* sailed into Lancaster Sound and anchored in Erebus Bay across from Beechey Island were dramatic and profound. This was where Amundsen's hero, John Franklin, the British Royal Navy officer, and his two ships and his men had been lost in 1845.

This loss was one of the reasons Amundsen was so motivated to find the Northwest Passage. Amundsen wrote:

I pictured to myself the splendidly equipped Franklin Expedition heading into the harbor, and anchoring there. The *Erebus* and *Terror* in all their splendor; the English colors flying at the masthead and the two fine vessels full of bustle. . . . Certainly these brave men had succeeded in discovering much new land, but only to see their expectations of accomplishment of the North West Passage that way brought to nought by impenetrable masses of ice. (*The North-west Passage,* vol. 1, 47–48)

John Franklin and his crew of 129 men succumbed to starvation; some of the men resorted to cannibalism. Their ships were crushed by the ice and lost to the sea. It must have been eerie for Amundsen to stand on those desolate shores, contemplating the path he and his crew in the *Gjøa* would choose.

I thought of following Amundsen and Franklin to Beechey Island, but it was a remote island connected to Devon Island by an isthmus. On Beechey Island there was a graveyard where some of Franklin's men were buried. Somehow it was just too bleak for me to swim near a graveyard, and Devon Island was so desolate that NASA sent its astronauts there to train to simulate a landing on Mars. What attracted me to loosely following Amundsen's route was that I would meet people in these far reaches of the world, have the chance to see how they lived. I got back in touch with Adam Ravetch, my friend who lived in Canada and who had spent a lot of time in the Canadian Arctic creating documentaries on polar bears and walrus and Greenland sharks. After discussing some options with him, it seemed like Pond Inlet, on Baffin Island, was the place to swim. Baffin Island, the largest island in Canada's Arctic Archipelago in the Nunavut Territory, was directly south of Beechey and Devon Islands. There were Inuit living near Pond Inlet and there would be much to explore.

The path Bob and I took was not direct. Flights to the Canadian Arctic were infrequent, weather dependent, and often delayed. From Montreal, Canada, I flew in an Aérospatiale two-engine turboprop to Baffin Island. The island is shaped like a lobster. We flew to the southeast coast of the island and landed on the lobster's tail in Iqaluit, a city of roughly six thousand people. While we were gathering our luggage, we met two strong middle-aged construction workers who said they had worked on many of the hotels and government buildings in Iqaluit. They offered us a ride to the Frobisher Hotel, where we would be staying. Bob and I eagerly accepted. What could be more exciting than having the men who built the town showing us around?

We jumped into their dark blue Ford F-150 and rode from the airport along a two-lane brown dirt road, past artist's studios and tourist shops, beyond which were some sled dogs tied off near a stream so they could be near a constant source of fresh water. The workers showed us the attractive bright-red-painted wooden Canadian government office buildings that they had built, the hospital and hotels that they had worked on, as well as the modern library and tourist center close to the bay. They said that with the opening of the Northwest Passage, and with the melting of the ice, there had been an acceleration of construction to accommodate the growing city of Iqaluit and to support development in the Arctic. There was promise of oil and mineral wealth in the north, and the Canadian government was supporting growth to ensure that the land remained Canadian.

The construction workers let us off at the hotel, and they wished us well as they drove off with a swell of dirt rising from their truck tires, trailing behind them and becoming airborne as a cold stiff wind ripped across Frobisher Bay, making the day feel like February when it actually was the second of July.

In the morning, we took off from Iqaluit in an Aérospatiale bound for Pond Inlet. Just beyond Iqaluit, Baffin Island was covered with a wavering carpet of soft golden grasses, a reminder that fall had been captured by a sudden white winter snow. And now in early July, with the extended days of Arctic sunlight, the hard, frozen land was thawing, softening like a down pillow, and the sparkling rivulets pulled by gravity were

*Flying above Baffin Island, named for William Baffin,
who searched in 1615 for the Northwest Passage with Captain
Robert Bylot aboard the ship* Discovery, *the same ship used by
Henry Hudson to try to find the Northwest Passage. The same
ship was used on other expeditions in search of the Northwest
Passage as well as the establishment of Jamestown,
in the colony of Virginia, in 1607.*

collecting in shallow basins, growing into silver and blue-black
ponds. There were patches of green grass and a feeling of spring.

As we flew farther north, Baffin Island looked like Greenland's cousin. Mountains rose abruptly from the sea, but they
were rounder and smoother than Greenland's glacier peaks.
The valleys below were more U-shaped, and they cradled
frozen rivers. The island was encased in a thick enamel of dark
glistening ice. There was something austere and troubling
about the scene. It looked as if the island had never awakened
from a winter's slumber.

We flew north of the Arctic Circle through bright blue skies
superinfused by brilliant Arctic light, along the craggy eastern

edge of Baffin Island, and above the silky blue waters of Baffin Bay. The pilot announced over the PA system that he would attempt a landing at Clyde River, a hamlet of 820 people, about halfway up the lobster-shaped island.

Attempt a landing? I thought. That didn't sound very promising. A robust woman in her fifties with a kind face, sitting across the aisle from me, must have noticed my puzzled expression. She explained that landings and takeoffs around Clyde River were always like that. She flew in and out occasionally. She was a psychiatric nurse, and she visited all of the communities on Baffin Island and provided medical care to the local people. The airport was often foggy, the runway short, and it was surrounded on all sides by mountains that made takeoffs and landings challenging. More often than not, she explained, the pilot had to fly over Clyde River and land somewhere else.

The pilot turned the aircraft west, directly toward the mountains. Within minutes they filled the horizon and loomed above us. Suddenly it felt like the aircraft had been shrunk to the size of a dragonfly, and we were riding inside the dragonfly, magically suspended between the craggy mountain faces, the deep blue fjords, and the wild white cresting sea.

We were heading for a long serrated cleft between two mountains. The hamlet of Clyde River was supposed to be at the base of the cleft, but all we could see were white clouds shaped like pinfeathers and smoky fog swirling on an updraft out of the cleft. The pilot apologized that the visibility was too poor to attempt a landing, but he said he would circle a couple more times, with the hope that the fog would lift enough for him to land.

What this told me was that weather conditions could change quickly around Baffin Island. But that afternoon the fog didn't lift. The pilot said that he still couldn't see the runway, and we began a gradual ascent as he turned the aircraft north toward Pond Inlet.

As the plane flew higher into the Arctic Circle, toward the top of the world, my excitement grew. I had been to remote places in the world, but few as remote as Baffin Island. To the

Flying over Pond Inlet, an Inuit town of about thirteen hundred people named in 1818 by James Ross for John Pound, the British astronomer.

left was the Arctic Cordillera, a snowy mountain chain that rose up seven thousand feet and ran along the northeastern section of the island. The Arctic Cordillera must have seemed like an icy fortress to the Vikings during their explorations around A.D. 1000. The stark glacial mountains looked unwelcoming, like frozen death.

The pilot lined the aircraft up with the two mountains on Bylot Island. He flew over Eclipse Sound between Bylot Island and Baffin Island. It was July 3, 2007, and the sound was frozen solid. The ice looked like a sheet of blown glass with whorling patterns of opaque white on a transparent blue background, and the patterns within the ice changed in different places. In some areas the blue ice was spotted with white ovals, cratered moons, and rings shaped like those around Saturn. In others it looked as if the sea had captured the globular clusters of stars from the sky and frozen them into the sparkling ice.

As we began our descent, I stared at the sound, trying to find a crack in the ice or a space of open water. All that spread before us was ice. As we descended I hoped to see thin transparent ice, but this ice was opaque and thick. How long would it take to break up? We only planned to be in Pond Inlet for nine days. Would the ice melt soon enough to swim?

We landed on a dirt runway, and we walked to the one-room terminal. Jared Arnakallak, the manager of the Sanuiq, the hotel were we'd be staying, met us in a beaten-up white van and drove us a quarter of a mile to the hotel, a single-story building painted chocolate brown that looked like a large double-wide trailer.

The rooms were clean, with twin beds and a bathroom with a shower in each room. Bob's room overlooked the dirt parking lot, and I had a view of wooden homes built on a slope and a wedge of the ice-covered sound and Bylot Island. Prices were high, around $250 per room, and more if meals were included, but this was the only place in town that served food, other than the Co-op store where people who lived in the hamlet bought food and day-to-day items, most of which were sent by barge once a year or flown up at an incredibly steep rate throughout the year.

Adam Ravetch suggested that I get in touch with David Reid, who ran a company called Polar Sea Adventures. David took photographers, adventurers, filmmakers, and tourists on wooden qamutiks—dog-pulled sledges—to the surrounding areas. Adam said that David was concerned foremost about safety when he ran these trips, and he was very open to new ideas and exploring.

We walked down the hill through one section of town, on a dirt road, past colorful single- and double-story homes, some recently painted, and others faded by the weather and wind. The town seemed vacant, although we could hear the sounds of construction: hammering and sawing. We passed the large new health clinic and turned right and walked to a white house with a van parked out front with POLAR SEA ADVENTURES written on the side.

The van had a flat tire, so we suspected that David was at home, but there was no sign of life or movement inside. We decided he must be asleep, so we reluctantly continued our walk around Pond Inlet. There was a large new blue-gray library overlooking the sound, and a small building housing the National Parks Department, where one small, lean Inuit man, wearing a park service uniform, was standing by the doorway.

He invited us in to see photos of Sirmilik National Park. There were photos of kittiwakes nesting in cliffs and old photos of the Byam Martin Mountains and their glacial peaks. By comparing the old photos inside the building and having us step outside and look at the Byam Martin Mountain glacier, across Eclipse Sound, the park service guide showed us how quickly the glaciers on Bylot Island were receding.

At that time of the year, the only way to land on Bylot Island was by helicopter, and while we were there, the helicopter was booked for the summer by geologists who were studying the glaciers and the Canadian Broadcasting Corporation, which was filming a documentary on global warming.

We continued our walk through town, noticing caribou skins hanging outside homes, snowmobiles parked beside houses, and beaten-up trucks. Two young children playing outside said hello and waved, and dogs fenced or tied up outside barked. It felt like a lonely place.

By the time we returned to the hotel, Jared had reached David by phone, and he joined us in the hotel cafeteria. David was a six-foot-tall Scotsman, with a buzz cut, sunburned cheeks, and the bluest eyes. He had just returned with a tourist group from the floe edge, which was about fifty miles from Pond Inlet, where the frozen waters of Eclipse Sound met the open waters of Baffin Bay.

Narwhales were waiting at the floe edge. They are called unicorns of the sea, or moon, or polar whales because of their white bodies. When they matured they could be thirteen to sixteen feet long. Male narwhales are known for the giant eight-to-ten-foot-long spiral tusk that grows out of their upper lip. Scientists believe that their tusks have a variety of purposes. Some think the tusks are sensory organs used by the narwhales to detect temperature changes, pressure changes, and salinity. Others believe that they are used for courting or displays of dominance. Often people observed male narwhales tusking—rubbing their tusks together to clean off crustaceans and other unwanted sea life, a form of brushing their tusks.

The narwhales were waiting at the floe edge for the ice to break up so they could migrate into Eclipse Sound, Oliver Sound, and the fjords, where they would spend the summer feeding on squid, halibut, shrimp, and redfish.

David explained in his lilting Scottish brogue that at the floe edge, there was a lot of activity. The edge was where polar bears hunted for narwhales and beluga whales and seals, and it was where Inuit hunted for these animals.

David's tourist group had camped on the sea ice near the floe edge, and they had to be cautious. There were polar bears. David's brow furrowed when he talked about the bears. On two separate camping trips, a polar bear had come into camp. He said, "Adult males can be from seven to nine feet tall and weigh up to fifteen hundred pounds. They are the world's largest predator on land. And they are very dangerous." He paused, and his voice grew more breathy as he recounted, "One large male, seven or eight feet tall, came to within a few hundred yards of our camp, and another time a different bear got near our tents. I carry a rifle for protection. And I hire a local Inuit guide whose job is to be on polar bear watch. He is a pro, but polar bears can be very stealthy. And often you don't hear their approach."

"Did you fire your rifle to scare the bear off?" Bob asked.

David shook his head. "No, a shot sounds like ice cracking, so it doesn't scare the bear. He doesn't know he should be afraid of the sound. There's not much that threatens a polar bear."

"Are there a lot of them around here?" I asked.

"Not usually, but a couple days ago, one came to the edge of town, and the parks people managed to scare him away."

"Are bears good swimmers?" I asked.

"Yes, they are. They have large front paws that they use like paddles. They swim a sort of dog paddle with their heads above water. They're suited for the cold water. They have thick fur coats, body fat, and black skin that absorbs the sunlight and warmth. I've heard of them swimming hundreds of miles off shore," he said.

"Will polar bears be something I should be concerned about during my swim?"

David frowned. "Normally, I wouldn't think so, but that bear that was just here could return. We'll have to check out the area thoroughly before you swim."

We discussed the best way to organize the swim. My goal was to swim a mile in the sound, four times farther than in Greenland, but I had one large concern: would the ice break up enough to swim in six days? I wanted to swim on July 9, Nunavut Day—a celebration of the signing of the Nunavut Land Claims Agreement in 1993, which led, in 1999, to the region's recognition as an official Canadian territory, allowing it to have some degree of self-rule and control over its own institutions.

David said that the floe edge was beginning to break up, and that with a few good winds, the sea ice would also begin breaking up. We discussed having David and Bob in a boat, but we couldn't be sure if there would be enough room for a boat to get through the ice, and the ice could damage a propeller. David said that he could escort me in a kayak. He often kayaked in the sound, and he could carry the rescue rope and clamp it onto my harness if I had a problem and tow me to shore.

This wasn't the ideal way to do a swim; it would have been better to have David drive the boat and Bob as the support person, but we were doing something different, and it was exciting to think about this in a new way. It would be a challenge to swim through the sea ice and see what my body could do. But I had some concerns.

I wanted to train, to try to acclimate or at least just work out, but the only place where there was open water was the Salmon River on the edge of town, where the current ran too fast to swim without a boat as protection, and we couldn't get a boat to the river area. There wasn't a gym, and so Bob hiked with me a couple times a day for two or three hours. We walked around the hamlet, past the government buildings, airport, and hamlet office, and to the outer areas of town. We paused at the cemetery, and wandered along the beach where sled dogs were tied up. We climbed the hills behind the town to see the freshwater pond that fed the hamlet's water system. We stopped at the ancient dump to look at cars and vehicles, and strolled across the tundra—a fairyland of miniature wildflowers, yellow Arctic poppies and delicate daisies the size of a thumbnail, tiny purple and yellow saxifrage, and fluffy Arctic cotton.

On each hike, we included a view of Eclipse Sound from the bluffs and from the beach, and we studied the surface of the sound, and for the first time, we watched the sky for clouds and hoped for really bad weather with strong winds that would roar across the sound and increase currents under the ice, creating enough force to encourage it to break up.

Between our hikes, we had our meals in the hotel cafeteria and met most of the construction workers, scientists, and engineers who were staying at the hotel. We became friends with Amy Chin, a traveling nurse from Newfoundland, and her friend Karen Nutarak, who was a nurse from Pond Inlet. They worked in the health clinic, but one day took a break to see the visitors' center at the same time I was there looking at exhibits. Karen gave us an insider's tour and showed us traditional clothing and equipment that had been made by her family and friends.

She also explained that she and some of the people in Pond Inlet competed in throat singing. It was an Inuit tradition. She had learned from her elders how to sing in the back of her throat and how to imitate the sounds of nature, like the calls of geese, the movement of the wind, and the flight of a mosquito.

Karen said that during a competition one person would sing a throat song, then the other competitor would repeat the song and add a variation. As they competed, the song would grow longer with each repetition and each variation. And the competition continued until someone ran out of breath or started laughing, and then the person who sang the longest without a mistake would become the winner.

Karen demonstrated throat singing. She drew in a very deep breath and sang in the back of her throat. It was not like any human song I had ever heard. She had great focus and amazing control, and she sounded like a goose, then the wind, and she transformed other voices from nature into her own.

Karen's song was beautiful, exotic, and powerful. She really enjoyed performing for us. She explained that it took a lot of training to keep her voice in shape. And then she offered to sing some *ajajaj* songs for us. She explained that they were traditional folk songs in the Inuktitut language. They were melodic and beautiful and equally exotic. Karen and Amy had to return to the clinic, and so I walked back to the hotel to have lunch with Bob.

During one lunch, we met Edward Little, who worked with the Geological Survey of Canada in Calgary. Edward had been studying the glaciers on the mountain on Bylot Island across Eclipse Sound. He had observed over the past two years that one glacier in particular was rapidly receding, and he was very concerned.

The hotel usually had people coming and going, but Pond Inlet always looked deserted. During one lunch, David joined us, and he explained that to the Inuit the normal state of water was ice. When it thawed, it became very dangerous, mostly because the majority of the hunters couldn't swim. It was already too thin for hunting, so many of the people had gone "on the land." They would camp out with their families in tents for most of the summer and hunt caribou and other game.

In Amundsen's time, the Inuit were nomadic, following the food source—the herds of caribou, Arctic char, seals, nar-whales, and polar bears—but in the 1960s, as a way to secure Canadian sovereignty, the Inuit were moved into government-built communities. For the most part, the people who lived on Baffin Island were still hunters and fishermen, and many of the families also received government assistance. Jobs were scarce, but the Baffinland mining company had recently applied to open an iron-ore mine a hundred miles south of Pond Inlet, a project that would involve the construction of a railway and a deepwater port to transport the ore to Europe. This port hadn't been considered until recently, when the ice began to thaw and areas that were once inaccessible by ship were opening up.

One day at breakfast, we met Richard Cook, who was working for a company hired by the mines to study the environmental impact the mine would have on the people who lived in Pond Inlet. In conducting this research, Richard had met with the local hamlet leaders numerous times and was welcomed into many homes where he was served traditional food: rotten walrus, which was one of the Inuit delicacies that probably originated when the Inuit had some extra meat, and wanted to keep it safe from bears. Richard explained that the Inuit dug a hole in the ground and saved the meat for three or four months.

When the meat was really rotten or, as the Inuit said, very tender, they served it to their family and guests. Richard was at a gathering and was offered the rotten walrus, and he didn't feel he could refuse or he would be considered ungrateful or rude. Richard looked at us and winced. "So I took a big breath before I put the rotten walrus in my mouth. And I don't know why, but I made the mistake of breathing just after I swallowed the rotten walrus, and I almost threw it up. My eyes were all tearing up, and I had to take a long drink to get it back down. It's hard, you want to accept their generosity, but sometimes, it's really difficult," he said.

"What about seal? Have you tried that?" Bob asked.

Richard pursed his lips together and nodded. "It's very oily and rich, and it has the tendency to clean out your system. I'm not a fan."

"The Arctic char looks good," I said.

"It is. It tastes just like salmon. It's delicious."

"Are there any unusual customs you've discovered here?" Bob asked.

Richard hesitated, as if he still couldn't quite understand, and he said, "The Inuit have open adoption. It seems strange to me, but it may be a way to keep the community alive. If you have a family, and you are expecting another child, and another husband and wife don't have any children, they may ask you for yours, and often, people give their children to other people in the community. The children grow up knowing who is raising them, and who their biological parents are."

Bob thought about it for a moment. Raised on a farm in Calloway, Nebraska, he was very practical. He said, "It must encourage a distribution of their resources and ensure the survival of the community."

It was good that Bob came from Calloway, where life was slower. It was hard for me to gear down to Arctic time, but Bob had no problem. For six days we watched the ice slowly crack. There were small leads, then finally larger ones, where the Salmon River flowed into the sound, but the open water was too far from shore, and we couldn't get out to the open water safely. Each day we watched a game that locals played to see who could keep a heavy snowmobile or qamutik dogsled on the ice the longest, without it falling through the ice and sinking to the bottom of the sound, and as we watched some snowmobiles start to sink, we realized that this was a signal the ice was melting.

Restlessly, we waited, and I thought of Amundsen in Antarctica on the *Belgica* waiting for months for the ice to break so he could sail back to Norway. This was nothing compared with his icy internment.

We met people working in the hamlet offices, their city hall, and we were introduced to the mayor and his friend, a former government representative named Paul, who was in his sixties and had traveled extensively throughout Canada and to New York City. When he asked me what I was doing in Pond Inlet, and I told him, he pushed his wire-rimmed glasses back against his face and looked more closely. "Aren't you afraid of the Greenland shark?"

"Are they a problem here?" Adam had filmed in Canadian waters, too. He hadn't told me that the Greenland sharks that lived in Canadian waters were different from the ones that lived off Greenland. He didn't tell me to be more careful.

Paul shook his head and said, "They must be different than the sharks in Greenland. In Canada, they're very aggressive. I've seen them attack boat paddles and each other. They're cannibalistic. And you have to watch out for stingrays, too. They're really large and they can really sting you," he added.

I was trying to figure out if Paul was joking or if he was serious. I glanced at Bob. He was smiling. He thought Paul was just kidding with me. But I wasn't sure. The following day, I asked David, and he said he had seen some small Greenland sharks six or seven feet long swimming close to shore. He said they didn't appear to be aggressive. He didn't think they would be a problem. But he said he never had to consider this before.

By Nunavut Day, sections of the ice had finally broken up. Near the center of Pond Inlet was an area of water about two hundred yards wide that had been created by the flow of the Salmon River. A mile and a half west, more water had opened up at the mouth of a fast-flowing stream. Beyond that, there were five-to-six-foot-high blocks of sea ice.

David Reid attaching the rescue rope and carabiner to the kayak, completely prepared and professional.

David carried his yellow kayak over his head down a steep embankment, past two wary sled dogs, and set it in the water. He was wearing a waterproof jacket and pants, a knit cap, and rubber-sole shoes. He was completely prepared. He looped the rescue rope around his waist, slipped into the cockpit, and covered himself with a spray deck to keep his lower body dry and prevent cold waves of spray from entering the boat; it was also an added safety measure, since if the boat tipped over, he could roll the kayak and right it without being tossed out. Then he paddled out into the sea ice.

David tied the water thermometer onto the kayak and took temperatures throughout the swim. I asked him not to tell me until I completed the swim. But when he held the thermometer up and looked at it, I saw it too. It read 28.8 degrees Fahrenheit, minus 2 degrees Celsius.

After he put the thermometer back into the water, his face became very serious, and he focused directly on me.

We had a plan. My first goal was to swim out to one of the chunks of sea ice beside David. If I managed that, I would follow him through the narrow passages between the ice. The only problem was that from shore we couldn't see if the channels were open or if there were ice shelves under the water that we might collide with or run aground on. I dragged my feet as I walked slowly into the silver-blue water so I wouldn't step on any stingrays. A chill ran up from my feet, through my legs and back, and out along my shoulders.

"This is great," I said, when I reached David. "Let's go to the right." The water felt as cold as it had in Greenland, but my breathing was much easier. The training had paid off. I put my face down quickly into the water; my hips rose, my body leveled out, and my swimming was easier. I looked under the white chunks of floating ice. There were no fins, thankfully, only crystal blue water and a small, delicate, white brittle starfish with long thin arms about five feet below me.

Quickly, I lifted my head; the water was too cold to put my face into it for very long. Swimming with my head up, I followed David around a small chunk of sea ice and entered an

Finally, the wind and water burst the sea ice, and I swim while friends watch from shore and help me gauge the distance yet to swim.

area where there were larger blocks of ice on either side of me. It was like entering a snowy sculpture garden, one that might have been inspired by Henry Moore—the ice had been rounded and smoothed by the winds and the waves and the tides.

To my right was a ten-foot-long block of ice that looked like a reclining polar bear with glistening white fur. On my left, another resembled a snowy white egret taking flight; another looked like a baby beluga. As I swam through the maze, I became a little afraid. There were ice ledges that extended under the water; David pointed to them with his paddle, but I still misjudged my position due to a current moving through the water and hit one. It hurt dully. I checked my forearm. Fortunately there was no sign of blood.

I caught up with David and gradually put my face back in the water. It was so much easier to swim that way—my hips and legs were not dragging, and I could see clearly below the water's surface. I checked for sharks. I couldn't get them out of my mind. But I also looked for narwhales and belugas.

As I followed David into deeper water, the supernatural Arctic sun saturated the sound and made the water resonate with energy waves. The sea became fire blue and searing cold. And where there was sea ice, the floating forms focused the sunlight into sunbeams that illuminated the soft, silty brown seafloor and three tiny brittle starfish. While I was swimming, I was gauging the distance we had traveled, making sure that I had enough energy to get back to shore. And although my outer body was numb and crimson red, my inner core felt warm.

I continued sprinting through the passage, watching David paddle on each breath. The small kayak was an extension of his body, he could move right between the narrowest sections of ice, spin the kayak around, and paddle backward. When I turned and wasn't paying attention, my right arm got hung up on an underwater ice shelf. David must have heard a change in my stroke rate, and glanced back to check on me before I shouted that I was okay and asked him how long I'd been swimming.

"Twenty minutes," he said. "One more crossing of the bay?"

Bob was standing near the edge of the shore with friends whom we had met at the hotel. They had come to show their support, as had a group of nurses and friends from the health clinic, people from the city government, and people from the neighborhood.

Bob gave me the thumbs-up sign, and I lifted my foot to signal all was well. Once I finished the loop, I headed into shore and found that I had been in the water for twenty-three minutes. Bob said the water temperature was 28.8 degrees Fahrenheit, and I had reached my goal of swimming a mile, a distance four times longer than in Greenland, in water 4 degrees colder than Antarctica. I was satisfied. Once out of the water I needed to keep moving, to hike back through town, and generate heat through my muscle movement, to see if I recovered more quickly than after the swim in Antarctica. After that swim, I was miserable and exhausted from the intense shivering. If it was possible to keep moving, my body would generate enough heat to compensate for the cooled blood on the exterior part of my body.

I got my sweats and shoes on and climbed the hills back to the hotel and continued walking for about forty-five minutes, then I climbed into the shower, turned on the warm water, and gradually added warmer water. Within fifteen minutes, the external part and internal part of my body were back to normal, and I wasn't exhausted as I had been for a couple days after the Antarctic swim. This was a much better way for me to rewarm.

Back in town, we joined the Nunavut Day celebrations. Community leaders were grilling hot dogs and hamburgers. Nearby a pair of caribou carcasses were lying on a tarp. Two others in the community were butchering the caribou and distributing the meat. Some large pieces had already been given

Using an ulu, *a half-moon-shaped Inuit knife traditionally used for skinning animals, cutting hair, and trimming blocks of snow and ice for igloos, a grandmother shows her granddaughter how to follow the ribs and cut caribou into smaller pieces.*

out. Men were holding big chunks of raw meat between their teeth with one hand and slicing off pieces of meat with eight-inch-bladed knives with their other hand. One slip of the knife and they would take off their lips. The women were holding the meat between their teeth with one hand and cutting off chewable parts using an *ulu* knife—a very sharp, half-moon-shaped blade. One woman sliced a white bit of meat, and she explained that it was part of the stomach. She was thoroughly enjoying it, and its bright green contents could have been moss.

Standing nearby, an elderly woman made a fire of a small pile of dried heather to heat water for tea. She had collected the heather earlier in the day, and burning it created a swirling stream of smoke that filled the air with a fresh and clean fragrance.

One of the nurses from the health center, who was originally from British Columbia, accepted a slice of raw caribou from an Inuit woman. They tried to entice Bob or me to try a slice of raw caribou and told us that it tasted like rare roast beef. They said that we didn't have to worry about getting parasites

An elder has the job of butchering the caribou and dividing it among the Inuit families.

Best friends standing in line on Nunavut Day waiting for hot dogs. The girl on the left is wearing a traditional anorak lined with fur made by her mother; the girl on the right is wearing a modern sweater and headband.

Brothers ready to participate in the traditional tug-of-war competition and footraces. They will celebrate with the community and dance and sing in the land of the endless sun.

from eating the caribou, although one could get trichinosis from raw walrus or polar bear unless it was aged in a cache for three or four months. But eating aged walrus or polar bear was an acquired taste. We passed. We watched a tug-of-war and running games, and that evening packed our bags. I thought again of Amundsen. When he left the grave site on Beechey Island on August 24, 1903, he sailed southwest, through Peel Sound and into unknown waters. He wrote, "Our voyage now assumed a new character. Hitherto we had been sailing in safe and known waters, where many others had preceded us. Now we were making our way through waters never sailed in, save possibly a couple of vessels, and were hoping to reach still farther where no keep had ever ploughed." But Amundsen almost lost the *Gjøa*.

In James Ross Strait—named for the British naval officer who reached the North Magnetic Pole in 1831 and later led the first search for Franklin—Amundsen awoke to the violent shock of the *Gjøa* running aground. He raced to the deck and found the ship was stuck on a bank. He and his crew set the sails and turned the engine on full speed. They managed to free the *Gjøa*, only to have her hit a shoal and splinter the false keel. And that same night, Amundsen heard a terrifying shriek as fire broke out in the engine room, near tanks holding twenty-two hundred gallons of petroleum. The crew desperately pumped water on the flames and managed to put out the fire.

CHAPTER 13

King William Island

By the time Amundsen and his crew sailed through the Rae Strait, more than five hundred miles from Beechey Island, they were completely exhausted. They hoped to find a place where they could stop and spend the winter. On September 9, 1903, on the sandy shores of King William Island, they found, Amundsen wrote, "A small harbor quite sheltered from the wind, a veritable haven of rest for us weary travelers."

Amundsen named the harbor Gjøa Haven: "The harbor itself was all that could be desired." He noted that the narrow entrance would prevent the intrusion of large masses of ice, and the inner basin was so small that no wind could trouble them there no matter from what quarter it blew. He noticed that there were a number of cairns and tent circles that indicated the Eskimo had been there, and he also noticed fresh reindeer tracks, a sign that there would be food. He decided that a spot on a hill above the bay would be a perfect place for the magnetic station where he and his crew would spend two years on his second objective—measuring and determining the location of the North Magnetic Pole. They also made astronomical measurements, as well as weather and temperature measurements.

During their stay in Gjøa Haven, Amundsen and his men became friends with the Eskimo who lived on King William Island, the Ogluli Eskimo who camped near Kaa-aak-ka Lake and the Nechilli Eskimo. Both were migratory peoples. They followed and hunted the caribou herds. In summer they lived in caribou-skin tents, and in winter they lived in igloos and traveled by dogsled. Amundsen and his crew learned the Eskimo dogsledding techniques and how to let the runners of the sleds become covered by a fine layer of snow so they would slide across the snow more easily.

The Eskimo also taught Amundsen and his crew how to prevent frostbite. They took their warm hands out of their gloves and applied them to frozen sections of their bodies until they warmed and blood circulated back into those areas. Amundsen became good friends with an Eskimo named Atikleura, who Amundsen believed was the most skilled among his tribe.

From Atikleura, Amundsen and his men learned the complex task of building igloos by cutting blocks of snow with a large knife that had a blade as large as a butcher knife and a handle a foot long. Atikleura cut blocks of snow that were about eighteen inches wide, twenty-four inches long, and four inches thick. Then he built the igloo up in spirals with one layer of blocks placed on top of another and each layer placed a bit farther inward. The blocks of snow were fitted together so they were seamless. Atikleura's wife, Nalungia, filled in any cracks with snow to make sure the wind couldn't penetrate. It took considerable skill. The last block that fit in on the top of the roof was usually a triangular block of snow. The door was cut in the igloo, and blocks of snow were cut and carried inside to create a bed that was covered with skins, and a table made of snow blocks was constructed inside the igloo.

Amundsen and his crew traded with the Inuit for reindeer and fish, and in return the Inuit were given sewing needles and knives. Amundsen invited the Inuit to join with them and celebrate Christmas and New Year's on board the *Gjøa*.

Nalungia made the finest reindeer clothing of all the women in the tribe. The reindeer undergarments that Atikleura wore were better for keeping warm in the Arctic than anything Amundsen had brought with him from Norway. Amundsen gestured and hinted to Atikleura that he would like to have some reindeer undergarments. Atikleura was pleased and produced some worn-out underwear, took off his clothes, put on the old underwear, and handed the ones he was wearing to Amundsen, expecting him to put them on immediately. Amundsen was surprised and hesitated. He said he wasn't accustomed to exchanging underwear with other people, and certainly not in front of Nalungia. But Atikleura insisted, so Amundsen covered himself the best he could and put on Atikleura's warm underwear.

There was on Amundsen's part a desire to understand Atikleura's way of life that proved to be critical for every voyage of exploration that Amundsen attempted in the future.

After eleven days Bob Griffith flew from Baffin Island home to California, and I flew to Gjøa Haven, a hamlet of about twelve hundred Inuit and a handful of government and medical workers from the Canadian mainland. I decided not to swim in Gjøa Haven, because I didn't have Bob there for safety. But I wanted to see the place where Amundsen spent two years of his three-year journey, so I flew across the frozen sea and still-frozen land to King William Island in the Central Canadian Arctic.

From the air, Gjøa Haven looked a lot like Pond Inlet, with the same layout of buildings, airport, and homes but without the hills or mountains. When I entered the one-room airport terminal, I looked around, trying to find a way to the Amundsen Hotel. I didn't see a hotel van or a taxi, and I listened to hear if someone was speaking English, so I could ask directions, but everyone was speaking the Inuit language. There's nothing quite like landing in a place where you don't know anyone and trying to find where you're supposed to go and not being able to speak the language.

I walked over to an older couple with their family and asked them in English if they could point me in the direction of the Amundsen Hotel. The woman pointed through the window and said they had a hotel van, and she had her husband talk to a man behind the airport counter who called the hotel. They said the van would be there in ten minutes.

After waiting half an hour, I decided to walk with my luggage the mile and a half or so into town. I was feeling a little down, being alone in such a remote place, but just as I stepped out of the terminal, an Inuit man, probably in his late twenties, pulled up in an enormous truck. He asked me if I was going to the Amundsen Hotel, and he offered me a ride. The elder couple said hello to him as they left the airport. And so I accepted his offer. He said his name was Samuel, and he drove the water truck for Gjøa Haven. I smiled. Of all the trucks I could get a ride in, I got the water truck. In a moment, I realized how doubly fortunate I was.

Samuel explained that because the ground was permafrost, the community couldn't use underground pipes. The pipes would simply freeze and burst. So the community had water trucks and sewage trucks. Everyone in town had a water tank and a sewage tank under their homes, and each day, he delivered water or removed the sewage.

Samuel jumped into the driver's side, and I climbed into the passenger's side. The ride to the Amundsen, unfortunately, took only a few minutes. Samuel was a bright spark of a guy, and he smiled so big when I asked him if he could show me how he drove the truck. He demonstrated the gearing, speed, and stopping distance based on the weight of the truck. He asked me why I had come to Gjøa Haven, and he pointed out different parts of the community, the central part where we were heading, and then the suburban area up out of town, and he mentioned where I could find the places where Amundsen and his crew had stayed.

Samuel stopped in front of the two-story-high Amundsen Hotel and explained that Jackie Flynn ran the hotel, and Leo, her husband, ran the town's co-op. They were from Newfoundland but had come north to work in Gjøa Haven until December.

Samuel lifted my swim bag out of the cab and led the way into the hotel's coffee shop and introduced me to Jackie.

Jackie explained that the hotel van had a flat tire, and they were waiting for a new tire to arrive, and it could take some time. Jackie was of Irish background with freckles and creamy white skin, a big smile, and great warmth. She was trim, probably from working hard, and moved and spoke very quickly with a Newfoundland accent and sweet Newfoundland colloquialisms.

She immediately asked why I was in Gjøa Haven and said that, in the nine months she'd been there, she'd never really had the time to explore much of the town, but she thought what I was doing was fascinating. So I asked her if she would take a break with me; she would be gone for only about an hour, so Leo wouldn't worry if he called and she wasn't there.

We walked along dirt roads, past new and rundown homes, many surrounded by rusting snowmobiles and old ATVs. There were four markers in and around town noting where Amundsen and his men had camped, but we discovered that the plaque on a distant hillside commemorating Amundsen's visit had been stolen, and the two old cemeteries in the town center had been vandalized, and the crosses were destroyed.

During the next few days, I wandered through Gjøa Haven, walking down to the tiny bay where the *Gjøa* had been anchored in clear blue waters. I walked to the site where the observation hut had been and imagined what it must have been like there in the dead of winter with temperatures plunging to 50 degrees or more below zero. I thought that many of the people I saw now must be descendants of those of Amundsen's time.

I noticed that there were several twelve- and thirteen-year-old girls with babies, and Jackie explained that this was the norm. She said that by the time the girls were in their twenties, they often had five or six children. And with the twenty-four hours of sunlight in summer, the children and teenagers stayed up all night playing unattended in the streets and hanging out in vacant homes. Sometimes they kept the hotel guests up late at night. The town looked so quiet during the day because most of the people were sleeping. Many were on government assistance. There were all kinds of problems with abuse: drug, alcohol, elderly, child, animal, and spouse. At the co-op the shoe polish and mouthwash had to be locked up. And there had been theft of yeast to make moonshine—home brews.

In spite of all this, the Inuit I met were very hospitable. They invited me into their homes, showed me how to play traditional Inuit games with dice, and served me hot tea. Through Rita Hummiktuq, a student-support assistant and the girls' soccer coach at the local school, I met Jimmy Qirqqut, Rita's uncle and one of the town's elders, who recounted an amazing story he had been told by his mother about the day his great-grandfather met Amundsen. Amundsen wrote about this encounter in his book, except Jimmy was far more dramatic when he described the initial tension between the Europeans and the Eskimo when they first met. Neither of the groups knew if the other was friend or foe.

They walked up to each other, standing close enough to see each other's eyes clearly. One of Amundsen's men had been carrying a gun, and when he set it down and put it aside, Jimmy said, the two groups realized they could be friends.

One evening, I joined Rita, Jimmy, his wife, and his wife's two sisters in Jimmy's home. The living room was sparsely furnished, with just one chair and a small couch. Jimmy sat in the chair, and Rita's tiny elderly aunt and her two small sisters insisted that Rita and I sit on the couch. They would sit on the floor. I felt uncomfortable doing this and asked them through Rita to please sit on the couch, and I would sit on the floor. They smiled and said it was more comfortable for them to sit on the floor. This was what they did when they were growing up. In the winter they had lived in igloos, and they sat on caribou skins spread on the snow floor, and in summer they had lived in caribou tents and sat and slept on the ground. They assured me that sitting on a couch was strange to them.

It seemed wrong for three elderly ladies in colorful skirts to be sitting on the floor. This was not the way I had been brought up to treat older people, so I sat cross-legged on the floor with them. They shook their heads. I was their guest, and they expected me to sit on the couch with Rita. They were three strong-willed women, and there was no way that they would give in. I laughed and thanked them, and they broke into smiles. Everyone was comfortable, and Rita asked if it was okay to let the questions begin. Jimmy wanted to know what fascinated me about Amundsen. Why had I traveled to Gjøa Haven? I explained that for four hundred years men from all over the world had attempted to sail through the Northwest Passage and Amundsen was the one who succeeded, partly because he knew that he would not be able to carry all the provisions he needed. He would have to hunt and fish and live off the land. One of the major reasons he succeeded was because of the people he met in Gjøa Haven, their ancestors.

Amundsen and his men didn't just survive when they lived in Gjøa Haven. They lived fairly well, and that was due to these people's ancestors. They showed Amundsen and his crew where to hunt and fish and how to train the dogs to pull the sleds and how to build igloos.

The elders listened to Rita and me, hanging on to each word. Their families were part of this history of great exploration; they had helped facilitate it. They had helped Amundsen and his crew accomplish their Northwest Passage.

But what Rita's family didn't know was that after finding his way through the Northwest Passage, Amundsen went on to the South Pole. Rita drew a globe with her hands and pointed to the bottom and talked about Antarctica. I was smiling because Rita and her family were from the Arctic, and they never confused where they lived with Antarctica, as so many other people in the world did.

Rita translated that the reason Amundsen succeeded in reaching the South Pole was because he had learned how to make garments from reindeer skin from their ancestors. Those garments had kept him and his crew warm on their way to the South Pole and back.

The elders smiled at the stories, and it was one of those memorable moments in life when one shares something about a loved one that was never known before. Rita continued translating, and she helped me pull everything together for them and let them know how important their families had been to opening the Arctic and Antarctica.

I told them, "Amundsen was so successful because he was open-minded. He learned from the Inuit people, and they helped him. It was because of your families who lived in Gjøa Haven and the Canadian Arctic, as well as your extended relatives in Greenland and their Greenlandic dogs that pulled the sleds with Amundsen's supplies, and that they killed for food, that Amundsen reached the South Pole."

My hosts nodded and smiled and recognized the great importance their ancestors had played. They sat up proudly, and we had tea together, and they told me about growing up in the Canadian Arctic. How they had lived like nomads, following the caribou and fish, and how difficult life was. Many friends and family members starved. They told me of great blizzards, of friends being lost on the ice, and of the day-to-day struggle to find food, especially in the winter.

Life was better for them now. They lived in heated homes in winter, and they had food. They didn't have to worry about starving as they did when they were younger. It was dinnertime, and they invited me to stay, but I knew that even though they had food, it was limited, and anything they purchased from the local co-op was extremely expensive.

For next five days I wandered around Gjøa Haven, trying to get a sense of what it must have been like for Amundsen and his crew to live there. It was a place they became very familiar with, a place where they felt almost at home. They had made celestial and magnetic observations of King William Island that had never been known by Europeans. They learned about the land and the sky and loved the protection the bay provided from the sea.

Each morning I stood on a rise where Amundsen's observation hut had once been and looked up at the heavens, wishing there would be darkness at night so I might have seen a little of what Amundsen had observed. And each day I stared across the bay where the *Gjøa* had been anchored. I wished I could see what it would be like to put into those waters.

When I first arrived, Prince William Island Sound was frozen solid, a three-foot-thick white blanket that stretched from shore to shore. As the days passed, the ice broke, and my energy and excitement grew. Floating on azure blue waters were fragments of silver ice, as thin and as transparent as glass, broken into rough-shaped trapezoids, rectangles, triangles, and squares ranging in size from six inches to six feet long. To a navigator, the ice shapes were telltale signals that soon the waters would be free for navigation.

I listened to the ice as the ice fragments rode across the tops of the tiny waves of King William Bay and collided with larger pieces of ice. The breath of the wind carried the song of the ice and waves across the bay, and the songs resounded off the sand berms—nature's amphitheater—and suddenly, out of nowhere, the wind increased in volume and stiffened to thirty-five knots, and the water rose into three-foot whitecaps that shattered the ice into tiny shards. The song of the bay grew louder, and the fine beige sand began to rise and swirl off each footstep. I leaned forward into the cold wind, sheltering my eyes with my hand from the blowing sand and feeling the tapping of the cold against my cheeks. And I walked down to the shoreline to hear and feel the day change from winter to spring. This song called to me as distinctively as the Sirens off Greek shores.

More than anything, I wanted to venture into the water, swim, explore, be where I'd never been, and learn something more. It had been only a few days, but I needed to swim as much as I needed to breathe, to stretch my arms, body, move through the water, balance within it, and find a path between the waves. I pulled off my sneakers and dipped in my toes.

It was cold—probably 35 or 36 degrees Fahrenheit. But the bay was shallow. Maybe it would be warm enough in a few days. I walked into the water up to my ankles. They hurt, and my feet felt like I had been walking barefoot though the snow. The distance across the bay was a mile or so. The water was transparent, and the bay didn't look deep. I could stop and stand up if I needed to. It would be okay to swim. But I knew that was wrong, that it would have been very foolish to go off swimming alone.

Jimmy shows off his hunting stick beside a polar-bear skin. Now he waits for the Arctic char to return to King William Island.

Still restless and feeling lonely, I walked by Jimmy the elder's small white home, hoping he would be outside working. He was. Jimmy was a medium-sized man in his seventies, thin and hollow-cheeked with bronzed skin from his genes and from working in the sun.

Jimmy showed me a fishing spear he was carving and filing down from a musk-ox horn. He held the horn up and showed me how he filed it down. His fishing spear suddenly reminded me of a picture I'd seen in Amundsen's book about the Northwest Passage.

Amundsen's best friend, Talurnakto, "the Owl," had stood knee-deep in a stream and used a spear that looked exactly the same as Jimmy's to stab trout. It was as if history had become the present within this artifact. And then I realized Jimmy must have thought about what I'd said to him, about how his ancestors had helped Amundsen learn how to survive so he could reach the South Pole.

Jimmy was teaching me how to make a fishing spear.

He turned the musk-ox horn on its side, held it with one hand, and filed with quick side-to-side hand movements with the other. He blew away the filed particles, ran his hand along the horn, and let me touch the spear so I could see how it felt.

For the next four days, I stopped by to watch him file the bone. He worked hard, taking in a deep breath, holding it as he filed, and then blowing it out. Each day the musk-ox horn was a little smoother, more refined, and the point a lot sharper.

And one day the musk-ox horn was just the shape Jimmy wanted; he attached the spear to a long wooden pole with a heavy rope. He turned the rope twice around the spear to make sure it was secure and tied it off on the bottom. He showed it to me as he worked so I would know just how to do it. We didn't need words to enjoy each other's company or to understand each other.

Sometimes words are just an embellishment for what is already known. On the day Jimmy finished the fishing spear, he showed it to me with great pride. I thanked him for teaching me and put my hand on my heart and said thank you in Inuktitut, the Inuit language. He smiled, and he said something; I couldn't understand the words, but when I turned to walk away, he said, "Good-bye." I couldn't leave like that. I walked back and extended my hand. His was large, and his long fingers wrapped around mine. We shook hands and said good-bye again.

As I walked back to the hotel I thought about what one of the local doctors had told me, that the elders like Jimmy were the ones who held the community together. They were all in their seventies, and they were slowly dying off. How would the next generation fare without their guidance?

On the way to the airport, I thought about the trip into town nine days before and how I hadn't known anyone in this community. And how much people had extended themselves, even though I was there for such a short time. It was hard to leave, and yet I was ready to go. It was much more difficult for Amundsen, I think. He had lived with the Inuit families in Gjøa Haven for two years, and when the ice finally broke, he sailed west toward Cambridge Bay on Victoria Island. I would follow him on the next flight out.

CHAPTER 14

Cambridge Bay

On August 13, 1905, Amundsen and his crew left Gjøa Haven, sailing 250 miles on the *Gjøa* through dangerously shallow and uncharted waters. There were many times the *Gjøa* nearly ran aground and days when Amundsen could not eat or sleep because he was so worried about the ship and his crew. On August 16, he entered Victoria Strait, and the following day anchored in Cambridge Bay on Victoria Island, the farthest point that ships traveling eastward from the Pacific had reached, thus completing, as Amundsen wrote, the last "unsolved link in the North West Passage."

I followed Amundsen to Cambridge Bay on Victoria Island and stayed only for a couple days, just long enough to see the sad remains of the *Maud* in Cambridge Bay, a ship that Amundsen would use on one of his future expeditions,

Ten days after Amundsen sailed out of Cambridge Bay, the *Gjøa* met with the *Charles Hanson,* a whaling ship that was sailing east from San Francisco. For Amundsen, the sight was magical. He wrote, "I could feel tears coming to my eyes." And he thought that he was now on the home stretch, but sea ice stopped the *Gjøa*'s progress at King Point on the Yukon coast. Amundsen had to anchor near shore and spend a third winter in the Arctic.

The following summer, the *Gjøa* sailed more than eight hundred miles from King Point until the sea ice forced a brief stop on Herschel Island, off the Yukon. Once the ice broke up, Amundsen set off again but made slow progress with the onslaught of more sea ice, heavy fog, and a dangerous un- charted sandbar. Finally he entered the smooth waters of Prud- hoe Bay, an inlet of the Beaufort Sea and the Arctic Ocean, covering more than 140 square miles.

In 1968, one of the largest oil reserves in North America was discovered there, and when the Trans-Alaska Pipeline was com- pleted in 1977, it was used to transport oil eight hundred miles south to Valdez. Today there are about five thousand transient workers in Prudhoe Bay who are involved in oil production. The oil field, which is owned jointly by BP, Exxon Mobil, ConocoPhillips, and Chevron and is operated by BP, produces about 150 million barrels a year.

There was something intriguing about swimming in Prud- hoe Bay. Part of it was that it was exciting to imagine swim- ming along the top of Alaska, and the other part was that Amundsen had found calm waters there. Through an Alaskan pilot friend who flew for BP, I contacted the head of security at Prudhoe Bay for permission to explore the waters, but my request was denied. I thought about it for a few days and decided that was the security man's job, to keep people out of the area. What I needed to do was to figure out who would understand my vision for this project, why it was important to follow Amundsen and learn from him and connect his story with the present by swimming in his wake. I contacted Francis McLaughlin, my nephew who had worked for Senator Frank Murkowski from Alaska. Francis and I discussed a number of ideas, and he helped me figure out the best person to contact.

I had spoken for Citigroup and met Charles Prince, the for- mer CEO. I e-mailed him and asked for his help. He had peo- ple who worked with him who knew the people at BP, and a few days later, I received a call from Alaska Clean Seas, an organization that is hired by the oil companies in Prudhoe Bay to be on call in case there is a spill and to be there to clean it up. Permission was granted.

Bob Griffith returned from California to join me, and Royce O'Brien and Tom Flynn, who worked for Alaska Clean

Seas, offered to pilot the company Zodiac and accompany me on the swim.

On July 29, at around 8:00 p.m., with the sun shining so brightly on the water that it seemed like noon, we gathered on the causeway on the west side of Prudhoe Bay, which extended about two miles out from shore. The air temperature was a balmy 50 degrees, and the bright blue bay was calm and clear and sparkling diamond light. I was eager to swim, but I noticed something rolling in the tiny four-inch surf. It was round, and the size of a golf ball, and it was the color of clear Jell-O tinged with plum, with inch-long tentacles extending from its base. "Tom, what is that? Is it some kind of jellyfish?" I asked, never expecting to find them this far north.

"I've never seen anything like that in my life," Tom said. Neither had Royce. And both were fishermen and had spent years fishing off Alaska.

For a moment, I wondered what other surprises could be in Prudhoe Bay, but I pushed that thought out of my mind and walked into the water. I swam parallel to the causeway, about fifty yards from shore, and each time I turned my head to breathe on my right side, I saw the elevated pipeline. At the end of the causeway was a seawater treatment plant, which processed seawater and pumped it back into the oil field. And as I swam, I pulled my hands through shoals of small plum-colored jellyfish. They didn't sting, but when I touched them they trembled, and so did I.

When I'd reached the thirty-minute mark, Bob called out to me and waved. I swam another minute. I still felt very strong, but the water was colder than I expected. I wasn't sure how cold it was, but I knew it was pulling heat from my body quickly.

I climbed out, and as I put my sweat suit on over my bathing suit and started walking along the shore to generate heat, Royce and Bob and Tom joined me. Royce came over and put a hand on my shoulder to feel my skin. "Wow, your skin's freezing. Tom, feel her back," Royce said.

"Yeah, my skin's cold. But my core's fine," I said. "I just need to keep walking."

Bob Griffith points and guides me across Prudhoe Bay while Tom Flynn keeps the motorboat on a direct course. Royce O'Brien watches the water for any unexpected visitors.

I'm swimming parallel to an oil pipeline and feeling strong in the calm 30-degree-Fahrenheit water.

Royce was walking beside me, and he said, "I've just seen you swim in thirty-degree water for thirty-one minutes, and from everything I know this isn't supposed to be possible."

Bob laughed, a big laugh—I loved his laugh—and he said, "That's part of why she does it."

Bob understood. He held the land-speed car-racing record on the Bonneville Salt Flats at 246 miles per hour.

Bob just smiled. And the conversation shifted to cars, and I kept walking trying to warm up back to normal.

In August 1906, Amundsen was almost at the end of the Northwest Passage, but three miles off Cape Simpson, about fifty miles from Point Barrow, he saw a big storm approaching. Amundsen wrote, "As the weather was still very hazy and the gale was stiffening to a hurricane, we sought shelter in the lee of some ground ice close by, and made fast to it."

According to Amundsen, the Arctic current raced off Point Barrow and flowed northeast at a torrential rate. Amundsen knew it was dangerous to let the *Gjøa* rest near ice. He had learned that it was easy to get caught inside a mass of ice, without an outlet, as he had experienced on the *Belgica* expedition, but one of the *Gjøa*'s propeller shafts warped, and the gaff, part of the ship's fore-and-aft rig, broke. They had no engine and no mainsail. But the crew raised the trysail, and Amundsen knew that they needed to push through the heavy drift ice off Point Barrow.

Finally in open water, under full sail, with the *Gjøa* increasing her speed, she violently struck the ice with her bow and parted it. Amundsen wrote:

It seemed as if the old *Gjøa* knew she had reached a critical moment. She had to tackle two large masses of ice that barred her way to the North West Passage; and now she charged again into them to force them asunder and slip through . . . a wild shout of triumph broke forth when the vessel slipped through.

Amundsen had reached the Chukchi Sea. I followed him west. Today, about forty-five hundred people live in Barrow, Alaska, which is 330 miles north of the Arctic Circle. More than 60 percent of Barrow's population is Inupiat, and the surrounding villagers are almost all Inupiat. Traditionally, many of the Inupiat hunted bowhead whale and fished in the Chukchi and Beaufort Seas. The Inupiat still have a traditional bowhead whale hunt. Today, most of the money coming into Barrow is from oil. Barrow is a large tourist destination, but increasing numbers of visitors are scientists who are working on global warming—studying carbon dioxide changes in the tundra and permafrost. They are observing the increasing speed at which the sea ice is melting and the erosion of the land around Point Barrow caused by the reduction of sea ice. Many of the scientists are based at the Barrow Arctic Science Consortium, a not-for-profit research organization established in 1995.

Three of the Barrow Arctic Science Consortium employees, Lester Suvlu, Vernon Kaleak, and Henry Elegak, volunteered to help me with a swim off Barrow. I had planned to do just a simple swim to complete the journey, only a mile. And we had waited for a calm day. Bob and I thought we had nearly reached our goal, and I felt more confident about swimming in frigid waters. But Lester told us about the polar bears, and he and Vernon and Henry were tremendously concerned. Lester told me he had seen more polar bears swimming ashore in recent years than he had in his whole life before.

The ice, he explained, was receding, and there was no place for the polar bears to hunt seals, their main food source, during the spring and the summer. In 2005, the ice was more than a hundred miles offshore, and he said that the wildlife management people found four polar bears that had drowned. They believed that they were so exhausted from swimming so far that they gave out. Recently, a mother and her cub had swum ashore and stopped, exhausted, on the runway at the old airport. Eventually, she got up and moved on, but polar bears were a real problem in town. While I was swimming, one of the crew would follow onshore, riding an ATV and carrying a rifle, in case we encountered a bear.

When I stepped into the Chukchi Sea on August 2, the water was far warmer than I expected—40 degrees. The wind and current would be at my back, and I felt like my swim would be all downhill. Bob and Vernon were in the Zodiac, waiting for me to start. I looked around. I didn't see any polar bears, but when I put my face into the water and started swimming, I realized I had entered a liquid hell of medusae—jellyfish—everywhere. There were large ones with purple-and-white-striped domes about three feet in circumference. They were inverted on the ocean floor ten to fifteen feet below me, their ten-foot-long tentacles splaying out around them.

I had been stung before by a variety of species, across the lips and face, on my chest, along the tender underside of my arms, down my legs, across my feet, and even through my swimsuit. Some species stung more than others. I didn't want to find out how much these stung. My muscles were tight as I braced myself for the soft brush of the tentacle that would suddenly become lines of searing pain.

In midstroke, I paused when I noticed a scarlet jellyfish the size of an apple moving right for me. The tentacles, fire red and as thick as spaghetti strands, trailed behind; they were six or seven feet long, and red in nature usually signals a warning that an animal is dangerous or poisonous. As I swerved right, my left hand grazed the red dome, and I recoiled and shot straight up in the water. I could see Bob looking at me totally perplexed. I was abruptly stopping and starting. He had never seen this behavior. But I was trying to do everything I could to avoid the jellyfish tentacles.

The wind was suddenly gusting to thirty knots, pushing the Zodiac and making it hard to hold a course. Bob and Vernon pulled two hundred yards away from me so they would not run me over with the boat. But Bob was concerned, and he yelled between cupped hands, "Are you all right?"

"Jellyfish," I shouted. They were signs that the water conditions were changing; the natural predators had been overfished, and so the jellyfish had multiplied at alarming rates.

"Do you want to get out?" he said.

"No, I want to finish," I said. But I thought, Oh, I really don't like this at all.

Staring down into the clear sea, I saw hundreds of red jellyfish. They were exquisitely beautiful, like flowers blossoming in an underwater garden. And they were terrifying. As some rose toward the surface, I pulled my hands in tight under my body to gain lift in the water so I wouldn't touch one of those searing tentacles.

A tentacle grazed the soft underside of my arm, and it felt like a combination of a bad beesting and fire burning my arm. Reacting to the sting, I swung wide and hit something else that wiggled. I jumped, turned, and looked. It appeared to be a small clear jellyfish, but it had four creased sides that were edged with deep purple and glowed. It looked magical. I stopped to examine it more closely, treading water as I tried to understand how it was propelling itself. I couldn't see any form of cilia or jet, but I saw another clear jellyfish. This one was edged with glowing pink, and another one was edged with neon green. I was concentrating so intently that Bob later told me that he was afraid that I might be going into an advanced stage of hypothermia, and he was on the verge of pulling me out. He had never seen me swim so erratically.

The red jellyfish were oscillating and swimming up to the water's surface. Their tentacles were fanning out. I swung wide and just missed one. Then I noticed the big purple-striped ones that were being flipped over in the Zodiac's wake. In a few minutes, I thought, these jellyfish would be on the surface.

"How long have I been swimming?" I shouted to Bob.

"Twenty minutes, but with the current you've swum much more than a mile. Do you want to go farther?"

"Let's go ashore," I said.

At Barrow, Amundsen turned the *Gjøa* south and sailed through the Chukchi Sea. He had traveled seven thousand miles, from Christiania to the Bering Sea. On August 30, 1906, he passed through the Bering Strait. The *Gjøa* and its crew had made it through the Northwest Passage. Amundsen caught sight of the Diomede Islands, and just when it seemed that the *Gjøa* had entered calmer waters, the ship was hit by a squall, and its gaff broke again. Then a dead calm set in, and the *Gjøa* sailed slowly into Nome, Alaska. Amundsen wrote:

> Suddenly a steam launch appeared in front of us, and we heard whistling, shouting, and cheering, the Americans' mode of expressing enthusiasm. Dark as it was, we could still discern the Norwegian flag floating side by side with the Stars and Stripes on the launch. So we had been recognized. . . . The Heartiness with which we were welcomed, the unbounded enthusiasm of which the *Gjøa* was the object, will always remain one of my brightest memories of our return. . . . The boat touched land. I really cannot say how I got ashore, but a jubilant roar of welcome issued from a thousand throats, and through the darkness of the night a sound burst forth that thrilled me through and through, bringing tears to my eyes; it was the strains of our national air.

As I climbed out of the Chukchi Sea, I felt a sense of elation. These weeks in Greenland, Canada, and Alaska had taken me into waters that few had ever entered or swum. I had traveled through the same Arctic world as Amundsen had, a place where one misstep could mean disaster. And at the same time I felt as though I were exploring a different place. I thought of the frozen waterways that were opening to exploration, the areas farther north than Amundsen had traveled, and they were alluring, but, as I thought about Amundsen and his Northwest Passage triumph, I realized that there was so much more to learn and understand about how he had built upon what he had done before, and how he had succeeded. At first I thought that I was mostly interested in his early beginnings, of how he became a great explorer during his early expeditions, but then I realized that following him through the Northwest Passage

*In 1906 Amundsen became the first to
sail through the Northwest Passage
but his success was overshadowed
by the San Francisco earthquake.*

wasn't enough. To understand him more fully, to see the challenges he had faced, and to see his successes and failures, and to understand how he had handled them, I needed to follow him through the course of his life.

In some ways, I realized, Amundsen's Northwest Passage success was like my first English Channel crossing. Those journeys were starting points and places where our learning curves weren't curves at all, just straight lines. So much was learned in the beginning for each of us. But there was much yet to achieve. Amundsen set the goal of becoming the first man to reach the North Pole, and he knew that he would compete with Dr. Frederick Cook, his friend from the *Belgica* expedition, and Robert Peary, the polar explorer who had explored Greenland with Cook shortly after the *Belgica* expedition.

When Amundsen returned to Norway after the Northwest Passage crossing, he received a hero's welcome, but he was still financially in dire straits, just as he had been when he first began the Northwest Passage journey with his band of "pirates." Amundsen had made an agreement with a London newspaper to write an exclusive for them, and in turn Amundsen would be paid for his reports, but his telegrams were intercepted and news of his achievement was transmitted around the world in numerous newspapers. With the exclusive broken, Amundsen didn't receive any money for his story, and when he returned to Norway, he went to work to pay back his creditors.

CHAPTER 15

South Pole

Amundsen's initial plan was to sail through the Bering Strait, drift across the Arctic Ocean, and become the first man to reach the North Pole, but he changed his plans without telling anyone, not even his greatest supporters, Nansen and the king of Norway.

Nansen had lent Amundsen his ship, the *Fram,* for his attempt to reach the North Pole. Amundsen reconditioned the *Fram,* secured provisions, selected a crew, and even chose an aviator for the attempt. But during these preparations, Dr. Frederick Cook, Amundsen's friend who had helped him survive the *Belgica* expedition, claimed that on April 21, 1908, he had become the first man to reach the North Pole.

Robert Peary, however, claimed that on April 6, 1909, he reached the North Pole first. This touched off an enormous controversy played out in the newspapers, in geographic societies, in court, and in public for years to come.

Amundsen sidestepped the controversy. He believed that the North Pole had been achieved, and he thought it would be more difficult to secure funding for his original plan. He decided to postpone that and do something far more captivating. He only told his brother, and Captain Nilsen, the commander of the *Fram.*

In August 1910, Amundsen and his crew sailed on the *Fram* from Norway to the Madeira Islands. They believed they would be sailing around Cape Horn to reach the Bering Strait and north to the North Pole, but when they reached the Madeira Islands, Amundsen announced that the North Pole had been discovered, and he had decided instead to go for the South Pole.

The crew excitedly agreed to the change of course. Amundsen sent a letter to Nansen and King Haakon dated August 22, 1910. Amundsen explained that in 1909, after he heard about Cook and Peary's successes, he believed the parliament would not give him the money he needed for the North Pole attempt, so he had decided he would go south instead. Amundsen wrote that he wished that he had been able to inform Robert Falcon Scott, the British explorer, about his decision so it did not seem like he was trying to sneak down to the South Pole ahead of him, and he hoped that he would meet Scott in Antarctica to inform him of his decision so Scott could act accordingly. Amundsen felt guilty for deceiving Nansen, but he wouldn't discover until later that he had done something even worse.

Amundsen laid out his plan: They would

sail south from Madeira to South Victoria Land and with nine men go ashore there, and let the *Fram* go out to do oceanographic examinations. The *Fram* will be able to take two trips from Buenos Aires and over toward Cape Verde when the *Fram* is leaving the ice, it will go east to Puenta Arenas and from there to Buenos Aires. Lieutenant Nilsen, who is in command onboard, will probably together with Kutschin be able to do a good job. I can not at this point make any decision as to where we will go ashore down there, but my intention is to avoid landing right at the same place as the English. They have the first right. We will have to be content with what they do not want. February–March 1912 the *Fram* will come back to pick us up. We will first go by Lyttelton in New Zealand to send telegrams and from there to San Francisco to continue the interrupted work.

Amundsen also sent a telegram to Robert Falcon Scott, the British naval officer and explorer who had attempted to reach the South Pole on the *Discovery* expedition from 1901 to 1904 and had begun the *Terra Nova* expedition to the pole (1910–13), to inform Scott of his plan.

Amundsen and his crew sailed southward on the *Fram* from Madeira through the Atlantic, then to the east, passing the Cape of Good Hope and Australia and arriving in the Ross Sea at the beginning of the new year 1911. Most Antarctic explorers believed that it was best to attempt the South Pole from McMurdo Sound, on the western side of the Ross Sea, but Amundsen had his sights on another start point. He had studied charts of Antarctica dating back to 1842, when James Clark Ross had first sailed with his crews aboard the *Erebus* and *Terror* into and discovered the Ross Sea. They had mapped the barrier now known as the Ross Ice Shelf (Ross called it the Victoria Barrier for Queen Victoria; later it was called the Great Ice Barrier).

Most explorers had avoided creating a base camp on the barrier for fear it would break off while they were camped there, but Amundsen had Ross's charts and noted that the barrier, the inner part of the Bay of Whales, had not moved in sixty-eight years. Amundsen also studied Ernest Shackleton's more recent account.

In January 1908, on Shackleton's second attempt to reach the South Pole, he and his crew reached the ice pack off Antarctica, and they sighted the Ross Barrier. They planned to go ashore once they reached Barrier Inlet, near King Edward VII Land, to establish a base station. But what they discovered gave them pause. Barrier Inlet had calved away. All that remained was a wide bay that Shackleton named the Bay of Whales.

Shackleton was convinced that the barrier was far too unstable for a base station. Instead, he headed west to McMurdo Sound and wintered over on solid ground on Ross Island. In October 1908 Shackleton and three of his crew, Jameson Adams, Eric Marshall, and Frank Wild, set out from Ross Island with four sledges and four Manchurian ponies for the

South Pole. The ponies died, the men had to drag the sledges themselves, and their food supplies dwindled. They crossed the Beardmore Glacier, and Shackleton and his men surpassed Scott's southernmost point of exploration, 82 degrees, 17 minutes, south. Shackleton and his crew reached the farthest south at latitude 88 degrees, 23 minutes, and longitude 162 degrees east, and they wisely turned back for McMurdo before their food completely ran out.

Amundsen thought that if Shackleton had sailed deeper into the bay, he would have recognized that at that point the barrier wasn't moving, and Shackleton could have succeeded at reaching the South Pole before Amundsen made his attempt.

There were additional factors that made the Bay of Whales attractive to Amundsen. The bay was a whole degree—sixty miles—farther south than McMurdo. If he started from the Bay of Whales, he was already closer to the South Pole before he began his journey than Scott was, about 350 miles to the west. From the unobstructed vantage point on the barrier, Amundsen believed he could easily monitor the weather and ice conditions. He knew from reading Shackleton's and Scott's accounts that the winds in McMurdo Sound were relentless and frigid, and that they often blew through the area at more than forty knots. He knew that these winds made working in McMurdo physically and mentally exhausting for Scott and his men.

After five months of sailing and struggling to get south and reach Antarctica, and years of preparation and planning, on January 11, 1910, at around 2:30 p.m., the southern sky brightened, and the sun illuminated the great ice barrier—the Ross Glacier. The edge of the Ross Glacier rose a hundred feet above the sea ice. This wall was nature's ice fortress, and to early explorers it seemed insurmountable. But Amundsen had read that there was an opening in the wall, about one hundred miles east of their position.

They arrived on January 14, a day earlier than they expected. From the high stable deck of the *Fram*, Amundsen looked across the sea ice and studied the juncture between the sea ice and the thick irregular wall of the Ross Glacier and saw the lay of the land: giant ridges and hollows spreading in every direction. He estimated that the ridges were up to five hundred feet high, but he wondered how much higher the ridges beyond this would be.

Amundsen and his crew of three skied into the bay with alpine ropes in the calm bright sunlight under a light blue sky to see what they would face. As they skied south on new light snow, they reached the connecting point between the sea ice and the glacier ice—the barrier. Would they be able to climb it, and what would it be like up on the other side?

Apprehensively, Amundsen and his men climbed from the sea ice up the edge of the Ross Glacier. It was only twenty feet high, and the edge had been softened so there was a gentle slope to the top of the barrier. Without any great effort, they climbed, and in those few moments, all their initial fears of the unknown dissolved. They smiled at one another. The shimmering silver and white world of Antarctica opened and rose gently before them.

CHAPTER 16

The Heroic Dogs

Amundsen knew from his experience in the Arctic that no crossing of Antarctica could be possible without the Greenlandic Eskimo dogs. He believed that one reason Shackleton and Scott had not reached the South Pole was because they had not carried enough food, and the Manchurian ponies that were used to pull their sledges weren't suited for Antarctica. The ponies were heavy, they fell through the ice and were injured so badly they had to be shot.

Amundsen figured that the Eskimo dogs were best suited for the job. Not only would they pull the heavy six-hundred-pound sledges laden with provisions, equipment, and sometimes the men, but the dogs would also be sacrificed along the journey for food. Amundsen calculated that each carcass would provide fifty pounds of meat to supplement their food supplies.

Ninety-seven Eskimo dogs that sailed aboard the *Fram* from Norway to Antarctica were selected for this purpose. Some dogs had puppies and by the time they reached Antarctica there were 110 dogs. The dogs had been handpicked, they were well trained, and each one of the crew had the personal responsibility to attend to ten dogs.

Tents were quickly set up on the barrier between Mount Nelson and Mount Ronniken, and the dogs were tethered to prevent them from fighting. Over the five-month-long voyage the dogs had gotten out of shape and had to be retrained. They were used to transport from the ship to the shore everything the party would need for the southward journey. They dragged the loads on sledges to the camp on the barrier while two crew members built a warm, well-ventilated hut that would serve as their winter quarters, which Amundsen named Framheim.

The crew was divided into two parties, a sea party that would be composed of nine men under Captain Thorvald Nilsen's command, and the land party composed of Amundsen, Kristian Prestrud, Hjalmar Johansen, Helmer Hanssen, Sverre Hassel, Olav Bjaaland, Jørgen Stubberud, Adolf Henrik Lindström, and Oscar Wisting. The sea party would conduct oceanographic studies, and sail to 78 degrees, 41 minutes, the farthest south a ship had ever reached, and then the crew would sail back to Buenos Aires while Amundsen and his land party remained in Antarctica. Amundsen needed to establish depots, places where they could cache food so they wouldn't have to transport the extra food to the South Pole and back, and so they would have access to the food on the return journey to Framheim. The nine men who made up the land party were divided into groups. Kristian Pestrud, Hjalmar Johansen, and Jørgen Stubberud would explore King Edward VII Land. Amundsen and Helmer J. Hanssen, Sverre H. Hassel, Oscar Wisting, and Olav Bjaaland and their dog teams would set out for the South Pole. Adolf Lindstrom would maintain Framheim.

On February 10, 1911, they began creating the depots to supply food for their journey to the South Pole the following austral spring. Prestrud, Hanssen, Johansen, and Amundsen, with three sledges and six dogs for each sledge, carried their first load of provisions to the first depot and then continued laying caches further south. The provisions included seal meat, blubber, dried fish, chocolate, biscuits, and margarine as well as black flags attached to long bamboo poles.

Their start was shaky. The dogs took off from Framheim at full speed, then the going got tough. Fog moved in, the snow was flat, and there were no landmarks or horizon to guide them and help them stay on a straight course. The compasses didn't work, and the sledge drivers were constantly checking their course by making astronomical observations. They established depots and used the long bamboo poles every ten miles to mark their route. Once they reached their predetermined last depot at 80 degrees they sledged back toward Framheim.

The route back wasn't easy to follow. Amundsen made an adjustment; he asked Prestrud to sit beside him on the last sledge and watch the sledge meter. Every time they had traveled a quarter mile, Prestrud yelled out, and Amundsen marked the position with a dried fish stuck into the snow. He knew that the dogs would be famished on their return journey from the South Pole and that they would smell the fish.

About three weeks later they arrived back at Framheim, and Amundsen was convinced his dogs were champions. On the last day of their journey to Framheim, the dogs had sledged sixty-two miles.

They wintered in Framheim and tweaked their clothing and equipment, improved the dog harnesses, repacked the sledge provisions, and removed extra weight from their sledges.

In early spring, on September 6, 1911, Amundsen and his crew noticed that the weather had warmed and the temperature was up to minus 7 degrees Fahrenheit. They made a false start. They harnessed the dogs and began their attempt for the South Pole, but the dogs did not obey. One dog team raced off without a driver; a second driver tried to catch them and lost his team as well. Hours later, the men got them under control, but the ninety-six dogs fought whenever they got a chance, and the temperature dropped again. By September 12 it was down to minus 61 degrees Fahrenheit. The dogs were so cold they were constantly shivering, and for the next three days Amundsen and the crew camped as the temperature dropped to minus 68 degrees Fahrenheit. On September 15, while Hanssen was in the tent he felt something strange. He took off his stocking, and a clump of flesh that had been his heel had frozen and fallen off. Stubberud realized that a chunk of his heel had frozen off, too. Amundsen decided that they had to return to Framheim for medical treatment.

On October 20, Amundsen, Hanssen, Hassel, Bjaaland,

and Wisting set out with four sledges and a total of fifty-two dogs (thirteen per sledge) for the real start for the South Pole. The going was anything but easy. On October 21 they were lost in a blizzard, they couldn't see their tracks or the depots, they couldn't tell where they were, and the area they were in was covered by crevasses. Bjaaland's sledge began to sink into a hole in the snow that would swallow the man, dogs, and sledge.

Instinctively, the dogs lay down and dug their claws in, but they were sinking deeper into the hole. Hanssen and Hassel snatched a rope and immediately tied it to the sledge; Bjaaland and Amundsen held on to the sledge, and the dogs and men were taken off while Hassel and Hanssen stood on the very edge of the crevasse. Just to the left of them, the ice crust was as thin as paper, and if they had stood there none of them would have escaped.

They continued south and built their first six-foot-high beacons. They would use these as landmarks for the journey back to Framheim. At the first beacon, at 80 degrees, 23 minutes south, they shot the first dog, Hanssen's dog, named Bone. The dog couldn't keep up, and he would be food on the return home. They placed the beacons every eight or nine miles as they continued south. In total they built 150 beacons from nine thousand blocks of snow. The dogs were in top shape, picking up speed and moving at four and two-thirds miles per hour.

On November 15 at 85 degrees south, Amundsen wrote that the distance from where they were to the pole and back was 683 miles. They were about to ascend into the mountains. They had taken enough food and equipment for thirty days, and they had forty-two dogs that would take them up to the polar plateau. And they would methodically slaughter the dogs until they had twelve that would take two sledges back to Framheim.

On November 17 they began their climb through the mountains. They saw the southern Mount Nansen and Mount Don Pedro Christophersen, and they used an aneroid to measure the height of a snow terrace. They had reached four thousand feet, and they continued to the Axel Heiberg Glacier. They climbed between the two mountains, sledged through deep loose snow, and when the sun warmed the snow and it melted, they ducked for cover as avalanches roared and spun around them.

When they rounded Mount Engelstad, Amundsen noted that the dogs seemed to know that this was their last big effort. They dug their claws in and hauled the sledges toward the southern side of Mount Engelstad. The men hoped they would see a smooth glacier ahead, but that was not to be. To the south were long ridges that ran from east to west and reached an altitude of 10,920 feet. They set up camp and shot more dogs for food.

On December 4 they were at 87 degrees latitude trying to navigate along a plain that was an ocean of drifting snow filled with sastrugi—hardened waves of snow—and heavy snow was falling from the sky blinding them and the dogs. Hanssen somehow managed to steer his course by compass, but every time he came to rough ground the needle flew around the compass. But when they managed to take an observation and use dead reckoning he was within a mile of where they expected to be.

Through December 7 the weather was very poor, with thick clouds, heavy snow, and fog. Amundsen hoped they would see the southern sun so they could make a solar observation and calculate how far they'd come and how much farther they had to go. Amundsen believed that they could get to the South Pole using dead reckoning, but he wondered if once they reached the South Pole, their claim would questioned. He really wanted to make a more precise observation. At 11:00 p.m. Hassel, Wisting, and Amundsen stood on the plateau, and they willed the clouds to part. Slowly, the sun melted the clouds, and they caught the sun at its highest point in the southern sky. Quickly, they made their measurements and realized that they had come up with the same results though dead reckoning and that if they had to use dead reckoning to get to the pole, they could do so. When they reached the farthest point south they continued on, past the point Shackleton had reached before he had to turn around. Amundsen was overcome with emotion, more than at any other time during the journey. Tears filled his eyes, and he wrote, "I find it impossible to express the feelings that possessed me at this moment . . . 88 deg 23' was past; we were farther south than any human being had been" (*South Pole*, 260). The crew cheered its accomplishment and realized how much Shackleton had achieved, too.

They continued their long march south across the nine-thousand-foot-high polar plateau, and at 3:00 p.m. on December 14, Amundsen, the crew, and seventeen of the dogs became the first beings to reach the South Pole. They planted the Norwegian flag, and Amundsen named the plain the King Haakon VII Plateau, after the king of Norway. Still, they couldn't be completely sure that they had reached the South Pole, and they didn't want their accomplishment to be doubted, as had occurred with the North Pole, so for the next three days they made a circle around their last camp with a radius of twelve and a half miles. And Hanssen and Bjaaland traveled four additional miles to make sure that somewhere within that circle they had reached the South Pole.

They planted a pole in an area they named Polheim, tied a Norwegian flag to it, and left a tent in a bag and a letter addressed to the king of Norway. Amundsen knew the return could be dangerous and something could happen along the way, so he wrote to Captain Scott, who he thought would soon arrive at the South Pole himself, asking him to carry the letter back to King Haakon. The crew wrote messages to Scott and his men on leather attached to the tent that said "Good luck" and "Welcome to 90 deg." Then they began their homeward journey, back to the *Fram*.

For the next month Robert Falcon Scott and his crew would endure horrendous conditions on their trek to the South Pole. On Scott's team was Thomas Crean, an Irishman who was one of the greatest unsung heroes of polar exploration. Crean had volunteered for Scott's *Discovery* expedition (1901–04). When the *Discovery* became icebound in the winter of 1902 in Antarctica and the crew's efforts failed to break her free from the ice, some of the expedition members left on a relief vessel, but Crean remained with the ship through the long dark Antarctic

Oscar Wisting with his dogs on the South Pole, December 14, 1911. The journey from Framheim to the South Pole and back took ninety-nine days, and they traveled about 1,864 miles.

winter until it was freed in February 1904. Crean earned Scott's respect and Scott recruited him for the *Terra Nova* expedition (1910–13), Scott's second South Pole attempt. Crean did everything he could to support the expedition's push to the South Pole. He saved the lives of crew members Apsley Cherry-Garrard and Lieutenant Henry Bowers when they drifted away on an ice floe. Crean managed to leap from one piece of sea ice to another until he reached the barrier and got other crew members to help rescue them. He was considered to be one of the strongest and most even-tempered of the crew, had a great sense of humor, and was always dependable, and he always went far beyond what was asked of him. He took care of the Manchurian ponies on Scott's expedition, and later, on Shack-

*Left to right: Roald Amundsen, Olav Bjaaland, Sverre Hassel,
and Oscar Wisting, South Pole, December 14, 1911.*

leton's *Endurance* expedition, he cared for the sled dogs and
sled dog puppies. Crean thought he would be chosen to make
the final push with Scott to the South Pole, but on January 4,
1912, Scott ordered him to return to base camp when they were
only 168 miles from the South Pole. Crean wept. But he
accepted Scott's decision and turned north with Lashly and
Evans, knowing that they had a seven-hundred-mile journey
back to Hut Point. They got lost on the return to the Beardmore Glacier. They were running low on food, and they were
struggling to survive. They had to move more quickly and
decided to risk sliding two thousand feet down the Shackleton
icefall on their sledges rather than walking for three days
around the icefall. Somehow they managed to avoid enormous
crevasses by only inches. They reached the barrier, but Evans
was weak from scurvy and he collapsed more than one hundred

miles from Hut Point. Crean thought he had died and Evans said that he felt Crean's hot tears on his face. Crean and Lashly strapped Evans on a sledge and dragged him until they were thirty-five miles from Hut Point.

At that point they realized that they had only two days' food remaining, and they couldn't move fast enough with Evans to make it back to the base camp before their food ran out. Crean left Lashly with Evans and set off on his own to get a rescue party. For eighteen hours he struggled across the ice, sometimes crawling to make headway, and when he finally reached the hut, he was so worn out that he was delirious and he collapsed on the floor. The crew revived him, and he volunteered to return to the ice to rescue Evans and Lashly, but he was too weak. The other expedition members found Lashley and Evans and brought them back by dogsled.

Scott and his party reached the South Pole a month after Amundsen, but all of them perished on their return journey to base camp. Crean was among the crew that searched for and recovered the bodies of Scott and his men.

Crean returned to Antarctica with Ernest Shackleton on the 1914–17 *Endurance* expedition and rowed alongside Shackleton for eight hundred miles in the *James Caird* from Elephant Island to South Georgia Island. He was key to the survival of Shackleton and the entire crew of the *Endurance*.

Amundsen and his men and eleven dogs arrived back in Framheim on January 25. They had traveled 1,860 miles in ninety-nine days and achieved what was then, and still is now, one of the most amazing journeys in the harshest of the world's environments. The men and dogs opened the continent of Antarctica for all further exploration. In spite of their great success, they did not receive the celebration they anticipated. Many people in Britain believed that the challenge created by Amundsen and his crew to reach the South Pole first had forced Scott and his crew to compete against them. And they ultimately blamed Amundsen for Scott's death. Amundsen did not accept that reasoning. He believed that he had prepared better than Scott and that was why he succeeded and Scott didn't.

Celebrating Amundsen, Nansen wrote an entire front-page story for the *San Francisco Chronicle* about Amundsen's magnificent achievement—reaching the South Pole. Nansen explained in great detail Amundsen's accomplishment. In the story he completely supported Amundsen for his decision to change his mind, to sail south for Antarctica rather than heading for the North Polar Sea.

Amundsen had explained to Nansen in his letter that he needed to achieve the South Pole in order to gain the support he needed to raise more funds and sail and do research in the Arctic Ocean.

When Amundsen returned to Norway, he immediately began working on raising funds for his attempt to sail through the Northeast Passage, and he followed up on promises that had been made by the Norwegian government to his crew. Amundsen was told that as a result of their success at reaching the South Pole, his crew would be awarded promotions, money, and jobs, but these promises were not being fulfilled.

Amundsen was relentless in his follow-up. He had not received the money he had been promised by the government to pay his crew or to fund the Northeast Passage venture. Amundsen began a series of two hundred lectures in the United States and Canada. He also wrote to Nansen to enlist his help.

Nansen wrote back and told Amundsen that he was focused on little things, and that he was afraid that Amundsen had lost sight of his big goal of exploring the Northeast Passage. Amundsen in frustration wrote back to Nansen and asked him again for his help. Amundsen felt he had not been fairly treated by Adrien de Gerlache on his first Antarctica journey, and he had learned from that experience and wanted to make sure that his crew, the one that had reached the South Pole and achieved that success, would gain the money and recognition that they deserved.

Amundsen wrote to Nansen that he felt that it would have a great effect on his plans for the future. He believed it was impossible to start the new expedition based on broken promises.

In a dramatic letter, on April 2, 1913, Nansen wrote back to Amundsen. This correspondence was different than any other between the two men. Nansen wrote that he was sad to hear that Amundsen was unhappy and his life had been stressful, and he wondered if Amundsen might give up the expedition. He asked Amundsen: "How would it look if you called off the expedition now?"

Nansen exploded and his writing changed; his words were scribbled, scratched out, underlined, and entire backs of pages were written on, and then scratched out. He wrote: "I have really done my best for you and your expedition."

Nansen continued that he had made a larger sacrifice for Amundsen than anyone alive. He said that he had planned to attempt to be the first to the South Pole. He considered this the completion of his life's work, but he realized that Norway couldn't support both of their expeditions. When Amundsen wrote to him and informed him that he had changed his plans to go to the South Pole before the Polar Sea, Nansen said that he and his colleagues worked to get more money from the government for Amundsen's Polar Sea expedition. Nansen said he did this because he believed that Amundsen's research in the Polar Sea would be of greater scientific importance than Nansen's own goal of achieving the South Pole.

Nansen wrote:

I with a bleeding heart gave up the plan that I for so long prepared, and which should have filled my life—to the advantage of your trip, because I regarded this as the most important thing to do, and by right Norway would contribute the most. You were younger and had this great life work in front of you, whereby you could contribute something considerable as I could seek other tasks. Yes that was how it was, but what it still cost me to cut off what I had planned for so long and became attached to. . . . Many regards, and [I] wish you were soon through with this exhausting lecture-life.
Yours Sincerely, Fridtjof Nansen.

The new prime minister, Gunnar Knudsen, wrote to Amundsen and gave him the impression that he was going to fulfill the government's promises. On April 26, 1913, Amundsen wrote to Nansen from Brainerd, Minnesota, and asked Nansen not to be angry with him. He would put all of his energy into the Northeast Passage expedition, and he asked if he could get instructions from Nansen for the Northeast Passage like he had for the *Gjøa* expedition. He wrote that he would really appreciate Nansen's help.

Nansen replied:

June 6, 1913
Dear Amundsen
   Your letter of April 26 made me glad. I see that I have taken your previous letter too heavy. But the case was that your letter scared me very much. I didn't understand what you meant, and if you really thought you were thinking of giving up the whole expedition, if the things you mentioned couldn't be arranged, and so I was afraid that you maybe were about to take a step that could ruin a lot of the honor you have won. I meant that it was my duty to take the matter so seriously and expose my view of this as I did, as I said in the letter I thought that in the exhausting life you lead you could easily lose perspective and the small could be too big. I see that this was superfluous, and my words could have been saved, but it looked a little dreary that you would stop all the preparations from the expedition.
   Now I will not write more live now really good, or at least as good as you can with all this stress, hopefully you are soon on your way home and a hearty welcome home. Hopefully I will see you here. . . .
   Yours devoted, yours sincerely, Fridtjof Nansen.

The emotional storm passed between the two men, and their friendship grew stronger. Without a hesitation Nansen did all he could to help Amundsen prepare for the Northeast Passage. But by 1914 it was too dangerous for Amundsen to leave port. It was the beginning of World War I.

CHAPTER 17

Darkness and Light

German submarines threatened all shipping in European waters. Amundsen delayed his departure, and he realized that the *Fram* was too old to attempt the voyage. He had the *Maud* built and purchased a Farman biplane to explore the Arctic ice fields from the air. The ship was christened on June 7, 1917, but the seas were still unsafe. A Norwegian merchant ship had been sunk without warning by a German submarine in the North Sea. In protest Amundsen returned the medals he had been awarded by the German kaiser for his success in reaching the South Pole.

By 1918 Amundsen had plotted out his course. He would sail north along the Norwegian coast, along the northern coast of Europe, past the northernmost tip of Asia, Cape Chelyskin, around the New Siberian Islands, and into the Bering Strait, but the threat of submarine attack had not diminished. Admiral William Sowden Sims of the U.S. Navy was aware of Amundsen's plans. He sent Amundsen intelligence about when the German submarines would be patrolling the Arctic Sea and when they would be returning to bases to resupply.

On July 15, 1918, Amundsen and his crew of ten Norwegians sailed north into the Arctic Sea. By September 9 they reached Cape Chelyskin, but by September 13, they were locked in ice in Maud Harbor. Here, Amundsen experienced a series of mishaps including one that nearly cost him his life. On a morning walk, while holding one of his dogs in his arms and

*Fridtjof Nansen, his daughter Liv Nansen Hoyer, and
Roald Amundsen, April 1918, Washington, D.C., after
the trade board gave license to the* Maud *expedition.*

walking down the ship's ramp, he slipped on ice, fell, saw stars, felt excruciating pain, and realized he had broken his shoulder. The pain, swelling, and shock were so intense that he was in bed for eight days.

A couple of months later, on November 8, Amundsen went for another morning walk with his dog Jacob, and he heard something strange nearby. He realized the sound was the heavy breathing of a polar bear. The bear had been chasing Jacob to divert his attention and get him away from her cub. When the bear saw Amundsen, she lashed out at him with her massive paw and took him down with a powerful blow.

Amundsen landed facedown on his broken shoulder and with gashes in his back. Unable to move, he waited for the bear to finish him off, but Jacob returned to play with the cub and distracted the bear. When she turned to chase Jacob, Amundsen managed to flee. Amundsen thought that it was the closest he had come to death, but a short time later, he had a more dangerous experience. He was working in a small observatory without windows making some observations. The room was heated and lighted by a kerosene lamp he had used on previous expeditions. He noticed that he felt sleepy and his heart was beating erratically, but he did not realize he was about to pass out. He dragged himself outside and got some fresh air. He was not sure what had happened, but he suspected that the flame used up the oxygen in the room or the fumes from the kerosene lamp had nearly killed him. For months after the incident Amundsen was weak, and his heart was seriously affected.

When the ice broke, Amundsen and his crew sailed past the New Siberian Islands and reached Aijon Island, where they befriended the Tsjuktsji people, who Amundsen noted were related to the Inuit throughout North America and Greenland, but spoke a different language. Amundsen bought caribou from them for his winter meat supply, and when the ice broke in July 1920, he sailed to Nome and became the second man to sail through the Northeast Passage.

While Amundsen was exploring the Arctic regions, Nansen was becoming more involved in humanitarian efforts. After World War I, Nansen was named the high commissioner for refugees by the League of Nations. He created the Nansen passport for refugees, and he helped 450,000 people resettle after the war. From 1921 to 1922, during the Russian famine, Nansen helped to feed up to 22 million people, and in 1922 he was awarded the Nobel Peace Prize. He continued his humanitarian work and became a pioneer in the study of oceanography and in fluid dynamics.

Amundsen had become convinced that the only effective way to explore the Arctic and Antarctica was by flight. In the spring of 1922, he began to fulfill this vision by discussing the possibility with the officers of the Curtiss Aeroplane Company. He purchased a Junkers, an airplane that had broken the world record for sustained flight of twenty-seven hours. He hoped he could use the plane to fly from Point Barrow, Alaska, to Svalbard, Norway. The aircraft was built from a new metal called duralumin, and it was supposed to be stronger than steel and lighter than aluminum. To make the Junkers more suitable for landing on snow, Amundsen tried something new. He had the wheels removed and substituted skis, but during the first test flight, the skis shattered on landing.

Amundsen thought about trying another aircraft and making another attempt, but he was financially strapped, his lecture series had not been successful, and he was exhausted and depressed. He was fifty-four years old, sitting alone in his room in the Waldorf-Astoria Hotel in New York City, and he was about to give up on any further expeditions when the telephone rang.

CHAPTER 18

Flying Boats

Lincoln Ellsworth, a wealthy American businessman whom Amundsen had met in France a few years before, called and told him he would like to join Amundsen on his upcoming expeditions. Amundsen told Ellsworth that he wanted to be the first to fly to the North Pole. He was well aware of past attempts and disasters.

Around the time of Amundsen's *Belgica* expedition to Antarctica, Salomon Andrée, a Swedish engineer and polar explorer, attempted to fly a hydrogen balloon from Danskon, an island west of Svalbard, to the North Pole. Andrée and two friends—Knut Fraenkel, an engineer, and Nils Strindberg, a photographer—launched the *Eagle* on July 11, 1897, and they managed to remain aloft for sixty-five hours, but it began to rain, and the rain turned to ice. The weight of the ice made the balloon drop from the sky like an asteroid. Andrée made an emergency landing on the Arctic ice pack.

They were prepared. They had three sledges, a boat, and enough food for three months inside the balloon. They trekked 295 miles across the Arctic ice, and in October they finally reached Kvitøya—White Island. There they died, probably from eating polar bear meat containing trichinella parasites.

This tragedy did not deter other men from dreaming of polar flight. Australia's Sir Douglas Mawson, a geologist and explorer who had accompanied Shackleton on his 1907 expedition, and who had turned down an invitation from Scott to participate in his *Terra Nova* expedition, decided to lead the Australasian Antarctic expedition in 1911. His goal was to explore King George V Land and Adélie Land, the region directly below the southern section of Australia. Mawson thought that flight was the way to explore Commonwealth Bay in Antarctica. His pilot used an airplane built by Vickers, an REP monoplane with a detachable sledge-runner undercarriage so the airplane could land on snow, but during a test flight in Adelaide, Australia, the pilot crashed the plane and nearly died.

Mawson scrapped his plans for Antarctic flight, but he sailed on the *Aurora* to Antarctica and established a base camp in Commonwealth Bay that he named Cape Denison and went on to explore Antarctica by sledge.

Amundsen and Ellsworth decided to attempt polar flight. In 1924 Lincoln Ellsworth purchased two Dornier flying boats, the N-24 and N-25, and Amundsen gathered a crew together: Hjalmar Riiser-Larsen and Leif Dietrichson, the pilots, and Oskar Omdal and Karl Feucht, the mechanics. Their goal was to be the first to complete a crossing of the Arctic Ocean from continent to continent over the North Pole. But as the crew discussed the plan, it was amended. They decided to use the N-24 and N-25 for making reconnaissance flights over the Arctic Ocean, to study the ice as far north as they could fly.

On May 21, 1925, Amundsen and his crew took off in the flying boats from Svalbard, an island off the north coast of Norway. Each airplane was built for water landing and taking off, and each carried enough fuel for a twelve-hundred-mile flight. As they flew toward the North Pole, Amundsen immediately realized that they could explore the polar regions much more rapidly than by ship or dogsled and far more exploration could be achieved by airplane.

They flew north across the Arctic Ocean, and when they reached 88 degrees north, six hundred miles from civilization, the N-25 suddenly developed engine trouble; they had to make a forced landing. They scanned the ice and water and knew they had to land immediately or they would crash, but all they saw were hummocks up to twenty feet high, which would destroy the aircraft. They continued their uncertain descent until they saw a small patch of open water between the hummocks and the sea ice. The pilot wasn't sure if the water runway was long enough to attempt a landing, but he had no choice.

The crews of the N-25 and N-24 splashed down in the small pool and hit the ice at the edge, which slowed their momentum. They thought they could relax for a moment, but the pool was turning into ice, and the crew had to work frantically to free the N-25 from the water and drag it up onto solid ice. But they were unable to save the N-24. They salvaged the provisions from the N-24 and loaded everything into the N-25.

They were six hundred miles from Svalbard and from any kind of help, with barely enough provisions to last them three weeks. Worse, the N-25 was designed to take off from the water, and they were on ice. The only way out of this situation, Amundsen decided, was to build an ice runway. For twenty-four days they worked frantically, flattening the hummocks and creating an ice runway that was as smooth as a skating pond. By then they were at the end of their food supply.

The six men crowded into the cockpit. Riiser-Larsen opened the throttles to the limit, and as their speed increased the crew was thrown violently from side to side. Amundsen feared that one of the wings would be crushed.

They reached the edge of the runway, and leaped over a small pool. The aircraft began to rise, but a twenty-foot hummock was immediately in front of them. They cleared it only by inches and began heading south, but they were not sure if they were on the right heading. They weren't sure if the fuel would last with the additional men on board. The fuel was burning fast, and they were down to only a half hour's supply. When they saw the mountain peaks of Svalbard, they cheered. They thought they were home, but they didn't know that Riiser-Larsen was forcing the lever for the aileron control, trying to make a wide sweeping turn, but the aileron control had stopped working. Riiser-Larsen had to land. Somehow a stretch of water magically opened before them, and they splashed down, at last back home.

CHAPTER 19

Amundsen and Byrd

After the flying boat experience, Amundsen was convinced that the best way to fly from continent to continent—from Svalbard, Norway, to Barrow, Alaska, over the Arctic Ocean—was with the N-1 dirigible *Norge*. Lincoln Ellsworth purchased the N-1 from the Italian government and employed Colonel Umberto Nobile, the N-1's designer, to pilot the dirigible for the flight. Tensions developed, however, between the Norwegian and Italian crews, as both groups vied to be in control of the expedition.

Amundsen clarified his position for Colonel Nobile and explained that he and Ellsworth were the commanders of the expedition and Nobile had been hired to pilot the *Norge*. Nobile believed differently; he was the N-1's designer and he would be the pilot and he wanted to be the commander of the expedition and receive all the credit. Amundsen would later believe that Nobile was pressured by Mussolini to do this to gain acclaim for himself.

Nobile kept focusing on the goal of flying to the North Pole. Amundsen clarified the continent-to-continent goal, but when Nobile heard that Richard Byrd and Floyd Bennett, the Fokker's pilot, were on the beach in Svalbard making final preparations for the *Josephine Ford,* a Fokker Trimotor plane, to attempt the first flight from Svalbard to the North Pole, Nobile told Amundsen that they could have the *Norge* ready in three days, and they could reach the North Pole before Byrd.

The Norge *flying over Svalbard with a combined crew of Norwegians, Italians, and an American. They became the first to fly from Svalbard over the North Pole and landed in Teller, Alaska.*

Amundsen, deeply fatigued after the challenge and stress of expeditions and financial concerns, 1924.

Amundsen explained that he had no interest whatsoever in racing Byrd to the North Pole. They were good friends, and they had different goals. When Byrd and Bennett returned from their sixteen-hour flight, Amundsen and his crew were there to congratulate them on their success.

Two days later, on May 11, 1926, a light breeze was blowing, and Nobile was nervous about how it would affect the *Norge*.

He told Riiser-Larsen, Amundsen's pilot, that if he took responsibility for the *Norge,* he could fly the *Norge* out of the hangar. Riiser-Larsen accepted the offer and at 10:00 a.m. they lifted off from Svalbard. They flew 3,391 miles, crossed the Arctic Ocean, and landed in Teller, Alaska. The flight took a total of seventy-one hours.

The disdain between Amundsen and Nobile grew as they vied for credit, and other disagreements ensued, until they would have nothing to do with each other.

Two years later, on May 24, 1928, Nobile and an international group of sixteen scientists and support crew attempted to fly to the North Pole on the *Italia,* an N-class airship. The *Italia* got caught in a storm on the return trip and on May 25 crashed onto the ice about twenty-five miles from Svalbard. Ten men were thrown onto the pack ice, and the *Italia* was swept skyward by the wind where it exploded, killing those still on board.

Many of the survivors were injured, including Nobile, who had a broken leg. The men managed to salvage a radio transmitter and a tent that they painted red to maximize visibility on the sea ice. They drifted on the ice toward Foyn and Broch Islands.

When Amundsen heard that Nobile was in trouble, as well as Amundsen's old friend Dr. Finn Malmgren, a Swedish meteorologist who had flown with him on the *Norge* and drifted with him on the *Maud* expedition, and that the Italian government had not initiated a rescue effort to save the men, Amundsen put all of his differences aside and joined an international team from Soviet Russia, Norway, Sweden, the United States, Italy, France, Finland, and Denmark to rescue Nobile, the scientists, and the crew.

On June 18, 1928, Amundsen flew with five aircrew on a Latham 47 flying boat, named for Hubert Latham, a French pioneer in aviation who had attempted to be the first to fly a powered aircraft across the English Channel. Latham's plane's engine failed when a loose wire was caught in the engine, and he made the first successful landing on the water.

Amundsen returned home to Norway to a hero's welcome, and his North Pole achievement was celebrated through the streets of Bergen, July 12, 1926.

Amundsen's home, Uranienborg, overlooking the fjord, as he left it. His study was filled with nautical charts and maps and books, a resistance cord to exercise his upper-body strength, and mementos, including a photograph of himself with the king and queen of Norway and one of Amundsen with Nansen. His study has a sextant and a bathroom designed like one on board a ship.

*Roald Amundsen, standing in front of the French navy's
Latham 47, before Leif Dietrichson, and the French aircrew of
Rene Guilbard, Albert Cavelier de Cuverville, Gilbert Brazy,
and Emile Valtte used the aircraft to search for Nobile.*

The day Amundsen and his crew took off from Tromsø, the
weather was very foggy. The Latham 47 disappeared somewhere in the Barents Sea. The crew's last radio transmission was
picked up on June 18, 1928, at 6:45 p.m., when they should
have been about nineteen miles south of Bear Island.

A month after the *Italia* crashed, Lieutenant Einar Lundborg, of the Swedish air force, landed a Fokker ski plane and
evacuated Nobile to Ryss Island, Svalbard, the base camp of the
Swedish and Finnish air rescue crews. Nobile had argued with
Lieutenant Lundborg to take the wounded men out first, but
that was not Lundborg's orders. When Lundborg returned to
evacuate another survivor, his plane crashed, and he was
trapped with them. The Soviet icebreaker *Krasin* ultimately rescued the survivors.

Amundsen's body was never found. Like the artifacts from
George Washington De Long's crushed ship that showed

The Fokker F-VIIA-3m Josephine Ford *flying over Kings Bay, Svalbard, Norway. Byrd and Bennett claimed to be the first to fly to the North Pole. It is believed that Amundsen is the man in the foreground, watching the flight, 1926.*

Nansen the way through the polar seas, a pontoon from Amundsen's plane rose from the depths and was discovered floating on Arctic waters.

It was as if the pontoon had been found as a way to under-score Amundsen's remaining vision—that flight was the way to explore the polar regions. Flight would give modern-day explorers the ability to see far beyond ships' masts and high above the dogsled trails. Flight would give them speed, allow them to cover expansive distances, and give them entrée into the unknown—the unexplored wilderness of Antarctica.

Amundsen shared this vision with Admiral Byrd on May 10, 1926, the same evening Byrd and Floyd Bennett returned from the first flight to or near the North Pole.

They had dinner with Amundsen and Lincoln Ellsworth, who were preparing to fly in a few days in the *Norge* over Byrd's route and land in Barrow, Alaska. Near the end of the evening,

Byrd and Amundsen standing side by side on Svalbard Island, Norway, before Amundsen attempted his flight over the North Pole.

Amundsen asked Byrd what he was planning to do next. Byrd told Amundsen that he wanted to fly to the South Pole. Byrd wrote that when he told this to Amundsen, he was half serious and half jesting, but Amundsen took him completely seriously. Amundsen told Byrd that it was "a big job, but it can be done" (*Little America,* 24).

Amundsen took Byrd under his wing, as Nansen had done for Amundsen. He told Byrd that flight was the way to explore Antarctica: "The old order is changing. Aircraft is the new vehicle for exploration. It is the only machine that can beat the Antarctic." He advised Byrd to purchase the *Samson,* a ship, to launch his expedition, which Byrd did. He later renamed her the *City of New York.*

Before Byrd set off on the South Pole expedition, he needed to complete a different objective. He had been competing with Charles Lindbergh to become the first to fly nonstop across the Atlantic. During a test run, though, Floyd Bennett crashed the Fokker Trimotor airplane, the *America,* and was badly injured.

On May 20 to 21, 1927, Charles Lindbergh began his

attempt and took off from Roosevelt Field, New York, in the *Spirit of St. Louis,* a tiny single-engine monoplane.

As a child Lindbergh had dreamed of flying across the Atlantic. He had taken flying lessons, worked as a mechanic, barnstormed, and wing-walked. And he wrote a letter to his father to convince him that this was what he had to do with his life, and he offered to help his father run for Congress by flying him around Minnesota, from one campaign stop to another. His father supported Lindbergh's aspirations,

Lindbergh joined the army, and in 1924 he began flight training in the U.S. Army Air Service in San Antonio, Texas, at Brooks Field (now Brooks Air Force Base). Lindbergh graduated first in his class, earned his pilot's wings and a commission as a second lieutenant, and continued to fly with the Missouri National Guard. He convinced Ryan Aeronautical Company in San Diego, California, to build the *Spirit of Saint Louis* for his attempt, and he invested his own money in the venture.

Lindbergh, in his unpressurized, unheated monoplane, flew into the unknown over Canada, to altitudes of more than ten thousand feet to avoid thunderstorms. When the wings of the *Spirit of St. Louis* became iced up, the airplane dropped from the sky to within ten feet of the surface of the Atlantic, and the wind off the ocean waves buffeted the plane. Somehow he managed to stay in the air, but when he flew over Greenland his magnetic compass stopped working. He completely lost his sense of direction and couldn't see where he was going. The fuel tank positioned in front of him completely obscured his view. He flew over what he thought was Ireland, over the English Channel, and landed on Le Bourget Field in Paris. He became the first man to fly across the Atlantic, from New York to Paris; he did it in thirty-three and a half hours.

In order to test out his Fokker F-VII, on June 29, 1927, Byrd made his own bid to fly across the Atlantic with Bernt Balchen, a former lieutenant in the Royal Norwegian Naval Air Service who had been on the Amundsen-Ellsworth *Norge* expedition. They took off from Roosevelt Field, New York, along with two other crew members, and on July 1, 1927, crash-landed on the shores of Normandy.

Byrd began to correspond with Amundsen and asked for more advice about his dream of becoming the first to fly to the South Pole. Amundsen took on the role of Nansen and wrote Byrd and told him the type of pemmican he would need, that he should hunt seals to provide fresh meat for his crew and the dogs. He told Byrd that he was trying to get all the equipment he needed, and he advised Byrd to bring chocolate and oatmeal crackers. He gave Byrd suggestions to wear good woolen underwear with a light windproof jacket over it. He cautioned Byrd against dressing too heavily and perspiring, and stressed the need to stay dry and warm. He also advised him to wear goggles to prevent snow blindness, and that they would make it easier to detect crevasses on sunny days.

Byrd and Amundsen continued exchanging letters and telegrams, and Amundsen did everything he could to help Byrd reach his goal of flying to the South Pole. Byrd wrote to Amundsen on June 7, 1928, to express his gratitude and friendship.

Unlike Amundsen, Byrd was able to secure the massive support he needed to cover the enormous cost of the South Pole expedition. His support often came from giants in the business world who had great vision; his backers included John D. Rockefeller Jr., Edsel Ford, Vincent Astor, the Daniel Guggenheim Fund, Harold S. Vanderbilt, Gilbert Grosvenor of the National Geographic Society, Adolph Ochs and Arthur Sulzberger of the *New York Times,* Joseph Pulitzer of the *St. Louis Post-Dispatch,* and the U.S. Navy.

Byrd required funds to pay for the cost and outfitting of three ships, the *City of New York, Eleanor Bolling,* and *C. A. Larsen,* and two aircraft, a Ford Trimotor and a Fairchild. He had to raise funds for the buildings that would be constructed at Little America—a mess hall, bunkhouse, photography laboratory, library with three thousand books, radio laboratory, hospital, and separate housing for the physician, geologist, meterologist, and physicist, as well as buildings for the magnetic observatory, weather station, radio storeroom, aviation workshop, and machine shop. Byrd had to provide twelve hundred gallons of gasoline, seventy-five tons of coal, enough food for fifteen months, and supplies and equipment for fifty-four men, eighty sled dogs, and Igloo, his small white terrier.

On September 1, 1928, when it was presumed that Amundsen was dead, Byrd wrote a letter for the *Aftenposten,* the newspaper in Oslo (as Christiania had been renamed in 1925), Norway, and the letter appeared in the newspaper on September 3, 1928:

> *Amundsen was my close friend. He was a lionhearted man and one of the greatest explorers of the ages. America shoulders this sorrow with Norway. He died nobly going to succor those in distress. In Amundsen's honor I shall carry a Norwegian flag with us to the Antarctic continent.*
> *R. E. Byrd*

On January 2, 1929, the *City of New York* reached Little America, Byrd's base in Antarctica on the Bay of Whales, on the Ross Ice Shelf, four miles north of where Amundsen had established Framheim. Byrd and his crew wintered over in Little America and discussed how they would achieve the first flight to the South Pole. They had to consider every detail: How much fuel and oil would they need to complete the flight, and how much of a reserve? If they had to make a forced landing, how much food and clothing, sledge equipment, and repair equipment would they need to carry for their survival?

They contemplated how they would attempt the flight: as a nonstop flight or with two stops. Dean Smith, one of the pilots, was concerned that if they hit a headwind, they wouldn't be able to reach the South Pole and return to Little America, and if they landed twice for refueling, in unknown places, they increased the risks of crashing by 20 percent. They decided to run fuel and altitude tests to see how the aircraft performed. Byrd also had his crew itemize and weigh everything they would be carrying on the aircraft—emergency food, sledges, medical supplies, tents, radio, scientific equipment—and they did the same for the sledges. They removed what was deemed unnecessary and reduced the weight of everything they could.

Byrd planned two flights: the first, to place fuel and supplies in a depot at the base of the Axel Heiberg Glacier for the return flight from the pole, and the second, to make the South Pole attempt. They would also lay down depots as emergency rations for the aircrew if they were forced to land.

The sled dog teams were essential to laying down the depots. They struggled alongside their handlers across the ice in the brutal cold and weathered numerous blizzards. To Byrd and his men, the dogs were far more than work animals; they were dear friends. Norman Vaughan, who was the expedition's best dog handler, had a favorite dog named Spry. Byrd noted that Vaughan loved Spry as a brother. Spry had worked so hard unloading supplies that his joints were so inflamed when he finished he could barely walk. Vaughan considered shooting Spry to put him out of his pain. Instead Vaughan and Byrd brought him inside, and Byrd kept him in his room where it was warm and gave him a canvas to sleep on. They fed him a special diet. A couple of days later, they took Spry outside for exercise just as his old dog team was running by. Spry saw his teammates Watch and Moody frolicking past, and he went after them in a burst of speed, overtook them, and summoned something from deep within to force his way to his position in the team.

Byrd wrote that it was one of the most beautiful things he had ever seen: "The whole camp stopped working at the sight, and watched with wonder how Moody and Watch muzzled the veteran, and laid their paws on him in a most extraordinary gesture. That these wild and untrammeled animals should be capable of harboring so deep and lasting a sentiment was beyond understanding." Spry gradually regained his strength, rejoined his team, and together with the men worked toward opening the Antarctic continent by dogsled and by aircraft.

Laurence Gould, second in command of the expedition, conducted the first geological survey of the Rockefeller Mountains from the air. Byrd and his aircrew photographed the first aerial survey of the Bay of Whales, and they monitored and tested the aircraft.

Throughout the expedition, the scientists, especially the magneticians and meteorologists, and the radiomen, were constantly problem solving and trying to determine the best day for the flight, and how they would maintain radio communications and help the aircrew navigate.

William Haines and his team of meteorologists made surface observations—temperature, wind, and so on—and sent pilot balloons up to thirty thousand feet, making some of the first observations of atmospheric circulation in Antarctica. They discovered that the upper atmospheric observations were the only reliable sources for indicating immediate changes in the weather.

And they also discovered that the earth's magnetism affected radio communications. Byrd's three radiomen, Malcom P. Hansan, Carl O. Petersen, and Howard F. Mason, created a radio system that operated on high and intermediate frequencies, which were less affected by physical disturbances, and they were able to provide the aircraft with a radio compass and a directive radio transmitting beacon for navigation. In a building they called Ochs Radio Station, the radiomen—along with Fred Meinholz, the radioman with the *New York Times*—kept the men in touch with the outside world, but after living months in cramped quarters, in the bitter cold and gray diffuse light, they longed for spring.

On October 9, 1929, Byrd and Russell Owen, a journalist with the *New York Times,* stepped outside their building, and, as Byrd wrote:

The air suddenly became charged with ice crystals, which fell like rain. The sun broke through the shattered cloud fabric which turned yellow and opalescent in its growing power, then arched more beautiful than any rainbow I have ever seen swept upward, curved, and in a moment the sun was crossed by two great shafts of brilliant light, in the center of which it burned with leaping

Portrait of Russell Owen (New York Times). *Owen's coverage in the* New York Times *of Byrd's Antarctic expedition won a Pulitzer Prize in 1930. Owen and the* New York Times *opened radio communications into the interior of Antarctica and from Antarctica to the world.*

tongues of flame. On either side could be seen the trembling halos of the mock suns, each impaled on its shaft of prismatic light. Directly opposite the sun was the anthelion, the reflection of the outstretched reach of the cross, a luminous pillar rising from the snows of the Barrier. For nearly an hour we watched this gorgeous display, while the ice crystals that caused it fell in sparkling showers. (*Little America,* 279–280)

Owen wrote that night, "We went indoors deeply affected by the beauty and grandeur of this great vision" (*Little America,* 280). They took this display as a favorable sign.

On Thanksgiving Day, 1929, Laurence Gould with the geographic party radioed that the weather was unchanged with perfect visibility. Harrison set off his weather balloons, and Haines checked the weather charts and told Byrd that he would never have another day as good as this.

Just after 3:00 p.m. on November 28, 1929, Richard Byrd, the navigator; Bernt Balchen, the pilot; Harold June, the copilot-radioman; and Ashley McKinley, the aerial surveyor–photographer, climbed into the Ford Trimotor *Floyd Bennett,* filled with rows of gasoline cans, piles of clothes, and sacks of food. They took off at 3:29 p.m. from Little America on the

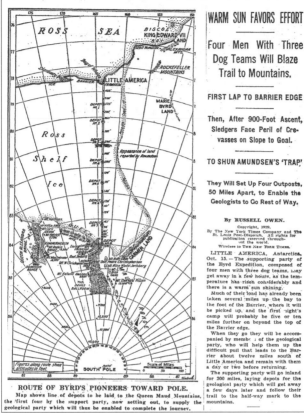

BYRD OPENS SPRING DRIVE OF DISCOVERY AS HIS SUPPORT PARTY GIRDS FOR START ON 200-MILE BASE-LAYING TREK SOUTH

WARM SUN FAVORS EFFORT

Four Men With Three Dog Teams Will Blaze Trail to Mountains.

FIRST LAP TO BARRIER EDGE

Then, After 900-Foot Ascent, Sledgers Face Peril of Crevasses on Slope to Goal.

TO SHUN AMUNDSEN'S 'TRAP'

They Will Set Up Four Outposts, 50 Miles Apart, to Enable the Geologists to Go Rest of Way.

By RUSSELL OWEN.

Copyright, 1929.
By The New York Times Company and The St. Louis Post-Dispatch. All rights for publication reserved throughout the world.
Wireless to THE NEW YORK TIMES.

LITTLE AMERICA, Antarctica, Oct. 15.—The supporting party of the Byrd Expedition, composed of four men with three dog teams, may get away in a few hours, as the temperature has risen considerably and there is a warm sun shining.

Much of their load has already been taken several miles up the bay to the foot of the Barrier, where it will be picked up, and the first night's camp will probably be five or ten miles further on beyond the top of the Barrier edge.

When they go they will be accompanied by members of the geological party, who will help them up the difficult pull that leads to the Barrier about twelve miles south of Little America and remain with them a day or two before returning.

The supporting party will go inland for 200 miles, laying depots for the geological party which will get away a few days later and follow their trail to the half-way mark to the mountains.

ROUTE OF BYRD'S PIONEERS TOWARD POLE.
Map shows line of depots to be laid to the Queen Maud Mountains, the first four by the support party, now setting out, to supply the geological party which will thus be enabled to complete the journey.

New York Times *(October 16, 1929) story and map of Amundsen's achievement of the South Pole.*

first flight toward the South Pole. Their major question was: would they be able to gain enough altitude to fly over the "Hump," the critical place in the route where they would have to climb to eleven thousand feet, high enough to fly above the Polar Plateau?

At 3:29 p.m. they took off from Little America and flew along the depot trail but lost sight of it off and on as they flew through a confusing haze.

The wind was gusting from the east, and Balchen had to correct 10 degrees to the left to maintain a straight line for the South Pole. He was calm, but eager to reach the Hump. June was working the radio, McKinley was using the mapping camera, and Byrd was studying the chart and navigating.

The men were shouting above the sound of the engines to communicate. They were hot in their bulky parkas and clothes, but a cool breeze blew through the cabin, and when the sky cleared, it was flooded with golden light.

Byrd noted their position and remembered that Amundsen had been delighted when they accomplished twenty-five miles per day; Byrd and his crew were now averaging ninety miles an hour over the barrier. Byrd also realized that in an aircraft he had the advantage of speed over Amundsen and his sled dogs, but if the aircraft had a mechanical failure or encountered strong headwinds, things beyond Byrd's control, these factors could destroy their attempt, and take their lives.

They spotted Laurence Gould and the geological party one hundred miles from the base of the Queen Maud Range. Gould radioed Byrd and he confirmed the aircraft's position. When they reached the Queen Maud Range, Balchen opened the engines up to full throttle—1,750 rpms. Byrd watched the altimeter and used a sun compass for navigation. The *Floyd Bennett* climbed steadily to forty-five hundred feet. When they arrived at the spot where the Axel Heiberg Mountains and the Liv Glacier came into view, they had to choose a direction, and they had to decide quickly—wasted time meant wasted fuel.

They recalled that Amundsen had said that the highest point of the pass on the Axel Heiberg Glacier was 10,500 feet. June calculated the fuel consumption and the weight of the airplane, and then they determined how high they could fly. They realized the towering peaks on either side of them, surrounding the pass, were higher than the aircraft could fly. But they weren't sure how wide the pass was, or if they would be able to fit through it or turn around if it was necessary.

Balchen noticed a thin cloud capping the Axel Heiberg Glacier, perhaps indicating a change in weather, so they chose to fly through the pass on the Liv Glacier, named after Nansen's daughter. Byrd judged it was not quite as high as the Axel Heiberg Glacier and perhaps a bit wider.

At 9:15 p.m. June tore open the fuel cans and poured the contents into the main tank and dropped the two-pound cans overboard to reduce weight. June calculated the fuel usage. They had encountered headwinds so the flight took longer and used more fuel than they expected, but they had taken aboard extra fuel just before they departed. They reached the face of the Liv Glacier and caught sight of what they thought might be the Polar Plateau.

Byrd noted that the glacier rose sharply in a series of terraces, some of which rose high above the altitude of their airplane. And there were glacial waterfalls up to four hundred feet high that were more beautiful, Byrd noted, than any stream he had ever seen. But beauty gave way to concern.

Air was rushing through the pass, and the airplane's wings were shivering and teetering and bouncing in the air. The air grew so rough that they had to change course over a scary sequence of crevasses and into downdrafts that nearly stopped their climb. The winds were so strong that they were creeping through the narrow pass, unable to turn around. They knew that if they lost power for a moment or if the air became violently rough, they could only go forward or down.

Balchen struggled to get the airplane to continue to climb, but it wasn't gaining altitude, and he shouted to the crew that they had to toss two hundred pounds overboard. Byrd had to decide between food and fuel. If it was fuel, they might not have enough to get to the pole and back; if it was food, and they crashed, they would have nothing for survival.

Byrd ordered June to throw a sack of food overboard, and the airplane began to climb again, but the downdrafts pressing on the aircraft increased, and so they threw out a second bag. The airplane immediately gained altitude, and they managed to clear the pass with five hundred feet to spare. They climbed

Admiral Byrd landing in Antarctica, 1929.

over the Polar Plateau and slipped past peak after mountain peak on the eastern horizon. And they continued their flight on the 171st meridian.

On the floor of the airplane was a drift indicator that showed the plane's drift to one side or the other. McKinley and Byrd were constantly checking it. Byrd was using that information along with a sun compass to guide Balchan.

Byrd took a sun shot, and at 1:14 a.m. Greenwich civil time their calculations showed that they had finally reached the South Pole. They crossed the pole a second time, and Byrd noted that they were over the spot where Amundsen and Scott had stood, and in their honor the flags of their countries were carried over the pole. Only a white limitless plain lay below.

They headed back toward Little America; the mountains that had been vibrantly clear were now covered in fast-moving clouds. Time moved slowly, but a tail wind pushed them along, and they flew at 125 miles per hour at an altitude of between 11,500 and 12,000 feet.

When they reached Mounts Ruth Gade, Nansen, and

Christophersen, Balchen smiled, and they flew between Ruth Gade and Christophersen. They were making great progress, but suddenly the mountains didn't look familiar to Byrd, and then he remembered what Amundsen had warned him about. The mountains change appearance from the position from which they are viewed. Byrd realized that they had been flying at a different altitude and suddenly recognized Mount Nansen and the Liv Glacier, where they landed smoothly and refueled. After taking off again, they finally saw the Bay of Whales and the radio spires of Little America. They landed at 10:08 a.m., November 29, 1929, and having completed the first flight to the South Pole in eighteen hours and forty-one minutes.

Richard Byrd coordinated four more pioneering expeditions into Antarctica, and in 1956–57 he commanded the U.S. Navy's Operation Deep Freeze I and established permanent bases in Antarctica at McMurdo Sound, the South Pole, and the Bay of Whales. The bases would open Antarctica for further exploration.

CHAPTER 20

Navigating

How could I explore Amundsen's vision and Byrd's legacy? Who would know how to fly to the interior of the continent and the South Pole? It occurred to me: the navigator that I'd met in Greenland before the swim in Ilulissat. Samantha East would know. I remembered she lived somewhere in New York State. I looked through my files. We had exchanged e-mails, but I couldn't find her e-mail address in my computer. I tried different name-and-letter combinations. The e-mails bounced back. I began searching, trying to find a scrap of paper with her handwriting and her e-mail address. I searched for hours and sat down and looked at the wall in front of my desk. There right in front of my face was a beautiful photo calendar of Antarctica. Samantha had sent it to me. She had sent a note. I had saved it. She said the calendar was to show me some of the places she flew with the 109th Air Wing and to remind me of the swim that I once did there. I had her home address! It was in a small pile of notes on my desk. I wrote to her and waited.

But time was passing. It was June 2008, and I knew that December and January were the months when people traveled to Antarctica. It was a narrow window of time, and I found on a Web site that the National Science Foundation had an office of polar programs for artists and writers who could propose various writing or artistic projects and compete for NSF grants that would enable them to travel to Antarctica and pursue their project. The problem was that it was too late to apply for the

2007–8 season. I couldn't fit in the NSF time frame, but I needed to go to Antarctica to write about the men and women who were fulfilling Amundsen's vision.

When I heard from Samantha East, she advised me to get in touch with Sarah Andrews, her friend who was an author and had been to Antarctica a couple of years earlier. Sarah immediately responded and suggested that I get in touch with Colonel Ron Smith, who was the in-theater joint task force commander for Operation Deep Freeze. Sarah explained that Colonel Smith was in charge of all the C-17s, LC-130s, icebreakers, and other ships that resupply the Antarctic bases and back-haul retrograde and waste materials.

The route the U.S. Air Force flies from McMurdo to the pole does not overlay Amundsen's route; he traveled farther east, but the LC-130 flies from the Ross Ice Shelf over the Transantarctic Mountains to the Polar Plateau.

Sarah wrote an introduction to Colonel Smith for me, and she gave me more details on his background. She said Colonel Smith was known as the Ice Ambassador. He was the U.S. Air Force representative as well as commander in Antarctica for Operation Deep Freeze. His mission was to work with the National Science Foundation and to support the scientists in Antarctica. He worked with the forty-four countries—their scientists, representatives, and support personnel—who operated under the Antarctic Treaty. The central theme of the Antarctic Treaty was that the Antarctic continent would be used only for peaceful purposes. No country could make new territorial claims within Antarctica, and there would be mutual cooperation. And the environment in Antarctica would be preserved. In addition, he was in charge of all U.S. Air Force rescue operations in Antarctica.

When I heard about Colonel Smith, I realized that he was the man fulfilling Admiral Byrd's legacy as the commander in Antarctica. It took me a while to figure out how to write to him.

On June 22, 2008, I was on the Seal Beach Pier in California, staring out across the choppy waters of the Pacific Ocean at sunset, watching bright orange-gold sunlight spread along the shoulders of the waves, and illuminating the larger three-foot-high waves that were curling and sliding onto the soft sand, releasing energy like an exhaled breath. I was trying to figure out how I could get to Antarctica to write about Amundsen and the 109th Air Wing when my cell phone rang.

"Hello, this is Ron Smith," a man said in measured way, with a wonderful Baltimore accent. It was the air force. I thought, I've got to tell him everything in three minutes or less. He's probably so busy. I told him that I needed to fly with the 109th and write about its mission in Antarctica and how it connected to Amundsen's vision. He asked some questions about the deadline for my book and understood that I could not make the NSF application deadline for the artists' and writers' program that year, and that the following year would be too late. He advised me to get in touch with the air force's public affairs office. If they thought it was a good project, they would send my book proposal to the secretary of the air force to request support for it. Thrilled that the air force would consider my request, I did a little dance on the pier.

As soon as I got home, I wrote the proposal and sent it off to the public affairs office and waited for its approval. On July 28 the approval came through from the Pentagon. I was elated. Piece by piece the project was coming together. I passed the approval letter from the Pentagon to the 12th Air Force public affairs office, and they in turn forwarded it to the National Science Foundation. Since Antarctica was a joint mission between the U.S. Air Force and the National Science Foundation, I needed approval from both groups.

Weeks passed.

Then one day I received a call from Ron Smith. He said that he had e-mailed a satellite photo of Antarctica. He wanted to know if I could open the file and take a look at the image.

He began by explaining that the LC-130s and C-17s that supported Operation Deep Freeze flew from Christchurch, New Zealand, to McMurdo Sound. The flight from Christchurch to McMurdo Station took ten hours. I looked at the

USAF colonel Ron Smith, left, and Lieutenant General David Deptula, the commander of Joint Task Force Operation Deep Freeze, landing in Antarctica, January 2006.

satellite photo. The Antarctic continent was the size of the United States and Mexico. Antarctica was shaped like an enormous stingray with the tail of the stingray pointing up toward the southern tip of South America. Ross Island, home of the U.S. base at McMurdo Station, was located on McMurdo Sound, and 730 miles south of McMurdo Station, near the stingray's head, was the South Pole.

From McMurdo Station, 920 miles to the left wing of the ray was the WSD, an acronym signifying the WAIS (West Antarctic Ice Sheet) Divide research site. On the right wing of the stingray was a new station for Antarctica's Gamburtsev Province (AGAP), a research project studying the Gamburtsev mountain range, which is buried under the glacier. It was in a very remote area. It had never been explored. I wondered if we knew more about the surface of the moon than we did the continent of Antarctica.

Emperor penguins with LC-130—flight through the water and flight through the air.

As Ron briefed me on Antarctica, I thought how fortunate I was to have a colonel who had spent eleven seasons there briefing me about the place, describing the satellite image and what I was viewing. Maps and charts always fascinated me. My experience, though, was with nautical charts. An aeronautical chart was so different; it was an entirely different perspective, looking down from space upon the Antarctic continent.

Ron knew Antarctica. Long before he was a colonel, he was an LC-130 navigator, and he was trained to be clear, concise, and descriptive to help guide the pilot and copilot. But he was also a poet, and he selected his words in a way that was very much like the way a fine artist mixed his paints to find just exactly the right shade of a color to apply to his canvas to share his vision. He was describing Antarctica to me as a vast breathtaking wilderness, an icy desert where temperatures dropped to minus 120 Fahrenheit degrees in winter, and where massive mountain ranges rose to more than fourteen thousand feet. It was an environment that was intensely harsh and unpredictable, and it could become very dangerous. One dumb oversight or stupid mistake could make life suddenly very tenuous.

Ron redirected my attention to the satellite map, to a place near the back of the stingray's right wing. This area was where McMurdo Station was built. It was on Ross Island, a volcanic island with two predominate mountains, Mount Erebus, an active volcano, towering 13,282 feet above McMurdo, and Mount Terror, an inactive volcano with a height of 10,597 feet. Mount Erebus constantly emitted a sulfurous plume thousands of feet into the air.

Ron explained that the United States shared Ross Island with the New Zealanders. The New Zealanders' Scott Base was located about four miles from McMurdo Station. The U.S. Air Force and the Royal New Zealand Air Force were great friends and colleagues. Within walking distance of McMurdo Station were the two huts Scott and Shackleton had built before they made their attempts to reach the South Pole. Because of the cold, dry air, both Shackleton's and Scott's huts were well preserved and looked pretty much as they had one hundred years ago, when the two men had camped out in Antarctica.

The main mission for the 109th Air Wing was to fly scientists, support personnel, and equipment to various research stations throughout the Antarctic continent. Critical to achieving the mission were the runways.

In most parts of the world, pilots preferred taking off and landing on runways that were free from ice and snow, but as a way to illustrate how different flying in Antarctica was, the only two runways that the U.S. Air Force used were made of either ice or snow.

Pegasus was a glacial-ice runway about a forty-five-minute drive from McMurdo Station, and it was used by C-17s, enormous cargo aircraft, and LC-130s, smaller aircraft. The C-17 and LC-130 landed on Pegasus on wheels. The other runway was Williams Field—a skiway where the LC-130s landed on the snow using their skis. Williams Field was about thirty minutes from McMurdo.

For years the U.S. Coast Guard supported Operation Deep Freeze by preparing the sea ice for an ice runway. The coast guard used an icebreaker to create a smooth path of open water that refroze and became the ice runway. But before the ice refroze, the coast guard played the critical role of "pathfinder" for the soon-to-follow tanker vessel and cargo vessel from the Military Sealift Command. Without the icebreaker there would be no bulk fuel or supplies getting into McMurdo to carry out the yearlong mission. Because of the low funding priority of the U.S. icebreaker fleet, the U.S. Coast Guard can no longer operate autonomously in the Antarctic mission and must rely on foreign-contract icebreakers.

At the end of our conversation, I realized how important it was for the United States to have more icebreakers for Antarctica and also for the Arctic. As the sea ice melts during the next ten years, Arctic waters will open and there will be an increase in shipping, commerce, and exploration. There will be increased pressure on the Arctic environment, and a dire need for the United States to be able to respond to potential problems. It also occurred to me that there would be a greater need for the U.S. Senate to ratify the Law of the Seas treaty, a treaty that defines the rights and responsibilities of the world's nations concerning the world's oceans and also sets guidelines for territorial limits for business, the environment, and management of the ocean's resources. The Law of the Seas treaty could help lead to mutual cooperation between the nations of the world, like the Antarctic Treaty, which focuses on scientific research, collaboration, and peace.

Sitting back in my chair, I realized how fortunate I was to learn about Antarctica from a man who had spent a large part of his career working on and above the continent and who was carrying on Byrd's and Amundsen's legacy.

CHAPTER 21

Antarctic Aviation

Admiral Byrd fulfilled Amundsen's vision of Antarctic flight as the way to explore Antarctica, and in doing so Byrd—along with many other explorers—opened the continent to discovery. Although the aircraft became more modern, and aircrews better trained and more skilled, the one factor that didn't change was the Antarctic environment.

Colonel Ron Smith explained that Antarctic weather conditions are constantly changing. The weather can change from flat calm to screaming hurricane-force winds in a matter of minutes.

Antarctica has its very own weather systems. Its weather originates off the Antarctic coast and over the high Polar Plateau, the area where Amundsen, Scott, and Shackleton climbed and traversed for months in their quests to reach the South Pole.

The Polar Plateau is shaped like a wedding cake, with the plateau being the smooth, high, iced top of the cake. The Transantarctic Mountains run between the Polar Plateau and the Rockefeller Plateau. As a result of radiational cooling, the cold, dense, heavy air on top of the Polar Plateau spills down the sloping terrain. The cold, heavy air, propelled by gravity, accelerates down the tiers of the wedding cake and tears out across McMurdo Station and out along the Ross Ice Shelf.

These are katabatic winds and are most commonly found

blowing off the large and elevated ice sheets of Antarctica and Greenland. The buildup of high-density cold air over the ice sheets and their elevation brings into play enormous gravitational energy, propelling the winds to well over hurricane force. These winds in Greenland are called Piteraq, and they are most intense whenever a low-pressure area approaches the coast.

Within twenty minutes, a katabatic wind could blow through McMurdo and ground all flights, making it impossible to land or take off.

Predicting the movement and the timing of storms approaching Antarctica is extremely challenging. There is one weather satellite that can see only one shallow angle of Antarctica. There is a twelve-hour gap between views that the satellite can capture.

Communications in Antarctica are also a challenge. There are communication satellites, but their use is also limited, and it is extremely costly to make a telephone call.

What really fascinated me was that navigation in Antarctica was different from in other parts of the world and full of challenges. Because of the magnetic variations caused by the South Magnetic Pole, compasses don't work in the area. And because of the geometric location of the South Pole, even the new systems for aircraft navigation don't work very well.

Ron explained that by holding up a globe and looking at the top or the bottom of it, you see that the lines of longitude converge at the geographic poles. When an aircrew climbs into a cold aircraft at the South Pole, the GPS can't get a position, and it spits out random numbers. To find the aircraft's position, the navigator uses a sextant and shoots the sun. The navigator attaches the sextant to a window in the ceiling of the LC-130, and takes a series of sun shots to calculate the position and direction the aircraft is heading.

There was something that was very beautiful to me in this—the air force navigators are as connected to the sun and to the stars for navigation as Amundsen was. The sextant Amundsen had used was very simple. The aviators' sextant is more refined and precise. It has to be. On a good day Amundsen traveled twenty-four miles, while the aircrews in the LC-130s travel at a speed of three hundred miles per hour.

The air force also uses a grid system for navigation in the Arctic and Antarctica. The grid is composed of a web of green squares, with one inch equaling sixty miles. The green grid is drawn on the aeronautical chart, and through a series of measurements and calculations, coupled with sun shots and calculations, and radar, the navigators can see where they are in the airspace and direct the pilots to their destination.

There is so much more to flying in Antarctica. Ron told me it is as much art as it is a science. More than anything, I wanted to see how the aircrews flew and the art and science of Antarctic flight.

I contacted the 109th Air Wing in Schenectady, New York, and requested a visit so I could do background research to gain a better understanding of how they achieved their mission in Antarctica.

Before I spoke with them I needed to be prepared. That was one of the reasons for my fascination with Amundsen. He was so pragmatic, and so organized. That was a large part of why he succeeded. He had my admiration, and I wanted to go to meet with the 109th Air Wing and learn from them. Socrates, the Greek philosopher, said that in order to ask a question, you need to know half the answer. I needed to know so much more before I could ask any questions.

Racking my brain, I tried to think who I knew that might know something about this world of polar flight. Ken Hansen, one of my old friends, had been a U.S. Marine who was an F-4 radar intercept officer in Vietnam (the RIO also acts as an aircraft navigator). He had the best stories about flight, about emergency situations, how pilots and navigators held things together and figured out how to save the aircraft and themselves. He taught me a lot about the g-forces that act on pilots and RIOs in F-4s and the G-suits they wore to pump blood up from their legs, back up through their bodies into their brains so they wouldn't pass out when they were "pulling g's." He gave me insights into their survival training, and we talked a lot about cold-water survival. He said that in training he was told that he would have a maximum of twenty minutes' survival time if something went wrong with the F-4 and he had to eject into the cold waters off northern Japan.

That bothered me because I didn't believe it was true. As in any case, so much about survival depended on the individual's conditioning and mental attitude, and what was going at the moment something happened. Thinking like that limited a person's chances of survival. Ken was one of those who inspired me to write, and he said, "All you have to do is to take what you do, experiences that most people will never have, and explain them in a way that they can feel it, they can experience it. If you can do that, you'll have succeeded."

Because Ken had been an F-4 RIO, I told him what I'd learned from Colonel Smith about the LC-130 navigators and the way they used sextants to navigate at the South Pole. This really piqued his interest.

Apollo 11 was the first to land on the moon; its crew was made up of Michael Collins, Neil Armstrong, and Buzz Aldrin. While Neil Armstrong and Buzz Aldrin touched down in the *Eagle,* the lunar lander, and walked across the Sea of Tranquility on the moon's surface, Michael Collins, the command-module pilot, remained behind in the spaceship *Columbia* and orbited the moon, waiting—as we waited, glued to the television—for Armstrong and Aldrin to return to the spacecraft.

Ken mentioned he had read that the Apollo crew had learned how to use a sextant for backup, in case the navigational systems went out during the flight, so they could steer by the stars. It sounded amazing and romantic. Astronauts who gazed at planet Earth from space could use the stars to guide them home. Armstrong, Aldrin, and Collins needed a patch to symbolize Apollo 11. Mike Collins knew the lunar lander was going to be called the *Eagle,* so he traced a picture of an eagle from a photo in a National Geographic book. Because the Apollo 11 was a mission of peace, he drew an olive branch, symbolizing peace, in the eagle's talons. He gave the design idea to the NASA team, and they used it.

Ann Collins, Mike's daughter, is a friend. She recently contacted me because Mike, at age seventy-eight, was starting to do triathlons. He was doing great with his running and cycling, but he needed some help with his swimming technique. She was also concerned about him swimming in Florida waters with sharks and with alligators.

When I called Mike to ask him about sextant navigation in space, at first all he wanted to talk about was swimming. It was something he wanted to perfect. He was warm, helpful, and inquisitive.

We talked about body position in the water; he said that he tended to be a sinker. It is all about the breathing, I told him. Try to think of your lungs as balloons: relax, draw in a deep breath, and the balloons fill with air, and you float. If you're tense, the balloons only fill partway, and you won't float as high in the water. Think of swimming as returning to space and to zero gravity, I told him. I gave him a drill to find his floating point, and we talked about finding his body position in the water. And then I asked him if he had used an aviator's sextant to steer the Apollo 11 spacecraft.

Mike explained that he and Armstrong and Aldrin learned the positions of fifty stars, and how to use the sextant to indicate their position, but only as a backup. In flight they used the sextant to sight on stars to update or make more accurate their inertial guidance platform.

Mike wanted to know why I was interested, and I told him what I'd learned from Ron about navigation at the South Pole. He was surprised GPS didn't work well at the South Pole.

He patiently described the global positioning satellite systems—GPS. He said that in the 1970s there were more than twenty medium earth-orbiting satellites that transmitted signals from space to GPS receivers, and this navigational system enabled astronauts and aviators to determine the spacecraft's or aircraft's location, speed, distance, and time. He added that the spacecraft crews primarily used inertial navigational systems—

INS. He explained that INS uses motion-sensing devices—gyroscopes and accelerometers—along with computers to help them navigate. He was intrigued that the INS system also didn't work well at the South Pole. What was wonderful in all of this was that I'd asked him one simple question, about using a sextant for navigation, and through that gained a better understanding of his mission with Apollo 11 and how he navigated through space. There was something really amazing in being able to learn this from the person who flew the first manned mission to the moon. While he had achieved so much, he was willing to share what he knew.

While astronauts and aircrews used different navigational aids, both were, at times, flying into the unknown: into outer space, or into unexplored regions such as Antarctica. I asked Mike if he knew of anyone who flew in Antarctica. His flight path had been so different. He didn't have friends or contacts in that area.

That was okay. I kept trying to think of who might know something more about flight. Greg Miller, a cyclist friend, was involved with the first human-powered flight. When we were in high school he invited me to drive with him at three in the morning in his VW van to Edwards Air Force Base to watch him attempt to fly the *Gossamer Condor,* the first human-powered aircraft.

Dr. Paul MacCready had recruited Greg for the project. MacCready wanted to compete for and win the Kremer Prize for the first human-powered flight. Greg was a national champion who had broken records for road racing. MacCready needed someone who had the power, strength, and speed to get the *Gossamer Condor* airborne and to satisfy the criteria for the award: to fly the aircraft a mile in a figure-eight course over two markers, and, at the end of the course, pedal hard enough to reach an altitude of ten feet.

MacCready had a group of friends, aeronautical engineers and designers from NASA and from Caltech who were working on the aircraft. It was so exciting to witness this event. What this group of aeronautical engineers and designers was attempting was something that had intrigued men and women since the time of the Greeks and their myth about Icarus and Daedalus.

There was something special about being there that day at Edwards Air Force Base with this team of researchers and aeronautical engineers who designed and built aircraft, rockets, and spaceships, and who had all come together to try to solve the question of human-powered fight using an aircraft that externally resembled the one that the Wright Brothers flew for their first flight. But internally the Gossamer didn't have an engine. Greg would power the *Gossamer Condor*. He would climb inside the fuselage and sit on a plastic seat holding on to a little steering wheel—parts MacCready had pulled from his son's Tonka fire engine. Greg would remember that MacCready always believed in simplicity, in doing more with less, and in using what exists to invent something new. Greg's seat looked like a recumbent bicycle. He would pedal as fast as his feet could move; the bicycle chain connected to a propeller that would power the aircraft.

Greg had practiced on other flights. He had crashed. The team had rebuilt and redesigned the plane. He had tried again. He crashed, but learned how to pace himself. He trained harder. He learned how to fly a fixed-wing plane. He watched birds in flight. He joined MacCready and his group numerous times at Edwards. They kept tweaking the aircraft, and he went back and tried again.

On the drive to Edwards in his VW van he talked about being able to hold a straight line during flight, but said that it was really difficult for him to make the turns. During the entire flight he had to maintain his pedal speed, and when he came to the turns, he had to steer more, and he felt the balance of the aircraft shift. He felt the speed drop, and he had to pedal faster to maintain flight. He had crashed ten or twelve times. He'd fallen ten feet out of the air. It didn't hurt too much. But it always hurt the Condor. And he didn't like to do that. He wanted to see it work. He really believed human-powered flight was possible, and he was going to be the one to do it.

We reached Edwards just before sunrise. The *Gossamer Condor* was on the runway, and poles had been set up to mark the course. There were a couple of bicycles on the runway, too, so the crew could ride beside Greg and coach him.

The air was still very calm. Greg climbed into the tiny fuselage. He had to be very careful that his elbows didn't tear the thin Mylar sheeting skin of the aircraft.

The team members positioned themselves along the course, and two held poles, one at the half-mile mark, the other at the finish.

Greg walked around to warm up his legs, took a few deep breaths, and then said he was ready. He began pedaling fast, and the *Gossamer Condor* lifted off the ground. It was amazing to see him gaining altitude. He increased his speed. I could see his feet were pedaling faster than I'd ever seen at any national championship. He was breathing so hard I could see the skin of the aircraft move in and out with his breath, and I could hear him. He was doing great. It was so exciting to witness the first human-powered flight and to think of all of the people who had been part of this moment.

Greg managed to fly half a mile, and we held our breaths as we watched him, transfixed by what we were seeing. But then he began to turn the *Gossamer Condor;* it was at too sharp an angle, with the left wing tilted directly toward the ground. He lost momentum. He pedaled harder and tried to hang on; he held it for a second, two, three, but the *Gossamer Condor* started to fall, wing first, as if in slow motion, and then crashed into the ground. The men on the team couldn't help themselves; they shouted, "Oh no," and they groaned. And then in the next moment they shouted, "Greg, are you okay?"

The Mylar wing was crumpled into an accordion shape. Snapped pieces of balsa wood stuck out like broken bones and the piano string that had held everything together tautly lay in the pile of wreckage. It looked so bad.

The crew got to work. They removed the broken wing and quickly attached a new one.

Greg smiled confidently and climbed back into the *Gos-*

samer Condor. I watched the same sequence as before, his feet pressing the pedals as rapidly as they would move. He lifted off the ground and gained altitude with the sunrise. The entire sky filled with red, orange, and yellow light and illuminated the wings of the *Gossamer Condor.*

He was climbing higher, six, seven, eight feet off the ground. MacCready had told him it would be easier to fly close to the ground—maybe from ground effect, which would provide lift and help him stay in the air—but he also needed to give himself some height, because if he made a mistake, there was more space for him to make a correction.

Greg reached the halfway mark, and then he began the turn. I think Greg was the only one breathing at that moment.

Over a walkie-talkie we heard the details moment by moment.

The *Gossamer Condor* began to shudder, but Greg made an adjustment; he made a wider turn. It took more time, and more energy, but he made it all the way around. The team cheered and threw their arms into the air. All he had to do was to fly back to the starting point. But "all" was still a lot.

He flew the *Gossamer Condor* quickly toward us, and the strong morning sun illuminated the aircraft. Everyone was focused on the aircraft and on Greg. The chase bikes were behind him, and the team's cheers were growing louder and more excited, sensing that Greg was almost there.

Greg had just one more hurdle; he had to climb into the air and fly to an altitude of ten feet to fly over a pole. But he was getting tired. I could hear him gasping for air. All he had to do was get up over that pole. Everyone was cheering. This was a vision they all had shared. And when Greg flew over that last hurdle, everyone cheered, applauded, or jumped up and down. It was one of most fantastic sights I'd ever seen. They had achieved the first human-powered flight.

Years and years had passed since that day, and I thought of Greg and Paul MacCready. Greg had broken more national cycling records, and he had become a mechanic for the Tour de France, helping Greg LeMond and Lance Armstrong keep their bikes performing at their best. MacCready had designed the *Gossamer Albatross,* and Bryan Allen became the first to fly this human-powered aircraft across the English Channel. Mac-Cready also designed the Solar Challenger, a solar-powered electric aircraft, and the solar-powered car, the Sun Racer (which Greg built the wheels for), which won the Race Across Australia. MacCready also developed drones and drone technology. MacCready's spirit had taken flight. He had passed away, but Greg was around, and so I asked him if he knew someone who might know someone involved with polar flight. He didn't off the top of his head, but he would think about it. And I kept thinking about it. Who else could I contact that might know something about polar flight so that if I got a chance to speak with the people at the 109th, I'd be able to ask meaningful questions?

As I continued trying to learn more about flight very unexpectedly Alan Williams called me. We had met years ago, in 1977, during my summer break on Dutch Harbor in the Aleutian Islands. Alan was then a pilot who flew Lear jets, and he had flown out to Dutch Harbor to transport customs agents there to check foreign ships coming into the port. Alan had saved my big toe. I had been on an expedition to the Aleutian Islands that had gone wrong, and I had gotten an infection in my big toe from a blister. I used that as the excuse to leave, but I later found out that if I hadn't I would have lost my toe from gangrene.

Alan said he was now flying a Gulfstream 5 for a corporate executive and traveling the world. His wife was a physician, and they had four sons, and the youngest was just graduating college. He asked what I was doing, and I told him I was planning to follow in the wake of Amundsen through the Northwest Passage. He immediately put me in touch with a friend of his who was a pilot in Alaska, and with her help, I was able to get the permission I needed to swim off Prudhoe Bay.

A couple of years had passed, but we'd stayed in touch, and when he heard that I was trying to learn more about polar flight, he said he grew up flying small planes throughout Alaska and that he was coming to California for work, and we could meet in Seal Beach.

Over dinner, Alan said his dad was an incredible pilot who had taught him everything about airplane mechanics and flight. He had soloed at fifteen and had flown into very remote areas of Alaska. Arctic temperatures were milder than those in Antarctica, but in either case keeping the airplane fluids warm was very important. Weather in the polar regions played a huge role in whether it was possible to fly or not. He also explained that an aircraft taking off at sea level performed a lot better than an aircraft taking off at altitude. He said he looked forward to reading what I learned from the 109th Air Wing.

Out of the blue, Pat Roberts, my good friend whom I had met just after college, who now lived in upstate New York, called to say hello. She asked if I would be coming out for a visit any time soon. I had never been to her home in New York to visit her family, and I had always wanted to, but we always met in California when she came to visit family.

I said I hoped to visit the air force base near Scotia and talk with the aircrews and maintainers at the 109th, but I needed to do background research first. Pat's voice filled with excitement. She said she lived half an hour from the base. She said that she knew two of the pilots from the air force who flew to Antarctica; one lived across the street, and the other, Gary James, was a close friend of hers and her husband. Gary would even be coming to her big birthday party in a few months. Pat would introduce them to me if I wanted to talk with them. And John, her brother who flew for the navy, had a friend who knew one of the Antarctic pilots. She wanted to know if I wanted to talk with them, and I said, "Oh yes!"

But Ron Smith suggested I first contact the public affairs office. I did and waited. And then I received an e-mail from the 109th Air Wing. They invited me to visit them in Scotia, New York.

Riding the train from New York City to Scotia, north along the Hudson River valley, was one of the most gentle and beautiful trips I'd ever taken. The Hudson River was silvery blue and calm. Trees, homes, and buildings reflected upon its surface. Waterbirds—ducks and geese—paddled across the water's surface. It was so soothing to watch the river slide past. I was excited and apprehensive about meeting people at the 109th. I didn't have much experience with the U.S. military. The only places that I'd visited on military bases, in addition to Edwards, were the cold research tank with the Navy SEALs on Coronado Island, the swimming pool at the Joint Forces Base in Los Alamitos, California, and the U.S. Marines' flight simulator in El Toro, California.

On October 6, 2008, I met with Samantha East (nicknamed Sam by her colleagues), and she brought me to the base to speak with the aircrews and aircraft maintainers with the 109th. I met with Colonel Tony German, the wing commander for the 109th; Senior Master Sergeant Ron Barnes, life support specialist; Major Mark McKeown, LC-130 aircraft commander/pilot; Senior Master Sergeant Glen Preece, loadmaster; Senior Master Sergeant Kevin Hubbley, flight engineer; Senior Master Sergeant Bob Thiverage, flight crew chief/aircraft superintendent; Senior Master Sergeant Chris Ricket, superintendent of command post/operations coordinator; and Major Sal Salvaggio, LC-130 navigator.

Throughout the day the aircrews and aircraft maintainers talked to me about their jobs. They gave me so much information about polar flight that I was afraid I wouldn't retain it all, but when Sam suggested that we head to the Y in nearby Scotia so I could help her with her swimming technique, I was eager to watch her swim and also have the opportunity on the drive to the pool to ask more questions.

CHAPTER 22

Parallel Planes

As I watched Samantha swim at the Y, I thought about flight through the air and flight through the water, and that reminded me of the small airplanes and private jets that my teammates and I used to wash at Santa Barbara airport to pay our way to water polo competitions with other universities. Most of the women on the team liked to clean the interiors of the planes, but I volunteered to wash the exteriors. This gave me the opportunity to feel the surface of the airplane—the wings, flaps, and rudder. The way the aircraft felt reminded me of swimming with dolphins and having them let me run my hands along their backs, tails, and fins. The shapes felt similar. When I turned the hose on an airplane's wing, I watched the water move as it did over the dolphins' flippers.

As Samantha swam, her hands become propellers, her body became the fuselage, and her feet gave her additional propulsion. She flew across the swimming pool. Her sense of balance and movement may have come instinctively from being a triathlete and from her experience as an aviator. Doc Councilman would have loved to watch her swim. Doc Councilman was one of the world's greatest swimming coaches, who coached Olympic greats Mark Spitz and Gary Hall. In 1978, when he was fifty-seven years old, he contacted me and said he wanted to become the oldest person to swim across the English Channel. Doc Councilman was the icon of modern swimming. It was hard to believe that he was asking me for advice. I was just twenty-one, but that didn't matter to him. He knew my swimming background. I gave him as much information as I could, but I was coaching another swimmer at the time, so I put Doc in touch with Tom Hetzel, a friend and former New York City cop who had swum across the English Channel five or six times. With Tom's coaching, Doc, at fifty-eight, became the oldest man to swim the English Channel. Doc was so far ahead of the curve in his thoughts about human potential at any age. He connected worlds where most people didn't see a connection.

Doc thought of swimming as flight through the water, and he applied Bernoulli's principle of fluid dynamics to analyze a swimmer's hand movement through the water. He compared a swimmer's hands moving through the water to a propeller moving through the air to generate a propulsive force.

Swimming is a learned skill, one that takes years to master, one that I am still learning. I wondered at Samantha's awareness of the movement through space of her hands entering the water, pulling pieces of water, setting them into motion, and finding new pieces of water, and pushing them toward her feet so she could move forward. She had a natural feel for the water. Her hands knew how to find new water, and to increase her feel, I asked her to do a series of sculling drills.

I had her lie on her back and scull her hands over her head, on either side of her face, then near her stomach, and, finally, beside her hips.

The drills helped her hands gain a greater feel for the water. The points where she sculled—over her head, on either side of her face, stomach, and hips—became waypoints for her hands. Maybe it was in part because she was an air force navigator that she knew where her hands were supposed to be. When she took a stroke, her hands automatically moved precisely from one point to the next.

She felt locations of still water, and her hands immediately locked into these places in the sequence of her pull from the entry point near the top of her head, out toward the side of the pool, back in near her waist, and out again by her hips. She traveled across the pool using a perfect S-curve pull. She stopped at the end of the pool and stood up with water droplets streaming down her cheeks. Her blue eyes were bright; she gave me the biggest smile and said, "I haven't had a swimming lesson since I was eight. I can feel that I'm swimming faster," and she wasn't even breathless.

Lieutenant Colonel Dean Johnson, an LC-130 Skibird pilot, avid triathlete, and swimmer said that there was an amazing parallel between polar flying and swimming. He said hydrodynamic efficiency depended on an awareness of the body's roll, pitch, and yaw. These same elements were crucial for aerodynamic efficiency to translate into a successful ski takeoff. The airplane became an extension of the pilot and accurate analysis of what the aircraft was telling you was the difference between mission success or failure.

All the concepts of swimming—lift, propulsion, and drag—were also integral to flight. Translation of these concepts to swimming might help improve her body position in the water to minimize drag and maximize efficiency.

Samantha's head was a bit high in the water, making her hips drop slightly, increasing her drag, and slowing her down. Dragging feet or landing gear considerably reduce speed through the water or across the runway. A similar kind of drag and speed reduction limits the LC-130's takeoffs and flights. Major Mark McKeown, one of the LC-130 pilots, explained that sometimes when the LC-130 moves to taxi or take off from the skiway—a snow runway that is used by ski-equipped aircraft—the movement of the aircraft's skis across the snow creates friction. This causes the snow to melt, and a very thin layer of water is formed. The plane glides on this film of water; otherwise the plane could not overcome the friction of the snow on the skis.

The water layer also creates suction. Sometimes if there is too much water, the aircraft does not have the power to overcome the suction to achieve the seventy miles per hour needed to take off. It's like trying to pick up a wet penny from a flat surface. Sometimes the aircrew has to attempt a takeoff a few

*Samantha East
in a LC-130 with
navigational chart.*

times, burn off fuel, and reduce the weight of the aircraft to let it move faster along the skiway and finally become airborne. Once in the air, they lift the landing gear into the aircraft and tuck the skis under the aircraft like a pelican pulls its feet up under its body to reduce air resistance and fly more efficiently.

The optimal position for the LC-130 to move through space depends on temperature and the aircraft's weight. It is the same in swimming, although each person's body is shaped and composed somewhat differently, so that each person has to find his or her own place in the water where he or she swims most efficiently.

"Samantha, your feet are down—it's like having your skis down in the air."

Swimming is about balance, and balance is equally important for the flight of the LC-130. The aircraft has to be balanced to fly, and the swimmer has to be balanced to move efficiently through the water.

Samantha was swimming smoothly, and she looked balanced, but she had overcompensated with her head position.

One correction changed everything else. Now she was burying her head in the water and making it difficult to turn and breathe.

To correct this, I asked her to look out over the top of her goggles at the black line drawn on the bottom of the pool—like the way she used the radar screen to navigate the aircraft. I suggested that she rotate her core more, roll more from side to side, so that she was reducing her profile in the water and thereby reducing the water resistance. Rotating this way would help her breathe, and that rotation of her whole body would take a lot of stress off her neck. She immediately placed her head in the right position. Her ability to take in new information and translate it so quickly to swimming must be an awareness that she had fine-tuned when flying with her LC-130 aircrew.

The LC-130 aircrews were constantly training and regularly being tested and evaluated by LC-130 instructors who seemed like coaches. The aircrews were always learning and adjusting to new situations. Samantha was able to move from flight to swimming by using a training process that linked two different worlds.

Head position was key to flight through the water and through the air. When Major Mark McKeown came in for a landing, he trained his eyes on the landing spot and did not move his head. Major McKeown checked his instruments, but when the aircraft was near touchdown, he would visually select a landing spot and kept his eyes focused on that spot, and he listened to the navigator, copilot, and flight engineer, one by one, provide information to help him land the aircraft.

Samantha continued swimming, but she was getting fatigued; she was falling off her pace; her stroke rate was dropping. Senior Master Sergeant Thivierage said that cold fatigued the LC-130 and caused the aircraft to break, in which case they had to ground the aircraft and work on it.

Samantha's stroke looked effortless, completely efficient, and she reminded me of Sandy Neilson, my roommate at UCSB who had the most beautiful and efficient stroke I had ever seen. Sandy had won the gold medal in the one-hundred-meter freestyle in the 1972 Olympic Games. She was swimming much faster at age forty-four than when she won the Olympic gold medal. She'd improved with age.

I wished Sandy could see Samantha swim. Sandy would recognize the natural feel that Samantha had for the water. Sandy would have gotten just as excited as I did. Samantha was a natural. I wouldn't be surprised if her friends from the 109th were good if not excellent swimmers. Flight through the air was, in many ways, like flight through the water.

CHAPTER 23

Discovering Greatness

As the months passed, I continued working on trying to obtain permission from the National Science Foundation to fly with the 109th Air Wing in Antarctica and write about their joint mission, but I wasn't making headway. One day, though, before I left home for a speech in Vancouver, I received an e-mail from Gary K. Hart.

Gary was a former California state senator; he had lived in the Santa Barbara area when I was at UCSB. We met then and he had followed my career. Gary had played football for Stanford University. He graduated and got his master's degree at Harvard, and became California secretary for education. He was still very involved in education and he loved exploration. Suddenly it occurred to me that maybe Gary would know whom I could contact to help me get approval from the National Science Foundation to fly to Antarctica.

Time was passing quickly. It was October 21. If clearance came through, the trip would most likely take place in January, when the weather was the best, and when there were often scheduled press trips or trips for distinguished visitors such as Congressmen, senators, foreign dignitaries, and officials from the Pentagon.

I explained to Gary that one of the reasons that I needed to go to Antarctica was to see with my own eyes and talk with people about their observations on climate change and global warming, as I had in the Arctic and in Greenland.

Gary offered to help. He called his old friend Phil Angelides, who had been California state treasurer, and Phil contacted Senator Boxer and Senator Pelosi's offices. They called the NSF and the generals at the Pentagon, who checked on my proposal. The generals assured Senator Pelosi that the air force had done all they could to support the project, but the NSF was not responding.

Every day and night I continued thinking of who else I could contact to help get NSF approval. Then it came to me: Arthur Sulzberger! Arthur was the publisher of the *New York Times*. We had met in 2000 when I gave a motivational lecture for the salespeople and executives at the *Times*. After the conference, he was introduced to me, and we talked for a few minutes. He was so approachable. He was an athlete, rock climber, scuba diver, and a tremendous supporter of Outward Bound.

A few months later, he invited me to have lunch with him, and I was so nervous about meeting with him. For as long as I could remember, I had wanted to be a writer, and this was the chance to meet the man who ran the best newspaper in the world, a man who had been a journalist himself.

During lunch we talked about our backgrounds and we discussed where we found our inspirations. When I mentioned to Arthur that I'd been a librarian after I graduated from UCSB, he immediately offered to show me his library. I love libraries, and I love to see what people read. It gives me insights into what is important to them, what inspires them, what they are curious about.

We climbed up a flight of carpeted stairs to the top of the old *New York Times* building, and I gazed at the bookshelves from floor to ceiling on the walls around the room. One section was filled with old books. The covers were faded from time and light, and the print on the spines was in heavy black. The covers looked brittle, like they needed to be opened with great care—with one hand supporting the delicate spine, and the other hand slowly opening the book and gently turning the page.

There were biographies, memoirs, histories, books on wars

and on current events by pundits and politicians. There was Barbara Tuchman's *Guns of August,* as well as books by some *New York Times* journalists and *New Yorker* writers, too. There was an entire section on Winston Churchill.

I was so involved in studying the books that I lost Arthur. When I turned around, he was standing behind me, slightly off to one side.

There was a whole section of books just on the Arctic and Antarctica!

Arthur was smiling. His hazel eyes were filled with light. I couldn't believe his collection. There were books by Amundsen, Byrd, Cook, Scott, Shackleton, and Peary. One at a time, I pointed to a book and asked Arthur about every author and every story. He knew them all. He explained that the *New York Times* for generations had covered the stories of exploration and human achievements.

A name on the spine of one book, Fridtjof Nansen, was new to me. This was the first time I encountered him. I asked Arthur about him. He said Nansen was a polar explorer from Norway and he had walked across the Greenland ice cap and attempted to be the first to reach the North Pole by dogsled. He said that Nansen was Amundsen's best friend, and that he lent Amundsen his ship, the *Fram.* Amundsen had used the *Fram* on his attempt to become the first man to reach the South Pole.

What a friend Nansen had to be, I thought, to lend Amundsen his ship. People never achieved great things completely on their own; there were always people who came before, who served as mentors, or who simply kept the dream going in the most adverse times. And that kept them going, and propelled them to achieve what had never been done before.

Neither Arthur nor I realized it at that time, but our meeting was like the one between Nansen and Amundsen, and between Amundsen and Byrd when they discussed their plans, and helped and inspired each other to attempt their great goals. By telling me their stories, and about their friendships, Arthur inspired me to write about them. Arthur immediately began helping me with research. He turned away from the bookshelves and said, "Would you like to see something that Admiral Byrd gave my grandfather?"

I couldn't believe his grandfather knew Admiral Byrd and I nodded very quickly.

Arthur led the way to his office and pointed to one of his most precious mementos—a silver dollar mounted beautifully in a large frame. Arthur explained that it had been handed down through his family. His grandfather had been a great supporter and fan of Admiral Byrd, and the *Times* had extensively covered Byrd's missions. His grandfather gave the coin to Byrd first when he flew to the North Pole in 1926. The second time Byrd carried the silver dollar with him was on his flight across the Atlantic. The third time Byrd carried it on the first flight to the South Pole. The coin's fourth trip was Byrd's second Antarctic expedition, and the fifth was Byrd's third Antarctic expedition. The last line in the story that is framed along with the coin is one Arthur's grandfather wrote—"A dollar can go very far in the proper hands." Arthur took the coin with him when he and his son made their first trip to Antarctica.

Arthur told me that Byrd continued his exploration of Antarctica with the U.S. Navy in Operation Deep Freeze, and there were enormous parts of Antarctica that still hadn't been explored.

That day was when I seriously began to think about writing a book about Amundsen and Nansen.

Anyone who does anything of significance faces obstacles.

What would Amundsen or Nansen have done? They went to the king of Norway. I wished President Reagan were still in office. He had invited me to meet him in the Oval Office after my Bering Strait swim. We spoke about swimming. He'd been a lifeguard in Illinois, and he had rescued more than twenty people. He also swam off Santa Monica Beach. He was fascinated with my Bering Strait swim. Maybe President Bush would be approachable. But he was leaving office; Senator Obama was becoming president, but it was too early to approach him.

Who else could I try? The father of Chris Murray, my roommate in college, was Dr. Bruce Murray. He had been the director of NASA/Caltech's Jet Propulsion Lab in Pasadena, California. Bruce had invited Chris and me to see the close encounters of the Voyager I and Voyager II with Io, Jupiter, Saturn, Uranus, and Neptune. We watched images on a television screen being beamed back live from deep outer space. Bruce understood the importance of relationships, whether they were between the planets or people. Maybe he could help, or maybe my friend Astrid Golomb's father could. Her father was Dr. Solomon Golomb, and he taught at Caltech, spoke twenty-six languages, and helped develop space communications. He was a fan of the Norwegian explorers and had offered to translate Amundsen's and Nansen's letters for me. Maybe he or Bruce would know someone at the NSF. But there wasn't much time remaining. Maybe there was a faster route.

The New Zealand air force had a great relationship with the U.S. Air Force, and the Kiwis flew to Scott Base, just four miles from the U.S. base. Maybe I could fly with the Kiwis and walk from Scott Base to McMurdo to at least have the chance to talk with members of the 109th Air Wing. But the New Zealander air force made fewer flights than the Americans and they had finished their season.

Finally I got a call from Gary Hart, who had spoken with Senator Boxer's office. The NSF had turned down my request.

For the next three or four days I thought hard about how I could accomplish what I needed to achieve, but in a different way. It wasn't clear which direction I needed to take. There would be a way to see Amundsen's vision and understand how it was realized. There was always a way. But I was stuck and heartbroken, and I still didn't know enough yet to ask good questions about Antarctic flight.

I sent an e-mail to Mary Thoits. She was a swimmer who swam in the ocean from the spring to the fall off the Southern California coast, and off Mexico when she took vacations. She taught world affairs at Long Beach City College in California, and for her eighty-fifth birthday, last year, she went skydiving. It was something she said she had always wanted to do. She went tandem and gave me a picture of herself with a handsome

*Mary Thoits, Women Air Service Pilots, entering an
AT-6 cockpit at Avenger Field, Sweetwater, Texas, summer 1944.
The new U-2 trainer aircraft are named for the AT-6, and
her WASP colleagues were awarded the Congressional Medal
of Honor, March 10, 2010.*

*Mary Thoits—celebrating her eighty-fifth birthday—and a
friend skydiving above Lake Elsinore, California, 2009.*

man behind her; both had arms outstretched like seagulls, and both had wide smiles.

Mary had initially contacted me five years before and asked me to speak at the college. At the time, I had been too busy, but Mary kept nudging me, and when I finally found time to speak, I discovered that she was one of the people I was supposed to meet in my life. She is a pioneer.

In 1944, during World War II, she flew with the Women's Air Force Service Pilots—WASPs. They were the first women who were trained to fly U.S. military aircraft and opened the world of aviation to women. These pilots were civilians, and they weren't permitted to be in the military, but they served the country. They trained in Sweetwater, Texas, where the first male African American pilots trained, too. The women pilots ferried aircraft across the United States. Some of the women learned how to fly up to twenty-seven types of aircraft. They also served as test pilots—they were the ones who often flew an aircraft for the first time, and they helped the engineers work out problems with the aircraft. During their training missions, they also dragged long targets behind their aircraft, so the army, on the ground, could shoot at the targets for practice.

Mary first learned to fly because her older brother charged her twenty-five cents if she needed a ride in the car. He wouldn't teach her how to drive, so she decided to fly instead. She saved Green Stamps, which were like coupons that could be redeemed for a gift or service. She was in high school at the time and convinced her friends to save stamps for her.

One entire booklet of stamps equaled fifteen minutes of flight. When she got four booklets, she had enough stamps for two takeoffs and two landings.

When World War II broke out, Mary decided that she wanted to fly in the service, for the country. She'd heard about the training program in Sweetwater, and asked her mother if she could go.

Before she entered flight school, Mary had to pass a physical, and she had to be five feet seven inches tall. She was only five foot one, so when she went in for the physical, she made her hair poof up on her head and she stood on her tiptoes when they measured her height. She passed the height requirement and the physical, and later, during flight training, she realized why there was a height requirement. She had a difficult time reaching the pedals in the aircraft with her feet, so she put three pillows behind her.

During one aerial maneuver, her instructor, in the front seat of the AT-6, rolled the aircraft over so Mary could learn how to feel the capability of the plane and learn how to get out of a spin. When the aircraft rolled over, the pillows that Mary had piled behind her back so she could reach the pedals flew out somewhere over Texas. She figured out how to strap the pillows in and hold them in place for her next training flight.

Early flight was all about feeling. When Mary was in the AT-6 racing down the runway, she felt the moment when she was supposed to pull back on the stick and fly. But she also had to learn how to fly with instruments instead of by feeling. The instructor sat in the front of the aircraft and the student in the back with a canopy over her head so she didn't have any visual references. The instructor did a number of acrobatic moves, and Mary couldn't tell if she was flying right side up or upside down. She had to learn to look at the instruments to figure out where the aircraft was, and she, like the other students, wore a string with a pencil attached to it, so they could tell if they were right side up or flying upside down.

Mary loved flying, and after the war was over, she became a flight instructor. A lot of the instruction she gave was on how to fly floatplanes that were a few generations newer than the one Amundsen used for the Arctic. The thing that made landing on water tough, she said, was that if the water was flat, it reflected the sky; it was hard to judge how far the plane was from the water, and that made landing very challenging.

Mary liked challenges. She thrived on them and loved to participate, so when I asked if she would come with me to the Los Alamitos Joint Forces Training Base to meet with General James Combs, she immediately said yes.

General Combs agreed to meet with us, along with J. D.

Brown, who was a Black Hawk instructor pilot and ran the airstrip connected to the base. General Combs spent an hour with us and gave us background on the base, mentioning that after he had served in Vietnam, he worked for the O'Neill wet suit company doing research on the effects of cold water on the body, and later he rejoined the army. The base he served on now was a training base for all branches of the military and offered programs for training at-risk youths and was a base for flying drones and served as a staging area for natural disasters, and the U.S. women's water polo worked out in the base pool also.

J. D. Brown offered to show us the helicopters and the airstrip.

With the rotors and all the moving parts that kept the helicopter aloft, J.D. made it very clear that the Black Hawk was challenging to fly. He let us climb into the cockpit, where there were buttons on the roof, instrument panel, and on the instruments. It was amazing how much a pilot needed to know to fly. J.D. said that the first time he climbed into a helicopter, it took him an hour to start it up; now it took him seven minutes.

I asked him what some of the most challenging conditions to fly in were. And suddenly he gave me the link between Black Hawks and LC-130s. J.D. said he had flown in Iraq and that it was tremendously difficult to fly in brownout conditions in the desert. This happened when there were sandstorms, and the visibility was reduced to nothing. He said that even when using instruments, it was difficult to judge where the ground was. If a landing wasn't done correctly, the helicopter could hit hard, bounce, and roll. He equated brownouts to whiteouts in Antarctica, when the winds were so strong that they blew the snow, and visibility dropped to zero.

Laura, my sister, knew how focused I'd been on this project. She suggested calling Troy Devine. Troy had played water polo with Laura and our sister Ruth. They were tremendous athletes, and when they played as a team, they were extraordinarily connected, and often their moves and plays, their passing and teamwork, were utterly beautiful.

Laura, Troy, and Ruth were selected for the U.S. national team; it was the equivalent of the U.S. Olympic team, but at the time women's water polo wasn't allowed in the Olympics. Many people thought water polo was a sport that was too tough to be played by women. Often the U.S. team scrimmaged against some of the best men's teams. Sometimes they won, sometimes they lost, but they always seemed to learn and improve.

The U.S. women's water polo team didn't have a manager, so I volunteered and helped out for six years. Laura, Ruth, and Troy were starters. Ruth once said that it took a lot of intensity to play on the U.S. team, but Troy had something more.

Laura reminded me that Troy was in the U.S. Air Force and that was why she had suggested that I contact Troy.

A few years before, I'd received an e-mail from Troy telling me she'd read my first book, and she thought it inspiring. She mentioned that she was in the air force and married to an air force pilot.

Laura told me that she remembered Troy had graduated at the top of her class and had become the first female U.S. Air Force U-2 pilot.

Through Troy's husband, Lieutenant Colonel Chuck Cunningham, who also flew U-2s out of Beale Air Force Base, I reached Troy, and we caught up quickly.

When Troy attended the Air Force Academy, she had swum the long-distance events for the team. She had met Chuck while they were in U-2 training, and after they graduated, they dated, married, and had four active children.

When Troy first graduated from the academy, women weren't allowed to fly combat aircraft, but when the politics changed, Troy tried out for the job. Pilots who tried for that position were given three flights, three chances to demonstrate that they were capable of doing the job.

Troy said that she didn't do all that well on her first flight, but she listened very carefully to her instructor and tried to take in all his suggestions, and she improved a lot on her second flight and did well enough on her third flight to qualify for the U-2 program.

She told me to call anytime to talk with her or Chuck about flying or anything else. Like great athletes who are often fascinated with other great athletes, they were intrigued with the 109th Air Wing, and when Chuck told me that the U-2 and the LC-130 were both built by Lockheed and that they had the same control yoke, I wondered if there might be a lot more similarities in their flight world.

Troy wanted to put me in touch with Cholene Espinosa. She said Cholene was an incredible person. Cholene was the second female U-2 pilot, but had now retired from flying U-2s. She was based in Dubai and flying for a commercial airline. She was a writer and a war correspondent for Talk Radio News Service, and she was philosophical, articulate, and had a lot of heart. She would be the perfect person for me to talk with.

When I called, Cholene immediately offered her insights. I explained that I needed to know more about flight to be able to understand the challenge and art of the 109th's mission and tell their story more completely. Cholene offered to help, but first we talked about swimming. She was more of a runner than a swimmer, but she had seen the tremendous need for public swimming pools in the South. It was then that I understood why Troy said Cholene had a lot of heart.

Cholene explained that when Hurricane Katrina occurred, she was compelled to do something to help. She discovered that many of the victims of the hurricane were African Americans, and most of them were the elderly and children. They had drowned in the floods because they had never learned to swim. They never had the opportunity.

During the 1950s, many of the public swimming pools were filled in and covered over and made into basketball courts because the white people in the community didn't want to share the swimming pools with black people. This act had kept several generations of African Americans from learning how to swim and had made them vulnerable to floodwaters.

Cholene wanted to do something that would change that. She saved money, bought property in DeLisle, Louisiana, teamed up with the YMCA, and through grants and donations raised enough additional money to have a new swimming pool built. A basketball court was donated by the NBA.

Cholene explained that the U-2 unit was very similar to the 109th, because they were specialty groups within the air force. Their missions were very different, but each unit dealt with the challenge of flying into uncharted areas. The 109th flew into unexplored parts of Antarctica, and the motto for the U-2 mission was "Toward the unknown."

The U-2 and LC-130 were very different aircraft. Cholene said that the U-2 was nicknamed the "Dragon Lady" because pilots never knew what to expect when they took the planes into the air, no matter how much experience the pilots had. This was because of the way the aircraft was designed. It had to be light enough to fly above seventy thousand feet and it was almost impossible to control. And at thirteen miles above the ground, the atmosphere is so thin that the envelope between stalling and "overspeed"—going so fast that the pilot loses control of the aircraft, which results in a unrecoverable nose dive— is razor-thin. Minor disruptions and turbulence could be as deadly as a missile. The aircraft also had a very long wingspan, like a glider, and was very susceptible to crosswinds.

There are real advantages to flying in the pilot's seat of a reconnaissance aircraft, though. She said that U-2 pilots could troubleshoot problems in midflight, creatively, in ways computers and remote-control pilots never could, and they could distinguish promising details that a drone would have missed.

She said that she would never forget the adrenaline rush of landing a multimillion-dollar jet-powered glider. Just before she touched down, another U-2 pilot followed her down the runway in a high-performance BMW or Mustang convertible and called out the plane's descending altitude, just as the navigator in the LC-130 assisted the pilots during their descent. And in each case, base operations monitored their entire flights and supported the pilots whenever they need help.

Cholene recalled what it was like for her to fly a mission. She said, "There was a sense of peace that began for me exactly one hour before takeoff. That is the time that a U-2 pilot goes on one hundred percent oxygen in order to prevent getting the bends during the mission. The closing of the double lock on the faceplate of the space helmet ushered the first stillness—the first sense that I was no longer of the world everyone else belonged to—surviving on oxygen from a tank and unable to hear anything except the sound of my own breath.

"The takeoff was more like a launch than a takeoff. Depending on the weight of the particular airplane, the U-2 can climb high enough to see the earth's curve in less than twenty minutes.

"I always wondered what it would be like to be in space—real space—and be able to look back at earth. I think that would be the ultimate 'perspective moment.' But for me, the U-2 was close for the simple reason that I was completely alone.

"Alone in my thoughts with distant images of war below, I would try to visualize what it was like for the men and women on the ground who were fighting and dying. The disconnect between those images and the images of the beauty I was beholding perched in the stratosphere brought tears at times.

"It was these days of being completely disconnected from life, human life, when I learned to fully appreciate the beauty and sanctity of life."

Because of that understanding of the sanctity of life, she was studying to become a physician. Most people told her she was ten years too old to become a doctor, but all through her life she had done things people said she couldn't do. She had created her own life, and she knew she would create her own course. She would find people who would support her dreams and become a physician and draw on her experience to fly to remote parts of the world and help people in need. She reflected again upon flying the U-2 and how important it was to her life. She had flown ten thousand hours in the U-2 and many other aircraft, including in C-130s as a passenger in the cockpit, and she completely appreciated the way that the aircrews worked together as a team. She said that at some point, for many pilots, the aircraft becomes an extension of themselves.

Finally, I felt like I understood more and could talk with members of the 109th and ask questions that would reveal their world of polar flight.

CHAPTER 24

AGAP

It would always be Antarctica. One hundred years could not change that. Antarctica was as remote, dangerous, unpredictable, and ever changing as it had been in Amundsen's day.

The 109th Airlift Wing, New York Air National Guard, under the command of Colonel Anthony German, knew that. They had flown eleven thousand miles from their base at Schenectady County Airport, New York, to support the U.S. science mission in Antarctica. They were the men and women fulfilling Amundsen's vision—using flight as the way to open and explore the wild and unexplored regions of Antarctica.

The U.S. Navy continued Admiral Byrd's legacy by establishing Operation Deep Freeze I under his command in 1955. The following year, Lieutenant Commander Gus Shinn, a U.S. Navy pilot, was given orders by Admiral George J. Dufek, the admiral commander of Operation Deep Freeze, to fly to and land at the South Pole. Admiral Dufek chose Shinn because of his reputation as a top-notch pilot and because of his experience flying in Antarctica. Shinn said that the navy wanted to prove that it was possible to fly to the South Pole and back. Their goal was to build a base at the South Pole. Shinn said that they knew that the South Pole was the coldest, windiest, and most remote place in the world, and no one knew if it was possible to live there. No one knew how the aircraft, the *Que Sera Sera*, an R4D, would perform. They knew the aircraft would be operating in conditions beyond its test specifications.

Shinn said things were different in 1956. The navy didn't do any advanced planning in Antarctica, and they didn't create any backups. There was no safety net if something went wrong. Shinn devised his own backups. He carried extra fuel aboard the aircraft, the *Que Sera Sera,* and he flew with Lieutenant Dick Swadener, a great navigator, and John Strider, a top flight engineer.

On October 31, 1956, as they came in for a landing at the South Pole, Shinn circled once, and he and Dick Swadener looked for a landing spot. They found one, and Shinn skillfully touched down on the rough surface of the Polar Plateau. When they stopped, the *Que Sera Sera'*s skis immediately froze to the ice. Shinn said that they had no idea this would happen, and while Admiral Dufek and some of the other six passengers climbed out of the plane, Shinn figured they only had one chance to get the aircraft off the 9,300-foot-high Polar Plateau. First Shinn dumped the extra fuel out of the *Que Sera Sera* to

Gus Shinn, the first man to land and take off from the South Pole, with the Que Sera Sera *aircraft at the National Naval Aviation Museum, Pensacola, Florida, 2009.*

reduce the aircraft's weight. Then he knew he'd have to fire the JATO (Jet-fuel Assisted Take Off) rockets just to get unstuck. When the passengers were back on board the aircraft, he ignited all of the JATO bottles, four at a time, until the last three remained. And the *Que Sera Sera* blasted free of the ice and built enough airspeed to lift off at sixty knots.

The ignition of the JATO rockets in minus 60 degrees Fahrenheit temperatures instantly caused ice fog and reduced Shinn's visibility to zero. It was a total whiteout. Shinn hadn't anticipated anything like this to happen, and he had never had a similar experience, but he relied on his flight instruments, and he got the aircraft into the sky. The aircraft was performing in an environment that was way beyond its limits. He wasn't sure if he would be able to get the landing gear up, but he said they were very lucky. They raised the landing gear and soon touched down at base camp. Their first flight helped to open the interior of the continent and helped the United States establish a research site at the geographic South Pole.

After the cold war ended and the military Antarctic operation was realigned under the U.S. Transportation Command, the 109th Air Wing was selected to take over the LC-130 operations as the single point manager of deep ski lift for the Arctic and Antarctic mission for the United States. Operation Deep Freeze continues to support the National Science Foundation with research and scientific exploration in Greenland and Antarctica with ski-equipped aircraft, heavy-lift C-17s, and naval support forces for ship operations.

The 109th were the pros of polar flight. They were the only military unit that specifically trained and prepared to fly in Greenland and Antarctica in LC-130s. The 109th studied the polar missions of those who had flown before, like Shinn and Swadener. This unit became so knowledgeable and skilled that they wrote the flight manual for the U.S. Air Force on polar flight.

The men and women in the 109th Air Wing knew that flying in Antarctica was different and could be more challenging than anywhere else in the world. Extreme cold played havoc on the aircrew, the maintainers—people who kept the aircraft in top shape—and the LC-130s. To function and survive in that environment, the maintainers had to have a heightened sense of awareness. One small mistake, such as touching a tool with a bare hand, could cause frostbite as quickly as touching a hot burner on a stove. The cold coupled with wind could cause hypothermia in a matter of minutes, and it could also kill.

The Antarctic cold made the aircraft metal more brittle, and that made the aircraft more apt to break. Breaking at JFK International Airport meant being delayed; breaking in Antarctica meant pulling out the survival gear.

The extreme cold could cause insulation, like aircraft door seals, not to seal completely. The cold could cause the hydraulic systems used to lift and lower the landing gear and control the plane to freeze. It made takeoff, flight, and landing very difficult and sometimes just plain dangerous. Below minus 58 degrees Fahrenheit, the aircraft fuel and hydraulic fluid could begin to turn into a gel-like substance, and that could make the aircraft unsafe to fly. Mechanics were specially trained for recovering aircraft in Antarctica, and sometimes it was so cold that the longest they could be outside was six to eight minutes, without running the risk of hypothermia or frostbite.

Surface conditions in Antarctica also affected flight. There

USAF Nansen sled carrying JATO bottles to a 109th Air Wing crew LC-130 on top of the Greenland ice cap, supporting scientists at NEEM doing ice-core research.

were "land sharks"—ice runways that could crack and crevasses and that could swallow an LC-130 and its aircrew whole. There were sastrugi and snow mounds that on takeoff or landing could chew off parts of an airplane. And there were "air sharks"—weather systems that struck so quickly they blew small granules of snow into the air and reduced visibility to a point where the aircrews felt like they were looking at the world through a bright white paper cup. Flying without any visual cues was very difficult. But that's why the flight crews trained, prepared, and did everything they could to put as much as they could in their favor before they flew. Amundsen would have been impressed with the 109th's research, training, and preparation, especially for their "put-in" mission.

A put-in was the first flight of the season to a remote camp or the first flight to establish a new research camp. The mission was inherently different, and far more challenging, than flying to an established camp, such as the South Pole Station.

The people in the 109th Polar Tactics Section spent at least one year doing research before they flew a put-in mission. They used satellite imagery, reconnaissance, ground-penetrating radar surveys, and satellite radar surveys to check conditions on the ground, and they made sure there weren't any crevasses or obstructions. Whenever they could, they first flew out to the remote area in a Twin Otter airplane and put someone on the ground—a ski landing area control officer, or SLACO, who was an authority on surface conditions. The SLACO walked around the area, tested the snow with a variety of scientific instruments, and sometimes used a large mallet and hammered the snow to test the hardness of the surface. The SLACO worked to get as much information as was practically possible.

All of this data was conveyed to Lieutenant Colonel Rick McKeown, pilot; Major Cliff Souza, pilot; Major Joseph DeConno, navigator; Senior Master Sergeant Mark Olena, flight engineer; Master Sergeant Glen Preece, loadmaster; and Master Sergeant Francis "Snow Dog" Czwakiel, loadmaster. They were the experienced aircrew selected to fly this season's

Clockwise from top right:
Colonel Anthony German,
Lieutenant Colonel Rick McKeown,
Major Cliff Souza, Major Joseph
DeConno, Senior Master Sergeant
Mark Olena, Master Sergeant Glen
Preece, and Master Sergeant Francis
"Snow Dog" Czwakiel. This aircrew
flew the AGAP mission (except
Anthony German, who was the
wing commander).

put-in mission to Antarctica's Gamburtsev Province project—AGAP.

The day before their flight, on November 19, 2008, the aircrew met, studied, and discussed all the research, including information about weather patterns and a satellite image that showed where the crew could land the aircraft.

They discussed the flight plan in great detail. They built in flexibility and contingencies based on their specific procedures.

McKeown, Souza, DeConno, Olena, Preece, and Czwakiel were confident that they could fly this mission. They knew one another very well, and they had flown together for years. They knew they held one another's lives in their hands: if the pilots made a mistake in flying the aircraft, if the navigator didn't know where they were at all times, if the flight engineer didn't completely check out the aircraft before they took off and monitor and control the systems in flight, and if the loadmasters hadn't balanced the load, the aircraft could crash. They understood the responsibility they had to one another, and with sixty years of combined flying experience, they had great confidence in one another. On this mission to AGAP, they would have to draw upon every bit of that experience to make it safely home.

Four hours before the flight on November 20, 2008, the loadmasters, Preece and Snow Dog Czwakiel, two tall, strong, and totally focused airmen, loaded the cargo in the back of the aircraft. Preece had studied the cargo a few days before to make sure that it would slide out of the aircraft quickly and in the right sequence. Everything was about efficiency. Every extra minute the aircraft was moving along the ground, it was burning precious fuel, fuel that they needed to fly back to McMurdo.

Olena, the compact "ninja turtle" and even-tempered flight engineer, entered the cockpit and went through his checklists, making sure that all the aircraft's systems were functioning correctly. He also inspected the aircraft for fuel or oil leaks.

Preece and Czwakiel calculated the weight and balance of the aircraft to make sure it was balanced and that they could take off. The weight of the aircraft was very important, but the balance of the cargo versus fuel was even more so. These calculations developed on takeoff and stabilized the aircraft aloft over the course of the long mission. The closest camp to AGAP where they could refuel was not around the corner; it was 330 miles away at the South Pole.

If they ran out of fuel at AGAP, they would be breaking out their survival gear: sleeping bags, long underwear, parkas, boots, and Meals Ready to Eat (MREs)—food packets containing meals over fifteen hundred calories each that would give them energy to help keep them warm. They would be building snow structures, which they had learned how to make during survival school in Greenland and in Alaska. These techniques were like the ones Amundsen had learned from the Inuit to stay warm.

The flight operations crew at McMurdo began the preflight check on the aircraft. Souza and McKeown, Olena, and DeConno were in the cockpit going over their preflight tasks and talking with one another. The crew communication in the LC-130 was different than any other air force aircraft. In the LC-130 the crew spoke and responded to one another like they were in a concert. They knew exactly when to speak, what to say, the flow of what they were doing. The navigator knew when to tell the pilots about course correction, drift, and speed. The flight engineer knew the moment to relay systems information. The pilots knew when to convey information and request support. They instantly recognized one another by their voices, and knew and understood every nuance. It was beautiful to listen to—this chorus in flight.

McKeown and Souza, the pilots, had been scheduled for the lightest LC-130 aircraft for the mission. This was very important, and they were pleased. They knew that if they got the lightest aircraft, they would be able to take an extra fifteen hundred pounds of fuel. And if they decided not to take the extra fuel, then they would be fifteen hundred pounds lighter, which could make the difference between getting stuck in the snow or not. The goal was to increase the potential of mission success.

The crew attached eight JATO rockets to the aircraft, four on each side. Normally the LC-130 didn't carry the rockets; they were put on for special missions, such as the one to AGAP; at a high-altitude camp, the rockets could be necessary for the aircraft to get off the ground. As a precaution the igniter wouldn't be put into the rockets until they were needed at AGAP. But the crew hoped they wouldn't need them, because if they had to put the igniters in the rockets, they would have to stop and shut the engines down in the open snow; if they had to do that, the built-up friction heat on the skis would melt the snow beneath them. When it froze again on the skis, they could be stuck in the snow—in the way Shinn was on his first landing at the South Pole—and have to dig out, and digging out at high altitude was very tough.

In the cockpit, Souza and McKeown, Olena, and DeConno were ready for takeoff. That morning's weather forecast was fair. And it was beautiful. The winds were calm, and the sky was clear blue, a radiant Antarctic sky.

The aircrew took off out of McMurdo, from Williams Field, and flew over Black Island and Minna Bluff, then above the Transantarctic Mountains over sheer white spires of rock, ice, and snow with peaks reaching over 14,800 feet. They sailed over the shimmering Beardmore Glacier, the treacherous glacier that Shackleton and Scott had trudged across on their ill-fated attempts to reach the South Pole.

Souza, McKeown, DeConno, Olena, Preece, and Snow Dog Czwakiel were going beyond the South Pole, beyond the ends of the earth, 790 nautical miles from McMurdo Station, and 330 miles from the South Pole, into the remote eastern interior of Antarctica, into a world far beyond Amundsen's imagination.

The aircrew was heading for the mysterious Gamburtsev Mountains, an invisible and jagged mountain chain the size of the Alps, buried deep beneath a two-mile-thick mantle of dense glacial ice and the pure white snow. In 1958 the mountains were discovered by Grigoriy Gamburtsev, a Soviet geologist, but due to their inaccessibility, more is known about the water on the surface of Mars than is known about the Gamburtsev Mountains. Scientists believe that they are one of the world's great mysteries, and they are a key to understanding the history of the earth and the birthplace of the East Antarctic Ice Sheet.

DeConno was navigating. The 109th Air Wing was one of the only C-130 units in the world where a grid navigator was still employed. DeConno was using the aviator's sextant, connecting it to a window in the ceiling of the aircraft to take sun shots, and he was also using radar and grid navigation to monitor their course. Grid navigation was the navigation system used by the air force in latitudes below 60 degrees south and above 72 degrees north, where compasses don't work due to the magnetic variations. DeConno's observations, plotting points on an aeronautical chart, and calculations enabled him to know where the aircraft was and where they were headed. His observations confirmed the information the pilots were getting from GPS and INS navigational systems. The crew needed the navigator. If the GPS and INS systems went down—for instance, if the electrical wiring to the navigation systems got too cold and the systems didn't work—without the navigator aboard, the crew would not be able to find the way home.

As a backup DeConno used a high frequency—HF—radio and stayed in touch with air traffic control in McMurdo and Charleston, South Carolina. Some of DeConno's communications were relayed through satellite to Charleston. He gave them the aircraft's position, altitude, and times. The information was for aircraft separation and search and rescue so that air traffic control center would always know where the aircrew was flying. If for some reason the aircrew didn't report in, search and rescue would do everything they could, like relay messages from other aircraft, and work to try to get in communication with the aircrew. As a backup, the aircrew also had a satellite phone so they could call back to McMurdo Station and let them know where they were, so they wouldn't have to send out a search and rescue crew to find them unless the crew truly needed help.

When the aircrew reached AGAP, they flew a box pattern overhead to thoroughly inspect the landing site. DeConno was studying the radar paint, a neon green image of the landing area on his radar screen. DeConno tweaked the radar and picked up the metallized flags near the skiway.

McKeown and Souza were also checking out the condition of the old skiway. They flew down and made a left-hand turn. The winds were very light. They made a low pass over the skiway so they could see what the flagging was like for the next crew so they would know what to expect.

Taylo, a civilian mountaineer on board as an adviser, came along to check if the camp area had survived the previous winter extremes. He looked out the window, studying where the snowdrifts were and if they were going to have to dig to get into their shelters. He was noting the location of the fuel drums and where they needed to off-load the cargo. There were remnants of the old skiway, a camp lab, and fifty-five fuel barrels.

McKeown and Souza visually set up the approach and kept a wide margin from the previous camp to make sure they didn't hit any flags or run over any fuel drums that might have drifted over during the Antarctic winter with wind and shifting snow. The flags could damage the aircraft, and the fuel drums could explode. They were very careful.

With clear skies and great visibility they landed the aircraft visually, using a long box pattern, and they touched down in deep snow. They faced the aircraft to the left of what remained of the old camp so they had a shorter taxi distance and used less fuel. They reduced the aircraft's speed and continued moving slowly across the open snow.

Preece and Czwakiel began unloading cargo. They were wearing full Antarctic gear and safety harnesses to ensure that if the aircraft hit a bump they wouldn't fly off the back of the aircraft.

Executing a combat off-load procedure, they slid the cargo

out of the back of the aircraft as it skied down the runway. Preece and Czwakiel were achieving one of the most important parts of their mission, the primary reason for the flight—off-loading cargo that would be used to build, equip, and supply the research camp, enabling scientists to survive in this utterly remote area of Antarctica and conduct studies that would help them uncover the mysteries of the continent, the Earth, and the universe.

Preece and Czwakiel were working at a pressure altitude of 13,500 feet, where the air was very thin. They had to pace themselves. When they needed to, they breathed oxygen from the aircraft system.

They knew their abilities. They had trained in an altitude chamber and learned about altitude sickness. They were constantly checking on each other for signs of hypoxia. They looked at each other's faces to make sure that that they didn't have blue lips or appear disoriented. DeConno was also serving as the safety officer, keeping track of Preece and Czwakiel from the bottom of the flight deck to make sure they were okay during the cargo off-load.

In the cockpit, everyone was scanning the ground to make sure that they didn't run over anything. Souza and McKeown were checking out the old skiway. They noted that there wasn't any difference between the snow conditions on the old skiway and the open snow, and the skiway flags appeared to be in good condition. They opted to make an open snow takeoff to take advantage of the headwinds and have enough space for a take-off slide. A two- to three-knot increase in headwind could make a difference between success and failure. A typical open snow takeoff slide could stretch over four miles at this pressure altitude. They wanted to stay within a ten-mile radius and that equaled a one-hour taxi or a one-day walk in deep snow.

They taxied between the flags across the skiway, and when they completed their checklist they started their takeoff slide. The pilots increased the throttles, but the LC-130 struggled to overcome deep undulating snow. The aircraft rose on the crests, fell into the troughs, shifted and tipped from one side to the other. McKeown and Souza were trying to keep the aircraft directed into the wind. Snow was dovetailing above the windows, reducing their visual cues, and the aircraft was ballooning and bananaing across the open snow. And with the pressure altitude of 13,500 feet, the pilots couldn't get maximum thrust out of the aircraft engines. The air temperature was minus 58 degrees Fahrenheit, near the limit for LC-130 operations.

Souza and McKeown kept working on different combinations of flaps and rudder to get the aircraft to accelerate, but it wasn't responding, and because the cargo had been off-loaded, the aircraft's center of gravity had shifted forward. This was not optimal for flight.

The weight of the aircraft was on the nose ski at the front of the craft. The pilots had to gain enough speed to get the nose ski up as quickly as possible and hold it off the ground. But the nose ski and the two main skis in the back of the aircraft were producing drag.

If they could just get to sixty-five knots, they could start to lift the nose ski off the ground; they could reduce the drag and accelerate. With more speed, they would get more lift off the wings because of the flap setting and the wing design; that would help take weight off the main skis so they could float the aircraft on the snow.

The LC-130 "Skibird" was sliding over two- to three-foot snow mounds that were like frozen waves. The plane was climbing over the mounds, riding over the crests, and pounding down into the troughs, and when the aircraft bottomed out, it slammed into the snow, boomed, and jolted the aircraft. The men inside were being pounded. Their heads jarred forward and snapped back with each impact. They clenched their teeth and held on.

The wings were starting to flex. Souza and McKeown knew they had to watch for larger snow waves. If the waves got too big, and the aircraft slid over them, the wings could start flapping and that motion could overstress them.

The aircrew stared ahead and got a glimpse of long rolling snow waves; they cringed and held on more tightly.

Long rolling snow waves were worse than snow mounds and if they skied over a sequence of them, the constant up-and-down movement could cause the wings to flex too much, and the aircraft could crack internally.

Souza and McKeown diverted their course, and steered clear of the long snow waves. They pulled back hard on the yokes. It felt like they were pulling one hundred pounds and that the weight was growing heavier as their muscles fatigued. Their biceps burned; their upper bodies were engaged in one unending isometric contraction. They were straining to lift the Herc off the snow. They worked the flap settings and moved them from 70 percent to 50 percent to 100 percent. Their minds were completely focused on the problem. They were trying every technique they knew to make the Herc accelerate.

But the aircraft wasn't responding. They were in what was known as a stagnant acceleration. The aircraft's speed was hovering between forty and fifty knots.

Souza and McKeown had to find a way to increase their speed to seventy-five knots.

Normally the loadmasters would off-load cargo or fuel to lighten weight, reduce drag, and shift the center of gravity of the aircraft from the front of the aircraft to the back. But they'd already dropped off the cargo, and off-loading fuel was not an option because they needed all of it to return to McMurdo.

McKeown and Souza changed the flap settings to lift the skis on top of the snow, but the pressure altitude was killing their speed. The air was too thin. The aircraft propellers needed to "bite" denser air to propel the aircraft forward.

As the pressure altitude increased, the aircraft performance decreased. The pressure altitude was what the wings and propellers were "feeling" as they moved through the air. At McMurdo Station, at sea level, the pressure altitude was at about one thousand feet, and there were a lot more air molecules, much closer together, so the propellers "felt" a lot of air and performed very well. At the South Pole the pressure altitude was at about ten thousand feet on a good day, and the wings and propellers "felt" fewer air molecules so the aircraft didn't perform very well. And at AGAP, at 13,500 feet pressure altitude, the aircraft's performance dropped even further.

The crew in the cockpit had to compensate for the high pressure altitude, too. They had to wear helmets and oxygen masks to be able to breathe.

The Herc was bouncing, shaking, wobbling, and slamming against the ice cap.

The pilots were working harder, and breathing harder. Their diaphragms, and the intercostal muscles between their ribs that helped to lift the ribs for inspiration and lower them for expiration, were overtaxed. Their lungs were working very hard to pull oxygen into their bodies and blow off carbon dioxide. When they managed to hold enough air in their lungs, they spoke in bursts. With the masks over their faces they sounded like Darth Vader.

Sweat streamed down their faces and dripped down their sides. Their flight suits that didn't keep them warm in the cold or cool in the heat weren't wicking the moisture away from their bodies, either. They were drenched. They could not let down, take a few deep breaths, blow off the carbon dioxide, and flush the lactic acid out of their bodies. They could not take a moment to recover. They kept working, trying different combinations of flaps settings. The aircraft pounded harder against the snow. The crew was holding on, taking care of their responsibilities and supplying the pilots with information and helping whenever needed.

In the backs of their minds, though, they wondered if they would ever achieve flight.

They recalled the warm day with fresh snow at McMurdo when they were on their takeoff slide and only had two feet left before they reached the end of skiway. In the final seconds, somehow the pilots got the aircraft off the ground.

They remembered Preece's story the day when he was on the Greenland ice cap with a different air crew at an altitude of ten thousand feet, and the sun was so warm that it had turned the snow to slush. They were sliding across the glacier, but the slush bogged them down, creating so much resistance that they couldn't get enough speed to take off.

His crew had to overnight in a tent in minus 49 degrees Fahrenheit temperatures. They were trained to go into survival mode, and they were completely prepared, but it still taxed their bodies. It was like trying to sleep in a freezer at an altitude of ten thousand feet. They were cold through the bone. They couldn't breathe well, and they didn't sleep. They waited until the next day, when the sun's angle to the ice cap became lower. When the snow did not absorb as much of the sun's energy, it remained frozen and they managed to take off.

If they couldn't take off from AGAP, they would be in survival mode, and this would be worse than in Greenland. They would be at a higher altitude, in colder temperatures, in one of the most remote parts of Antarctica. If this happened, it set up a whole list of complications and complexities for them, and for those who might have to go in and help get them out.

They had another option if they couldn't take off. Souza and McKeown could slow the aircraft down, turn it around, return to the starting point, and attempt another takeoff. By then, they would have burned off more fuel. The aircraft would be lighter, and they would have a better chance of taking off, but they didn't want to make second attempt unless they really had to. A second attempt would burn off a lot more fuel, which this meant that they might not have enough fuel to return directly to McMurdo, and instead, they would have to fly to the South Pole to refuel. That would extend their flight time, and they knew the weather would only hold for so long. A change in weather would change everything. They had to get back to McMurdo before the weather deteriorated.

At McMurdo, they had Pegasus, the ice runway, and Williams Field, the skiway. If the ceiling dropped and the visibility was reduced to the point where they couldn't see the runway, they would have to land only using instruments in a specially designated whiteout area near McMurdo. The area had been checked out at the start of the season with radar and by personnel on snowmobile and cleared of all obstructions. Landing in whiteout conditions, totally blind, was something that no one liked to do. It was their last option.

McKeown was straining against the yoke. Sweat was stinging his eyes. He gave it his maximum effort and groaning and was so fatigued he had to ask Souza for help.

McKeown was pulling harder on the yoke with one hand and guarding the throttles with the other, in case the engines failed on, or low to, the ground. He had to be completely aware of what Souza was doing, so if something went wrong, there wasn't any confusion. Each knew exactly who had to take which task.

The aircraft slid for two miles.

McKeown was trying to baby the nose ski and to keep more aft pressure on it. His arms, shoulders, and neck burned from exertion.

The air was filled with the roar of the LC-130's engines. The aircraft was bouncing, galloping, and booming, and every time the aircraft bottomed out, it hurt. The crew felt the aircraft going *bam, bam, bam, bam.* The impacts compressed the vertebrae in their spines and snapped their heads back and forth. It felt like their spines were working up through the roof of their skulls. They braced themselves for each impact. They had now covered four unrelenting miles.

McKeown and Souza were working to create that perfect moment when the speed and balance of the aircraft were just right, when the aircraft defied the force of gravity and lifted off the ice. The crew was keeping the pilots informed, checking out the terrain, and anticipating the next impact.

Suddenly, after 4.2 miles, they felt that moment of elation when the skis broke free from the friction of the snow, and they lifted off. They felt the miracle of flight. As the aircraft climbed into the cerulean sky, high above the sparkling white dome of the Gamburtsevs, they felt their spirits soar. They grinned. They were flying. They were relieved. They were thinking about the flight back to McMurdo, hot meals, warm beds, and deep sleep.

Those thoughts abruptly ended.

When McKeown raised the landing gear, he noticed that a red light came on. The light indicated that the nose ski was not locked in the up position.

This sometimes happened in open-snow operations. McKeown was not overly alarmed, but he informed the crew.

Olena, the flight engineer, began thinking about how to solve the problem. He knew that they were operating in minus 49 degrees Fahrenheit and that with everything open under the plane on their takeoff slide, snow could have gotten into the aircraft and impacted. That might have affected the nose ski.

Under the flight deck was a small glass window used by the loadmaster to scan the nose gear and ski assembly. Preece looked out the window, but couldn't see what the problem was.

The crew had three and a half hours to discuss the issue, and they began to troubleshoot it.

McKeown and Souza reduced their airspeed in accordance with the standard operating procedure.

Once they reached their cruise altitude and completed their departure checklist, the crew double-checked the remaining fuel. They calculated that they would have enough for the return to McMurdo.

For the next two and a half hours DeConno continued to shoot the sun, whose path throughout the day and night would create a halo over the South Pole, but whose harsh light filled the cockpit.

The crew went through their procedures and tried to figure out what the problem was and how they could solve it. They couldn't tell why the red light wouldn't go off.

When the aircrew reached the McMurdo area, McKeown determined the best time to lower the landing gear and he told Souza to lower the gear. Souza lowered the gear handle, and the crew anticipated the gear to come down and lock, but when the loadmaster looked out the window and inspected the nose ski position the crew was expecting to hear Preece say to the pilot, "Nose ski down and level. Loadmaster." Instead, what they heard Preece say was, "Pilot. Loadmaster. Unable to confirm nose ski is level."

The pilots could tell the landing gear was down, but it wasn't locking in place. This was a big problem.

If the aircraft was going to land, the nose ski had to be locked in place. If they attempted to land with a drooping nose ski, the ski could catch and they could crash. They knew that they had to get the nose ski level.

Souza radioed McMurdo and informed air traffic control and skier ops that they had an emergency situation. The supervisor of flying and Colonel Ron Smith, the deployed commander, as well as a support team and the mechanic who specialized in nose ski repair, began working on the problem. The mechanic stepped outside and looked up at an empty sky. He listened hard for the Skibird's engines.

The aircrew checked to see how much fuel they had remaining. That told them how much time they had to figure out what to do.

The aircrew went through their emergency procedures and stayed focused on their tasks, but with the uncertainty, they felt their tension increasing in the cockpit.

Skier ops and the aircrew kept an eye on the weather.

If clouds moved in, their landing would be even more difficult. Clouds over Antarctica often made it impossible for the aircrews to distinguish the difference between the sky—the horizon—and the ground, and get a surface definition. It was like looking down on a flat piece of white paper in noon sunlight. The whiteness of the surface and the whiteness of the sky coupled with diffuse lighting confused their spatial orientation, and made landing the aircraft very challenging. And if the katabatic winds started blowing, it could make landing an aircraft with a dropped nose ski very dangerous. The mechanic and ground support crew heard the Herc's engines. In the cockpit, Olena was continuously monitoring the aircraft systems and DeConno took sunshots, and checked radar, and navigated.

When base ops reported fair weather at McMurdo, McKeown and Souza took deep breaths and they were somewhat relieved. Now they knew their best option was to attempt a wheeled landing on Pegasus ice runway. This was the only runway in the area where they could do a wheels-down landing. With a drooped nose ski, a landing at Williams Field would have been much more difficult and potentially dangerous. The mechanic saw the Herc and confirmed the LC-130 had a drooped nose ski. He took a photo. He and the base crew held their breath, hoping they would be okay. Some said silent prayers.

As McKeown and Souza made the final approach, the crew heard the tension in the pilots' voices. The crew at skier ops and the mechanic strained to watch the aircraft. The entire aircrew executed the emergency procedure. The pilots and crew made the LC-130's skis come up and the wheels go down. They held their breath. The nose ski hit the belly of the aircraft, and that helped to keep the ski somewhat level. They landed perfectly, and rolled along the ice runway until the aircraft came to a stop.

The base crew and the aircrew broke into smiles.

It had been a long twelve-hour day, and the aircrew was exhausted and cold, but they walked to the day room where they debriefed and caught a second breath.

Everyone who wanted to hear about the mission joined them in the day room. They were there to listen and to learn.

The air crew shared their experience in the same tradition in which Amundsen had guided Byrd, and Nansen had coached Amundsen. The knowledge, skill, and wisdom was transferred from the great explorers to the next group of great explorers, men and women who would learn from their experiences, and with that knowledge be able to reach further into the unknown. They, in turn, would bring back a better understanding of these newly explored worlds, and of human beings' desire and ability to reach, strive, and to believe that things that are thought impossible can be achieved.

Afterword

As the pilots reduced the LC-130's speed and began their descent onto the Greenland ice cap, I zipped up the green parka the air force had loaned me and felt a surge of excitement.

Only a few months before, after I had interviewed the aircrew at the 109th Air Wing's base in Scotia, New York, about their AGAP mission, I had walked into Colonel Gary James's office to thank him for giving me the opportunity to learn from the men and women of the 109th about their Antarctic mission.

At the end of our conversation, Colonel James asked, "Would you like to fly to Greenland with our aircrews and watch them train on the ice cap for our Antarctic mission?"

It took a moment for his question to register. Two years before, when I met Samantha East and Brian Gomula they were returning from their spring training with the 109th on the ice cap, and when I was on my way to swim in Disko Bay, I silently wished that I could go there. Now Colonel James, and Colonel Anthony German, the wing commander, were officially inviting me to Greenland to see how the aircrews trained and honed their skills for polar flight.

"I would absolutely love to do that," I said with so much enthusiasm that Colonel James grinned, and his blue eyes grew bright. He explained that there would be a press trip in June, and I would be traveling with the media. He said that travel in Greenland was weather dependent. If the weather was good, we would fly to three different locations on the ice cap: Summit, at an altitude of 10,000 feet; Raven, at 6,960 feet; and NEEM, at 8,038 feet. The 109th would also be carrying supplies to the support people and scientists doing research at the stations.

Sitting sideways on orange nylon bench seats with net backing, I stared out of the porthole-shaped window at the searing bright white below. The air suddenly grew thinner, more difficult to breathe, as the flight engineer depressurized the cargo area to diminish the effect of the altitude on our bodies when we stepped out of the aircraft and to make sure the door didn't blow out when it was opened upon landing. The flight engineer also cooled the cargo area to prevent a meltdown when we landed, to prevent icing and possibly breaking the ramp.

I put on my cap and knitted mittens and put leather mittens over the top of them, like Amundsen had done on his South Pole quest.

As the LC-130 gently touched down on the main skis, I felt my excitement grow. The weight of the aircraft shifted forward onto the nose ski, and we slid in the ski bird along the skiway until the aircraft began to slow, and then the pilot reversed the aircraft's roaring engines and brought the aircraft to a stop.

The cargo door was opened, and the air seemed thinner. We ducked through the cargo door and walked down three steps, and touched the snow. There were support people waiting for us on snowmobiles pulling Nansen sleds—they were smaller than the sleds Nansen used when he crossed Greenland more than one hundred years before, but the shape of the sled was the same design.

The day, and the remaining days that followed, were equally amazing and filled with memorable and reflective moments.

The next day, June 20, our media group was invited to fly on a training mission to Raven Camp. Lieutenant Colonel Marc LeCours, the navigator, explained that the last fifteen to twenty seconds before landing and the first fifteen to twenty seconds after takeoff were the most interesting parts of flight.

*Left: USAF Colonel Anthony German, wing commander,
109th Airlift Wing. Right: USAF Colonel Gary James.*

The transitions would be what the aircrew would focus on during their training.

When we arrived at the aircraft, I was given a turn to be in the cockpit for the takeoff. Lieutenant Colonel Mark Armstrong and Captain Wayne Brown, the pilots, were busy, going through their checklists; the flight engineer sitting behind them was clicking switches on the ceiling; and Lieutenant Colonel LeCours, the navigator, was in the back of the cockpit beside a computer screen covered with a section of Greenland, and beside that a folded paper chart, focused on the same area.

The empty and silent cockpit that Samantha East had shown me when I first visited the 109th in Schenectady was now filled with life and activity and energy. The engines were so loud that we had to wear earplugs, and the aircraft vibrated so much that if I'd been holding a cup of coffee, there would have been waves in the cup.

When Lieutenant Colonel Marc LeCours handed me a pair of headphones and I put them on, I heard the aircrew speaking in clear, abbreviated sentences. It was wonderful. They were

A dream come true: flying low over the Greenland glaciers en route to Kangerlussuaq after walking on the Greenland ice cap and visiting research camps.

saying numbers, directions, and wind speed, and the pilots were talking with a man from Greenland in the control tower, who was speaking to them in English.

There was no way for me to understand what they were saying or what they were doing, but they were all working together, and it was a beautiful thing to watch. It was so exciting being with them in the cockpit. I loved being there and feeling that moment when the aircraft suddenly lifted off the earth, peering down through windows that arched around the front of the cockpit, watching the rocky terrain slip away, looking between the pilots to see the mountains dropping below us, and listening to the crew as they talked with one another and flew the aircraft toward Raven Station. I didn't want to leave, but there were other media friends waiting for their turn and I returned to the main cabin.

We landed on skis on the snowy skiway at Raven camp. The

landing was as smooth as riding in a boat across flat water. We were dropped off on the ice cap while the aircrew began their training mission.

A billowing cloud of snow rose behind the silver LC-130 as it thundered along the skiway, flashed its bright orange tail, and lifted steadily off the ground.

Someone suddenly shouted, "Prop wash!"

And I wondered what that meant, until a snow cloud completely enveloped me like a blizzard, and the world went totally white, and the air temperature dropped instantly, way below zero degrees Fahrenheit. I shook my head and laughed. Now I knew what "prop wash" meant. What incredible fun. I pulled the fur on the brim of my parka hood over my head, and smiled. The same Inuit-designed parka with the fur hood was what Amundsen wore through the Northwest Passage and to the South Pole, and that parka design was successful and is still being used by the U.S. Air Force. It was so warm. The aircraft became a dot in the sky, disappeared into a white sky, and circled back. The aircrew landed twice and took off twice in an open snow area. Their takeoffs and landings looked smooth and effortless. And when the training was over and I heard the aircrew talking, they were pleased with the work they had done.

The following day, June 21, 2009, while on the bus to breakfast at the airport café, I noticed a group of about thirty people standing in a semicircle, with three men wearing white, standing immediately in front of the flagpole. They were raising the red-and-white flag of Greenland. This was the day when the way Greenland was governed changed from "home rule" to "self rule," which gave the country greater autonomy from Denmark, though not quite independence. This was what Lars-Emil Johansen, the former prime minister, and his colleagues had been working on for many years.

The celebration continued at the airport café in Kangerlussuaq. The cashier lit four small candles, and she smiled at me. She said her name was Enoksen, like the prime minister who had just left office. On the radio, a choir was singing in Greenlandic,

Lieutenant Colonel Mark Armstrong flying over Greenland while his daughter is in the United States doing swimming workouts.

and when the choir finished, I heard a man's familiar voice, and pointed to the speaker and asked, "Lars-Emil Johansen?"

She stuck her thumbs up in the air and nodded. Two years before, Lars-Emil and I had talked about Greenland gaining its independence from Denmark. And now, after thirty years of work, it was closer than ever.

How were they celebrating this peaceful transfer of power, I wondered. Walking to the lobby, I noticed the receptionist at the airport hotel. She said people were celebrating with picnics and, in the afternoon, there would be a soccer match between Greenland and Denmark. In the early evening children would do traditional Greenlandic dances, and later at night the adults would do traditional dances, too. She said Hans Enoksen, the former prime minister, was speaking on the radio and she said that this freedom from Denmark would give Greenland the ability to determine its own future.

We entered the aircraft and flew to NEEM, about a three-

*Colonel Gary James on a LC-130 training mission taking off
from the Greenland ice cap passing the old DEW line.*

hour flight from Kangerlussuaq. We landed on the Greenland
ice cap at NEEM and climbed down metal stairs and into a
snow cave. Jørgen Peder "J. P." Steffensen, a scientist who has
been conducting ice-core studies for the past twenty-nine
years, met us in the snow cave where the research team was
drilling ice cores and carefully extracting them from the ice cap.
The ice cores were frozen time capsules. and they were exquisite frosty white crystal cylinders.

J.P. introduced us to the group of scientists who were cutting cores into various shapes and sizes. This group was collab-
orating with fourteen other scientists from around the world.
They were studying changes through time in the earth and the
earth's atmosphere. J.P. noted that the earth's climate was
always changing, but what was more significant was the rate at
which climate changed.

Just before we climbed out of the ice cave, a tall, strong-
looking, rosy-cheeked scientist came over to me and said that

she was from Switzerland and was a long-distance swimmer, and there in the snow cave, within the Greenland ice cap, we talked about our shared experiences of swimming across Lake Geneva and other favorite Swiss lakes. Our time, though, was too short, and soon we were back in the LC-130.

During our return flight to Scotia, New York, I asked Lieutenant Colonel James Powell, the navigator, if he would demonstrate the way he used the aviator's sextant.

Lieutenant Colonel Powell carefully lifted the sextant out of a heavy black case, stepped on a pullout stair, attached the sextant to a window in the ceiling of the aircraft, and focused it on the sun. We were flying south over Canada, over the St. Lawrence Seaway and a carpet of puffy clouds.

Lieutenant Colonel Powell let me stand on his chair and look up through the eyepiece. In the center of the image was a beautiful bright orange ball, smaller than my fingernail, and I thought, This is like the navigational instrument that Amundsen and Byrd used to find their way to the South Pole, and this was what the LC-130 navigators were using to find their way far beyond that and home. There was something so beautiful in the way the sextant connected the great explorers to the sun and the universe, and linked the history of polar exploration and brought that exploration into the future.

Lieutenant Colonel Powell turned his attention to the radar screen and how to interpret what he saw. The screen no longer looked like a photo of an alien to me, as it had first time I saw a radar image; now I could see the wide St. Lawrence Seaway and where it forked, a dot that was a ship sailing across the water. A small island, close to the city of Quebec, glowed brighter than all the other images, and Mark explained a building on it was made mostly of metal.

"Do you think it's beautiful?" I asked Mark.

"Yes, very beautiful," he said, and smiled.

"So do I." There was something so wonderful in seeing and understanding the world in a new way.

When we landed at Schenectady, the ground surrounding the base was vibrantly green and lush. The wide-branched maple, oak, and birch were in full leaf, with knee-high grasses and Queen Anne's lace shimmering in the sunlight after a sudden summer shower.

It surprised the senses to fly from the stark silence of the Greenland ice cap to a place where the air was filled with birds singing loudly overhead and bees and dragonflies buzzing by.

Glancing back at the LC-130 parked on the tarmac, I smiled. Amundsen would have loved flying with the 109th, too, and he had been right: aircraft were a much better way to travel over and explore the polar regions than dogsled.

When I arrived home in California, I thought I would write about the 109th and complete this book, but one of my friends in the gym, Margee Ralston, asked me if I wanted to go outrigger canoeing, along with Ted, her husband, and their outrigger crew. After workout, during breakfast, they listened to my stories about flying with the 109th and about their Greenland and Antarctic missions and how incredible it had been to watch them train. Ted asked if they flew C-17s to Antarctica, too. Ted and Margee had told me the United States Air Force flew them out of Tacoma, but I hadn't had the chance to fly on one. Ted smiled, and one of their outrigger friends said that they had to get me into a C-17. She explained that they worked for Boeing, and they wanted to know if it would interest me to see how the aircraft was built.

Former air force colonel James Schaffer met us at the Long Beach, California, Boeing offices and explained how the C-17 was used in Antarctica. It was built to fly long distances with the capability to refuel in flight and was able to carry heavy cargo into Antarctica. He guided us on the tour to see how sheet metal was transformed into wings, fins, and a tail and how the C-17's structures were reinforced and constructed. Outside on the black tarmac we were invited to climb into the enormous cargo area of a new C-17, and Tech Sergeants Tracy Gray and Robert Tenorio explained how efficiently and accurately paratroopers and cargo deploy from the aircraft and how everything is done with precision timing and computers. Tommy Schueler, a former instructor pilot and evaluator pilot for the air force and now a Boeing test pilot, gave us a tour of the cockpit and let me sit in one of the seats. I was awed by the number of buttons and computer displays and the multiple systems that had been developed to fly the C-17.

When the tour was complete, Tracy checked with Lieutenant Colonel Keith Guillotte at March Air Reserve Base, and he invited me to join him and Lieutenant Colonel Tim Harris in the Boeing C-17 flight simulator there. They let me sit beside Tim in the mock cockpit, and fly the C-17. Mostly I watched Tim, who was an instructor pilot and an open-water swimmer. He programmed the flight course from Los Alamitos Joint Forces Training Base to Tacoma, Washington, and during our flight Lieutenant Colonel Harris asked the flight simulator operator if he could simulate snow and zero visibility like what they might experience in Antarctica, and I asked if he could simulate loss of one engine, and then the loss of a second. Lieutenant Colonel Harris adjusted to the changes; his focus was complete and intense. In the background Lieutenant Colonel Guillotte commented on how amazing Tim was doing. He said that most young pilots would be bouncing around in the air, but Tim kept the C-17's flight smooth and level. A few weeks later, after contacting their colleagues in the Air Force, Lieutenant Colonel Guillotte and the secretary of the air force invited me to fly with them and see how they achieved their C-17 missions, and we're now working on unrestricted clearance so I can go.

As time has passed I've been asked by Jeremy Piasecki, a chief warrant officer in the United States Marine Corps whose unit is Marine Corps Forces in Stuttgart, Germany, and the head coach of the Afghanistan National Water Polo team, to help him bring the team to the United States to compete here and on the international level. Jeremy believes that building an Afghanistan water polo team will be a way to unite people in Afghanistan and build cultural bridges between the nations of the world. Jeremy is teaching Afghan soldiers how to swim and play water polo at the Pol-e-charki and Helmand bases, and I've been working to get him support from the State Department and Department of Defense to help him and the Afghanistan National Water Polo team realize their dream.

While writing and reflecting upon the significance of the one hundredth anniversary of Amundsen's and Scott's attainment of the South Pole, I've been creating a South Pole celebration. I have written the White House to request Vice President Biden lead a group of American explorers in December 2011 to the South Pole to join the official representatives from Norway, Britain, and New Zealand that will be arriving at the U.S. South Pole Station to celebrate the historic anniversary of Amundsen's and Scott's achievements. By honoring Amundsen and Scott, we also remember Charles Wilkes, the American navy lieutenant who discovered that Antarctica was a continent and set the stage for all Antarctic exploration.

It is autumn now in the Northern Hemisphere and spring in the Southern Hemisphere. I imagine the preparations that are being made by modern-day explorers. They will be departing for Antarctica in time to celebrate the centennial of Amundsen's and Scott's success. What a legacy these modern explorers will follow and what a legacy they will create. What new worlds will they open on the continent, and what will they discover in the heavens?

Soon Brigadier General Tony German will be talking with Colonel Paul Sheppard, the commander for Operation Deep Freeze, and with Colonel Tim LeBarge, the wing commander on the challenging task for the 109th Air Wing on their upcoming Antarctic mission. Soon they will be flying south with the sun.

SOURCES

Amundsen, Roald. *Belgica Diary: The First Scientific Expedition to the Antarctic*. Huntingdon, UK: Bluntisham Books, Erskine Press, 1999.

————. *My Life as an Explorer*. Garden City, NY: Doubleday, Doran, 1928.

————. *The North-west Passage: Being the Record of a Voyage of Exploration of the Ship Gjoa, 1903–1907*. 2 vols. Elibron Classics, 2006.

————. *The South Pole*. McClean, VA: IndyPublish.com, n.d.

Amundsen, Roald, Archives. Manuscripts Collection, National Library of Norway, Oslo.

Amundsen, Roald, Collection. Picture Collection, National Library of Norway, Oslo.

Bomann-Larsen, Tor. *Roald Amundsen*. Stroud, UK: Sutton Publishing, 2006.

Bryce, Robert M. *Cook and Peary: The Polar Controversy, Resolved*. Mechanicsburg, PA: Stackpole Books, 1997.

Byrd, Richard E. *Little America*. New York: G. P. Putnam's Sons, 1930.

Cherry-Garrard, Apsley. *The Worst Journey in the World: Antarctica, 1910–1913*. New York: Dial Press, 1923.

Cook, Frederick Allen, Papers. Manuscript Division, Library of Congress, Washington, DC.

Curtsinger, Bill. *Extreme Nature: Images from the World's Edge*. Italy: White Star Vercelli, September 27, 2005, www:whitestarpublications.IT.

de Gerlache, Adrien. *Voyage of the Belgica: Fifteen Months in the Antarctic*. Norwich, UK: Erskine Press, 1998.

Delgado, James P. *Across the Top of the World: The Quest for the Northwest Passage*. Vancouver, Canada: Douglas McIntyre, 2009.

Fram Museum. *Fridtjof Nansen, Scientist and Humanitarian*. Oslo: Fram Museum, 2008.

Lewis-Jones, Huw. *Face to Face: Polar Portraits*. Cambridge, UK: Scott Polar Research Institute, University of Cambridge, 2008.

McGonigal, David, and Lynn Woodworth. *Antarctic and the Arctic: The Complete Encyclopedia*. Willowdale, Canada: Firefly Books, 2001.

Nansen, Fridtjof. *Farthest North*. New York: Modern Library, 1999.

————. *The First Crossing of Greenland*. Honolulu: University Press of the Pacific, 2001.

Sources

Nansen, Fridtjof, Archives. Manuscripts Collection, National Library of Norway, Oslo.

Nansen, Fridtjof, Collection. Picture Collection, National Library of Norway, Oslo.

New York Times archives, NYtimes.com.

Peat, Neville. *Antarctic Partners: 50 Years of New Zealand and United States Cooperation in Antarctica, 1957–2007.* Wellington: New Zealand Ministry of Foreign Affairs and Trade, 2007.

Scott, R. F. *Tragedy and Triumph: The Journals of Captain R. F. Scott's Last Polar Expedition.* New York: Konecky and Konecky, 1993.

INDEX

Page numbers in *italics* refer to illustrations.

279

Index

Index

Index

A NOTE ON THE TYPE

This book was set in Adobe Garamond. Designed for the
Adobe Corporation by Robert Slimbach, the fonts are based
on types first cut by Claude Garamond (c. 1480–1561).
Garamond was a pupil of Geoffroy Tory and is believed to
have followed the Venetian models, although he introduced
a number of important differences, and it is to him that we
owe the letter we now know as "old style." He gave to his
letters a certain elegance and feeling of movement that won
their creator an immediate reputation and the patronage of
Francis I of France.

Composed by North Market Street Graphics,
Lancaster, Pennsylvania
Printed and bound by Berryville Graphics,
Berryville, Virginia
Designed by Virginia Tan

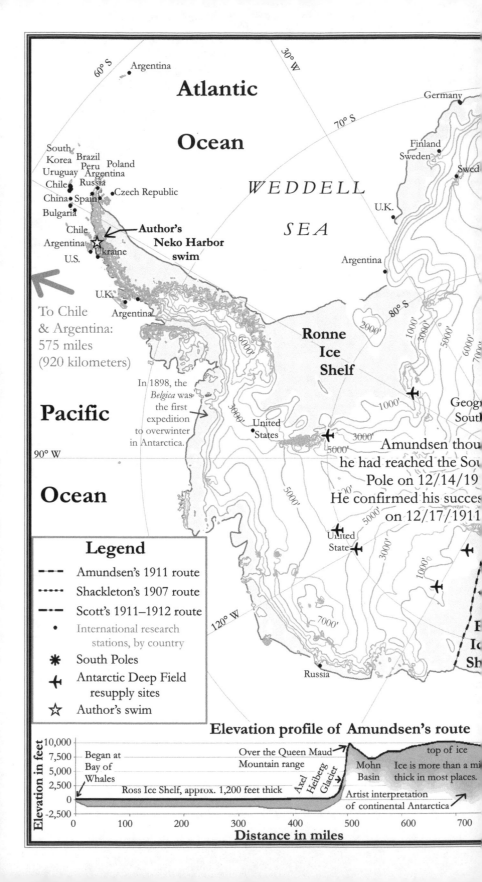

60° S　Argentina

Atlantic

Ocean

30° W

70° S

Germany

Finland
Sweden

Swed

South
Korea　Brazil
Peru　Poland
Uruguay　Argentina
Chile　Russia
China　Spain
Bulgaria
　Chile
Argentina
U.S.

Czech Republic

Ukraine

W E D D E L L

U.K.

S E A

Argentina

80° S

**Author's
Neko Harbor
swim**

U.K.
Argentina

2000'
1000'
3000'
5000'
6000'
7000'

To Chile
& Argentina:
575 miles
(920 kilometers)

**Ronne
Ice
Shelf**

6000'

In 1898, the
Belgica was
the first
expedition
to overwinter
in Antarctica.

Pacific

90° W

Ocean

3000'

United
States

1000'

Geog
Sout

3000'
5000'

Amundsen thou
he had reached the Sou
Pole on 12/14/19
He confirmed his succes
on 12/17/1911

5000'

70°

5000'

United
State

120° W

5000'

70°

7000'

I
Id
Sh

Russia

Legend

- - -　Amundsen's 1911 route

· · · · ·　Shackleton's 1907 route

- · -　Scott's 1911–1912 route

·　International research
　stations, by country

✳　South Poles

✈　Antarctic Deep Field
　resupply sites

☆　Author's swim

Elevation profile of Amundsen's route

Elevation in feet

10,000
7,500
5,000
2,500
0
-2,500

Began at
Bay of
Whales

Ross Ice Shelf, approx. 1,200 feet thick

Over the Queen Maud
Mountain range

Axel
Heiberg
Glacier

Mohn
Basin

top of ice

Ice is more than a mi
thick in most places.

Artist interpretation
of continental Antarctica

0　　100　　200　　300　　400　　500　　600　　700

Distance in miles

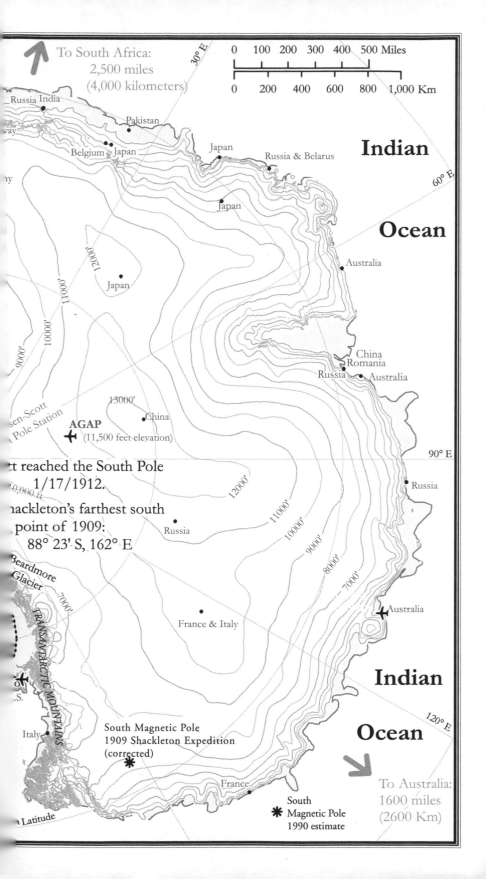

To South Africa:
2,500 miles
(4,000 kilometers)

30° E

0   100 200 300 400 500 Miles

0   200   400   600   800 1,000 Km

Russia India

Norway

Pakistan

Belgium Japan

Japan

Japan

Russia & Belarus

Indian

60° E

Ocean

Australia

Japan

China
Romania
Russia   Australia

90° E

13000'

China

Amundsen-Scott
South Pole Station

AGAP
(11,500 feet elevation)

Russia

...t reached the South Pole
... 1/17/1912.

10,000 ft

...hackleton's farthest south
... point of 1909:
      88° 23' S, 162° E

Russia

Beardmore
Glacier

7000'

TRANSANTARCTIC MOUNTAINS

Russia

France & Italy

Australia

of
...S.

Italy

South Magnetic Pole
1909 Shackleton Expedition
(corrected)

France

Indian

120° E

Ocean

To Australia:
1600 miles
(2600 Km)

...a Latitude

South
✳ Magnetic Pole
1990 estimate

12000'
11000'
10000'
9000'
8000'
7000'

13000'
12000'
11000'
10000'
9000'